"This brilliant memoir, a debut no less, has the insights, the epiphanies, and the ability to let the reader really *live* the life being documented. Not only is this an extraordinary narrative about a family challenged by mental illness and foster care, it gives voice to a greater sense of displacement and alienation. It also offers hope, love, and forgiveness. It is a book for our time—for all time—in that it's heartbreakingly beautiful and genuinely unforgettable. This memoir is absolutely not to be missed. There are not enough thumbs-up to give it. Read it! Now!"

—SUE WILLIAM SILVERMAN, AWARD-WINNING AUTHOR OF *HOW TO SURVIVE DEATH AND OTHER INCONVENIENCES*

"*When I Was Her Daughter* is a gripping, visceral, page-turning memoir. With humor and heart, Ferguson tells the story of growing up with a seriously dangerous mentally ill mother, navigating the sometimes-terrifying-often-lonely foster care system, and ultimately finding a home. Unflinching, powerful, lyrical, and raw, this memoir is both heartbreaking and triumphant."

—MARNI FREEDMAN, CO-FOUNDER OF THE SAN DIEGO WRITERS FESTIVAL

"*When I Was Her Daughter* is a powerful and compelling memoir. Ferguson's gifted storytelling transports the reader to her childhood, a time filled with confusion, imagination, grief, and hope. This is a story that will break your heart and put it back together again."

—HOLLY KAMMIER, BEST-SELLING AUTHOR OF *LOST GIRL*

"In this haunting and heroic memoir, Ferguson captures the reader with her intense storytelling skills and invites us to cheer her on every step of the way. The book leaves inspiring moments of strength and resilience throughout to be captured and called on for our own forever. Brilliant breakout book!"

—SUNNY REY, OWNER AND CREATOR OF POETS UNDERGROUND AND POETS UNDERGROUND PRESS

When I was her Daughter

A MEMOIR

LESLIE FERGUSON

FROM THE TINY ACORN...
GROWS THE MIGHTY OAK

When I Was Her Daughter is a work of creative nonfiction. The stories in this book have been reconstructed from memory with the intent to present them as truthfully as possible. The conversations in the book are not meant to represent word-for-word transcripts but to portray mood, tone, and meaning as experienced by the author. In all instances, the essence of the dialogue is accurate. To reconcile gaps in memory, for brevity and clarity, and to protect privacy, some events and timelines have been compressed and some names have been changed.

For my brother
who kept me safe

And for my mom and dad
who never gave up

chapter 1

Summer 1980

AGE 6

MY EARLIEST MEMORY IS OF DROWNING.

Mom squints and smiles at me. Holding my hand, she guides me into the ocean. I'm on my tiptoes and intoxicated with excitement. I want her to take me farther so I can float like a buoy. The cool water lifts me up, makes me weightless under the blasting summer sun.

I'm six years old, wearing my pink and white floral two-piece with the ruffles over the chest and across the hips. The water's surface rises under my chin like a blanket, and a lukewarm chill trickles along the back of my neck.

Auntie Philys and William wade at the shoreline behind Mom and me where the water rushes in and tugs at the land. Auntie's polyester pant cuffs are rolled up, so I know she's expecting to get wet even though she can't swim. William is only five, and he can't swim either. The sun makes the top of his blond head shine.

Mom tells me, "Not too deep," but I pull her toward the horizon, where all I can see is water and sky.

Then a ragged voice rings out. "Help! I can't swim!"

When I look back to the shoreline, I see the surf has knocked my aunt down, and the water and sand take her, as if with fingers, into the sea. Like an overturned beetle, Auntie kicks at the air. Then, William falls, and the whitewash yanks him into the surf, too.

It all happens so fast. I think I should go back and save them, but when I turn toward Mom to tell her, water gushes into my mouth and floods my ears with its *whoosh, glomp, whoosh,* and then I'm like a bundle of clothes in a washing machine. I don't understand the thick scent that fills my nose—mushed strawberries mixed with salt? My eyeballs sting like a burn, but I keep them open. I need them to find the light because that's where the surface is.

Mom lets me go. I inhale ocean and flail around for her—a hand, a body, something to anchor me. I'm slammed into the sea floor. It's a scratchy, sickening drag along the bottom before I'm tossed again and tumbling. I strain toward the surface, teaching myself how to survive already. Something scrapes my thigh. Mom's fingernails? No, her ring. The yellow topaz one with the prongs that stick up like needles.

I reach for her but come up empty.

I open my eyes after drowning to see Jesus looking down at me. He holds me in his arms, carries me to my towel. Seawater drips like honey from his long brown hair and beard. The sun behind him creates a halo around his head.

William lies on his belly on a towel, whimpering. I rest my hand on his trembling back.

Jesus leaves but returns soon, carrying Mom. He leaves again, and when he returns, he has Auntie Philys in his arms. He lays her gently on a towel.

"You're an angel," Mom says, her breath heavy like sadness. "You saved us. An angel sent straight from heaven."

"It's Jesus, Mom," William says.

Jesus laughs.

"Where did you come from?" Mom says. "The beach is practically empty except for those two fucking lazy excuses." She points to a man and woman sitting as still as mannequins in low chairs about fifty yards away.

"I was just out on my board," Jesus says. "The undertow took you."

Mom's mascara streaks her cheeks, and her short auburn hair sticks to her temples and forehead. "Damn Communists." She shakes her head. "They're everywhere."

Auntie squints. "Roberta, knock it off." She coughs into her hand, then gropes around the towel for her purse. "I need my glasses. And a cigarette."

I sink into my warm towel, floating on being alive. I look up, but Jesus is gone.

"Lazy bastards!" Mom shouts and shuffles through the hot sand toward the lounging couple. "Kids are drowning, and you just sit there?"

They ignore her, staring straight ahead in their sunglasses. Maybe they *are* mannequins. Or Communists, whatever *that* is. Auntie puts her hand on Mom's arm, but Mom kicks sand at their legs before giving up.

Towels over shoulders, we drag ourselves to the car. Boiled hotdog and coconut suntan lotion smells replace the scent of drowning. Soaring seagulls let squawks fall from their beaks. A cloud-gray bird lands at the edge of the sidewalk to peck at breadcrumbs.

We drive home in Auntie's Ford Mustang with the fuzzy white dice hanging from the rearview. Lungs small and tight, I fall asleep and dream about how staying close to the surface keeps me safe.

On the sidewalk in front of our Paramount apartment, I turn

the crotch of my swimsuit inside out to release clumps of sand. I should have died, but instead, I feel how soft the sand and I are, and how hard, too. I'm mad at the ocean for tricking me, for being so inviting when all it wanted to do was swallow me.

We moved in with Auntie shortly after we almost drowned.

One night, I awoke because Mom was sitting next to me, leaning over me where I lay on Auntie's loveseat. Mom seemed to be concentrating on something with all her might.

And then my throat was straining to break free of something constricting my neck, rubbing it raw like a rope burn.

Something glimmered. Mom's topaz ring.

I'd struggled to find her hands that day at the beach. Now, here they were, but I wanted them as far away from me as possible, those hard hands and the ring that pretended to be pretty.

Clawing, I scratched myself with jagged fingernails but couldn't loosen the material wrapped around my neck, couldn't make Mom stop killing me.

"Shh. Go back to sleep," she whispered. She tightened the noose again, and her eyes went deep, dark, and mean. She eased up as if to get a better grip.

"You're hurting me." The room came alive, and the pressure of her body made me hot. I shrank, became tiny, lost in the couch's velvety green ivy pattern.

My feet were so cold. Didn't Mom know they peeked out from under the blanket? And how I needed them covered? Didn't she know how blurry she became, how cloudy and cotton-like? And how good she was at making me disappear?

A dim, warm glow emanated from the hanging lamp in the corner. The wall beneath it shone as if someone had painted it with a clear coat of nail polish. I closed and opened my eyes, fluttered my lashes like a butterfly kiss, but instead of seeing me, Mom tightened her lips into a small *o*. Her eyebrows lifted and lowered.

Crying, William sat cross-legged on the always-deflating pool raft bed where he'd been sleeping. He leaned toward us and put his hands out. I thought he was going to pull Mom away from me, but he was too small to do that. He cupped her leg and begged her to stop hurting me.

I raked Mom's arms and my neck, pawed her wrists and forearms. I kicked the couch cushions, which only jostled her a bit. The taste of metal spread into my mouth like the time I stuck my tongue on a 9-volt battery terminal. But I could hold a battery in my hand and pull it away from my lips. This was something else, something out of my control.

Mom blinked and shook her head from side to side as if exiting a trance, a wicked spell cast by an evil witch. "Oh, Leslie." She sounded disappointed in me for not dying fast enough. "It was supposed to be over really quick." I coughed. She eased her grip again, releasing one end of the strangling thing, and slid it out from under me as if it were a scarf.

Then I recognized it—one of my red knee-high socks. My favorite pair. The socks I always wore with my fancy navy blue dress with white polka dots and a Peter Pan collar.

"You weren't supposed to feel it. Mommy's sorry. Go back to sleep."

My skull throbbed from the pressure, lack of oxygen, and the thought I'd done something wrong that caused Mom to hate me.

"Why did you do that?"

She shushed me and slid from my side. "Go to sleep."

On a Saturday, we drove to Seal Beach, where we almost drowned less than a year earlier.

"Don't worry," Mom said, "we aren't going swimming. We are visiting someone."

William and I stayed in the car while Mom traipsed up the walkway to a blue house. I couldn't see the person who answered the door and stayed behind the screen. When Mom got back into the car, she said, "Your father is a son-of-a-bitch, good-for-nothing bastard, too good for his own kids and just turns us out on the street and starts a new life." Her eyebrows got low and close over her eyes.

He'd left before I was two years old—before William's birth. And I never saw him or thought about him except when Mom brought him up. From Mom's reaction to being turned away at the door, I guessed my dad was not going to be involved any more than he'd ever been, which was too bad because I got the sense we needed him to save us.

1980

AGE 7

I WAS SEVEN WHEN WE STARTED RUNNING FROM the government.

We had moved in with Auntie Philys again after living in apartments and sometimes with Gramma and Grampa. Mom, William, and I slept in the living room of Auntie's tiny place. Mom slept in the cushioned rocker, and William and I alternated between the couch and the pool raft, which fit lengthwise in front of the door. When I slept on the raft, cockroaches crawled the still mountain of my body in the dark, and after they fled, their ghosts scurried along my arms and in my hair. William admitted he had trapped roaches on his arm in the night, but he always let them go.

Convinced Auntie Philys's place was bugged with listening devices planted by the government, Mom searched ceiling corners with her eyes and ran her hands along tables and under lamps, cursing the Communists. "Damn Russians. Sent to torture us," she said when I questioned her. And then she lit a Marlboro 100, puffed on it until the smoke streamed smoothly from its tip, and cleared a tobacco fiber from her lip.

Next to me on the couch in the daylight, Mom sat close. I ran my hand over the velvety ivy pattern and shuddered, more from the memory of what Mom did to me that one night than from her urgency about running from the government.

"What's Communism?" I asked.

Mom scowled, shook her head, and took a drag off her cigarette like she was sucking it dry. Her disapproval and her refusal to answer my questions made me feel like I'd done something wrong. Mom's disdain had fangs—it sat inside her face, behind her eyes, always ready to inject its venom.

We were poor not only because Mom had no job and no savings, but also because she often refused to cash her welfare checks or spend actual money. When William, Mom, and I walked to Pizza Hut from Aunt Philys's, William found a dollar on the sidewalk. He always found money.

Once, a van almost ran him over in the Coin-Op Laundromat parking lot. He had crouched to scoop up a twenty. Mom yanked him out of the way, saving him just in time.

But this dollar foretold our fate, and it also showed the government where we were, so Mom held out her hand. William placed the dollar in her palm.

"Don't pick up anything," Mom said. "I've told you before it could be a trap. Now they're watching." She eyed the buzzing wires above and squinted to focus on far away things. "Always think." She poked her temple. "You hear me?" She squeezed our chins to make sure we understood she was serious. Then, after a complete scan all the way around at the sky, street, and buildings, she squinted again at the telephone wires. I listened but couldn't hear what they said.

I tugged on Mom's hand. I didn't want to hear what she might say next. Hunched over and jutting her head out in front of her like a cartoon buzzard, she walked slowly, the crumpled dollar bill in her hand at her side. She stopped again. "Don't ever pick up anything." She turned toward William and then toward me, and her eyes turned from icy blue to gray as if clouds had settled in them.

"We know, Mom," I said. "Let's just get pizza." She didn't scare me. I felt annoyed at being lectured about a stupid dollar.

"Don't take anything that isn't yours." She flattened the bill and held George Washington's dirty face to the sun, mumbling, her orange lipstick dark in the cracks and worn in the fleshy parts. "L00307506," she read from the bill, with trembling lips. "You see that?" She showed William and me the front of the bill. "You know what this means?" We shook our heads. "That L stands for Leslie." Mom pointed to the letter. "And the seventy-five represents the year William was born." She scanned her finger over the ink in an intentional, smooth stroke. "And the number three. There are *three* of us." She pointed to us and then to herself. "They're going to take you. And you. And me. And the zeros." She paused, circling them lightly. "They symbolize rape." She didn't say anything else for a minute but focused her attention on the dollar.

Then she told us what rape was.

I didn't understand why someone would want to do those terrible things to us.

She hit the bill against her other hand. "And that's why we can't spend a lot of the money we get."

"But if we spend it," William said. "It won't be ours anymore. They can't track us with it if we don't have it." Mom hugged him against her. A steady stream of cars rolled past us.

"Why would this dollar just happen to have these particular

numbers? Huh? You think it's just a coincidence?" She glared into my eyes like she was reading my soul. A sick feeling rolled through my gut. Why would she lie? Mom turned the dollar bill over in her hand and ran her fingers under the phrase, "In God We Trust." Then, she ripped the bill to shreds and stuffed its snowflake bits into her macramé purse. Mumbling buzzed in her mouth like an insect.

She thundered, marching toward the Hut, mumbling incoherently. She puffed up her wild, auburn hair with her hands, cigarette still between two fingers. Clinging to the strap of her purse, I sped up until I could feel the warmth of her body.

Inside Pizza Hut, standing on my tiptoes, I watched Mom move money across the counter—money she must have inspected earlier. I wondered what a "safe" dollar looked like.

Back at the apartment, Mom tossed the pizza box on the white Formica table. In the small kitchen, Dawn dish soap and stale cigarette smoke rose together in a bubble of scent mixed now with oregano and mozzarella. Auntie's canary, Lemon, twittered and pecked at birdseed. His cage was so small, but it protected him.

Not even money was safe in Mom's hands.

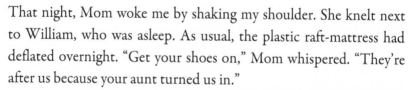

That night, Mom woke me by shaking my shoulder. She knelt next to William, who was asleep. As usual, the plastic raft-mattress had deflated overnight. "Get your shoes on," Mom whispered. "They're after us because your aunt turned us in."

The darkness in my aunt's living room told me it wasn't morning yet. Mom and William were fuzzy blobs. The sticky swish of plastic trash bags and the unlocking of the door disturbed the silence. Mom stood in the doorway like a shadow, backlit by the yellow porch lights of the apartments in the small complex. William and I followed her outside. On the sidewalk in front of the apartment building, Mom handed me one of the trash bags and lit a cigarette. I held the bag in front of me with both hands, gripping the top, strangling it shut, and twisting it like a bag of bread. It bobbed up and down, hitting each knee alternately as I walked.

"It's cold," William said.

Mom stuck one hand into my bag and took out the multi-colored afghan Gramma had crocheted for her when she was pregnant with me. She threw it across William's shoulders like an old lady's shawl. The blanket hung to the ground, swallowed his feet, and slowed him down. I walked behind him at first, and I was like Pac-man and he a blue ghost I could gobble up for two hundred points. We walked along Clark Avenue, past the Pizza Hut and past the school I had almost attended in the fall.

On that first day of school, Mom had driven me there, and I sat in the passenger seat, excited and in my new ivory-and-fuchsia-striped shirt with the scratchy tag. "I'm not taking you there," she said and flipped a U-turn in the middle of the street. "They'll brainwash you." I begged and kicked the glove box, but her eyes scowled at the road, and there went the second grade.

Seeing the school now made me long for ordinary things—math worksheets, spelling quizzes, and tetherball and handball challenges at recess. The cold, misty air landed on my skin as we hiked away from the sidewalk a bit and up a slight hill. My bag weighed more with each step up. I held it against my tummy like a sack of groceries.

Mom stopped us and lowered herself to the grass. We had walked down the road, past the lighted intersections—not far from Auntie's. I wasn't sure how we would hide from the government outside, only a short distance from the street, where anyone could drive by and see us. There was a Shell gas station across the street. And farther up, the grass stopped where a huge, vacant parking lot began.

Mom took the blanket from William's shoulders and laid it on the grass like a picnic blanket. She sat on it cross-legged and patted the ground next to her. "Lie down here and sleep. It'll be fun. Like we're camping."

We were caught in that space between dusk and dawn that laces the dewy air with a crisp chill. Street and car lights made a kaleidoscope of colors. We lay down, William on one side of Mom and me on the other. I'd never been camping before, but on TV, camping meant a tent, a campfire, and marshmallows roasting at the end of a long stick. It was supposed to be cozy, and maybe we'd sing songs, and everybody'd laugh and have a good time.

This was not that.

The starless sky, midnight-blue with gray layered in it, peeked through the tree branches. Pine trees dropped needles on us like prickles of rain. I shivered, and my teeth chattered. The wet grass poked my skin through the holes in the afghan.

In the morning, worms, roly-polies, and ants crawled in the grass. Had I slept with them all night or had they only just arrived? Pine, sap, dirt, and asphalt scents surrounded me, and cars zoomed by on the street below. I stretched my stiff, cold face and hands to the air.

"We heard from Philys," a voice said from down the grassy hill. It was Gramma, and the sound of her words made me panic like I'd done something wrong. Her short, wide body bobbed toward us as she climbed the slope. She and Grampa were there to help. I relaxed. Gramma shook her head and sighed.

"We've been driving all over Hell and back," Grampa said, "trying to find you." He didn't look at us but surveyed the street, hands on hips. The light from behind him made his face too dark to read. But his voice was sick and tired of dealing with Mom and us. Grampa jerked his head like he did when the Dodgers were losing—a quick, restrained shake. "Come on, Roberta. Don't be difficult. This is no life for children." His deep brown eyes had a glimmer in them, as if from tears about to fall, though I'd never seen him cry.

"I suppose you'd rather see us dead," Mom said. She folded her arms across her chest. Maybe she meant to stay there for a while, but I knew we would be leaving with Gramma and Grampa. And I was glad.

Gramma clucked her tongue. Seeing her downhearted stung me. Grampa shook his head again, and when I put my hand out to him, he closed his fingers over mine with a warm, gentle pressure that gave me permission to breathe.

"I'm sorry," I said. I needed to apologize since I should have resisted Mom more, should have refused to follow her into the night. But she was my *mom*, and I wasn't an expert at standing up to her. And didn't William, Mom, and I belong to each other like three sections of the same thread?

Mom looked into the distance, scowling as if deciding her next move. She mumbled and shook her head, gnawed her fingernails and spit out the bits.

At Gramma and Grampa's, William and I settled into the den, the room at the back of the house. Small, backless couches against perpendicular walls became our beds.

A square black table inset with a mother-of-pearl mosaic fit in the corner between the beds like a puzzle piece. I ran my fingers over the shell table, admiring it for how smooth and bumpy it was at the same time—and how iridescent, so many different colors at once.

That morning was the start of the three of us living with Gramma and Grampa so they could keep an eye on us.

chapter 3

1981

AGE 7

GRAMMA AND GRAMPA'S DEN BECAME A BEDROOM I shared with William. Mom routinely lifted the cushions with her bony hands and ran her fingers along the inner rims of lampshades and behind the furniture. Her whispers barely audible, she tried to explain herself. "Communists are everywhere, and everyone is brainwashed not to see it." Mostly, she didn't speak at all because, she said, the government listened in on our conversations. She accused Gramma and Grampa of ignorance. "You just don't understand. The government has brainwashed you against us."

Except for the TV and the arguing that went on between Mom and my grandparents, the house was hushed. Grampa rocked in his chair, furrowing his brows, ticking his tongue or digging a toothpick between his teeth, and shaking his mostly bald head.

Gramma sighed her disappointment and disapproval as she slowly blinked her blue eyes and wiped her sweaty forehead with a paper towel. I preferred Gramma and Grampa's to the streets, so I stayed quiet and out of the way. William did, too. Other than time spent outside playing, we both carried on like baby lambs, following the path set before us, doing what we were told.

In the backyard, we tried not to bounce the ball over the brick wall into the neighbor's yard or into Grampa's camellias. Mom stayed in her room, which was the middle bedroom, for days on end, so the slam of the screen door announcing her presence startled me. She sat without a word on the back porch and smoked cigarettes while staring off into space as if she were contemplating the various unsolved mysteries of the universe.

Grampa refused to let her smoke in the house, which made me glad. "It's a filthy, disgusting habit," he said, scrunching up his face and shaking his head.

On the porch, Mom sat in the white metal chair, one leg crossed over the other. She faced William and me, but her stare seemed a million miles away.

One time, I thought she was admiring me, watching me hit the ball against the wall. I tried to hit it perfectly, so she'd applaud and smile, but when I smiled at her, she didn't smile back. Her eyes shone empty as holes. She tightened her mouth, opening it only to slip her cigarette inside. And when she was done, she smashed it into the ashtray on the patio table and vanished into the house before the trail of smoke died out.

In the middle bedroom, I plopped next to Mom against the headboard. She raised her wine glass to avoid spilling. Then, she gazed into the distance, twirled her hair, and sipped from her glass.

On the wall above her head hung the scary ghost boat painting that put eerie feelings of loneliness deep within me. Mom didn't mention it, but I wondered if the artist put brainwashing messages in it on purpose. Framed in solid, carved walnut, it depicted a remote lake alcove with bushes, lily pads, and blush pink flowers. On the lake rested a small hull, empty of everything but its oars. Where did the boater go? Maybe a lonesome woman wearing a flowy white dress paddled across the lake to her destination. Maybe a large bird or some terrifying sight overtook her and caused her to fall overboard. Her lungs took in too much water, nobody arrived to save her, and she suffered a wet, bloated death.

"I wonder where the person rowing the boat went," I said, but Mom didn't answer.

William trotted into the room and jumped onto the other side of the bed next to Mom. I pointed at the muted painting.

William's eyes widened. "It's spooky."

The dark colors recalled old, haunted things that made me long for something I couldn't describe. If I walked into the painting, maybe I could discover a new world—haunted or not—because wherever a sliver of light crept in, there was potential for secrets, mystery, and horror. Why would anyone paint a picture of a lost boat unless to announce that someone who had been in the boat was also lost? It chilled and comforted me at the same time because becoming lost in an unknown world seemed like such an easy thing to do.

Mom caught William and me pretending to smoke camellia branches, so she taught us how to smoke.

The cigarette was more fragile than I'd expected. The sheer act of trying not to drop or crush it made my hand tremble. Mom laughed. I put the filtered tip to my lips. Pretending to smoke was much more comfortable than the real thing. Even though I had practiced many times with my candy cigarettes, smoking the real thing didn't feel natural to me. I fumbled and tried to be as graceful as possible with the cigarette between my straightened fingers, delicately placing it there with my other hand. Mom flicked the wheel of her neon green Bic lighter. A flame spurted from a series of sparks, and a blue-white cone of light shuddered up to my cigarette. Nothing else happened.

Mom said, "You have to light it by sucking in. Then you *puff, puff*. Like this." She struck another flame and made it kiss her cigarette. She sucked on the filter like a straw, and her cheeks caved in, emphasizing her high cheekbones. She blinked fast behind the smoke.

I puffed at uneven intervals as the tip burned orange beneath my nose. The glow made me shudder. I held *fire*. I couldn't drop the thing and prove I was too young to be smoking. A dumb girl who can't hold on to a cigarette certainly couldn't smoke one. She'd burn the house down.

Mom lit William's cigarette, and as always, the first burn smelled so good. The three of us smoked like chimneys next to Grampa's truck. I coughed. William made a face as if he'd tasted sour milk. Then he coughed, too. Mom laughed and pointed at me with her orange frosted fingernail. "Now maybe you won't be so curious. Smoking's horrible for you." She took a long drag on her cigarette and exhaled at the sky.

The heat of the fire near my skin startled me, and I dropped the cigarette on the cement. I heaved and choked before stamping out the burning body with my shoe.

"You're only supposed to smash the tip with your toes, like this." She pressed the tip of her sandal onto the cigarette as if she were pointing to something on the ground with her foot.

William got a few more puffs in. Then, shaking his head, he held the cigarette up to Mom. His face reddened, his cheeks puffed up, and he exploded in a thunder of cough. Mom took the cigarette from him and bent over to rub the hot tip on the cement. She stuck it back in the pack.

Cigarettes and Mom went together like peanut butter and jelly. Like Batman and Robin. I couldn't imagine her without Marlboros. She needed them. I understood the idea of needing something. But what if the things you think you need aren't good for you? How do you train yourself to need something else? I was attached to Mom and to her cool skin and sparkly laughter—and to her cigarette scent. I wanted to be like her—hoped I'd grow to be tall and thin with bright eyes and a straight smile.

When I curled up next to her and she caressed my forehead and hair with soft fingers, I sank into her love. But was she the lake and I the drowned girl? I lived somewhere between fear of her and fear of being lost to her. I needed her to be a boat so she could always be the one to save me.

The more Mom talked about being harassed by the government, the more Grampa felt harassed by Mom.

One night, he'd had enough, so he kicked us out. We went to Auntie Philys's, but soon, Mom accused her of being brainwashed by the government. The more Auntie tried to defend herself, the more convinced Mom became that Auntie was spying on us for the Russians. So, we drove to a motel.

In the car, Mom sang our favorite lullaby, "You Are My Sunshine." Her voice rose and fell into the lyrics, lifting me up because I was her sunshine, and William was, too. I closed my eyes and imagined a smiley-faced sun bouncing in the sky between puffy clouds. When Mom sang, my world stopped spinning. And it was enough.

William and I joined in. We existed as each other's sun—not even a storm could annihilate us.

In some spots, the motel stairs' white paint was scuffed black like someone had tap-danced all over it. Chipped parts revealed many layers like a jawbreaker. The peachy-brown underneath made me think about how things on the inside can sometimes be shockingly different from how they seem on the outside. Even Mom was layered like that.

When she unlocked the door to our motel room, Mom propped her suitcase against a wall, said, "I'm tired. Good night," threw back the scratchy floral bedspread, and climbed in.

It was still daylight, and William and I weren't sleepy. We rummaged through our black trash bags of belongings for our swimsuits.

At the pool, a chlorine smell filled my nose, and my lungs grew tight as I inhaled. I jumped in first and somersaulted backward and forward. After pushing off of the pool tiles with my feet, I glided through a clear blue lagoon, a mermaid fantasy creature with long hair that tickled my shoulders and back as it snaked behind me. It made a gauzy weblike mess in front of my face and went into my mouth when I inhaled.

William dog-paddled at the edge of the pool. I rushed from one end to the other, underwater, holding my breath longer and longer, wishing I could transform into a real mermaid. The water stung my eyes, which burned so hot I thought they might explode. Pressure filled my chest until my face and lungs were about to pop and all my brains could burst out like clots of jelly.

I scanned the pool for William. He wobbled in a blur of color at the deep end. His arm shot up. I laughed. His hands flapped at the surface like bird wings. He sank. Then, for a moment, his mouth came up. He was so quiet, I thought he was playing dead. I laughed again, but as I got closer, nothing was funny anymore.

"Grab the side," I yelled. But his head was underwater. I reached for him, but the more I tried, the weaker I grew and the slower I swam. I shouted and splashed and flailed, swimming toward him in the deep end. One hand touched him briefly, which gave me hope, so I scratched and clawed at him. He clung to me, and I pulled him to the surface.

All he had to do was *reach* for the wall. "I'm *drownding*," he said, frantically dog-paddling." He went under again. I slipped under for leverage to shove him with all my strength. He was so heavy. Locking onto my neck with his fingers, he pressed into my throat and pulled me down. He kicked my legs. We got tangled. He climbed my body, drowning me.

I sank.

Underwater, I focused on the wavering blue tile lining the inside of the pool. Then William clobbered me over the head, and almost as if by magic, the burden lifted, and I shot to the surface.

"Don't ever do that again." I gasped. William clung to the side of the pool, his chest red and rashy against the cement.

"I was *drownding*."

"You were *drowning*," I said. "There's only one 'd.'" I had to teach him *everything*, and now I had to protect him, too. I was so mad at Mom I wanted to scream. She should have been there. But I knew we could never tell her what had happened because she would have blamed us for going swimming without a lifeguard on duty. And she would've been right. It was our fault.

We slowed our panic, got out of the pool, and trudged upstairs, slapping our wet feet along the painted walkway. As a trickle of water dripped from my ruffled bikini, I recalled the time I almost drowned in the ocean and thought about how I was doubly lucky to be alive. For some reason, that made me remember the time

Mom squeezed my throat with my sock, and it made me shiver. Triply.

Back in the motel room, the blackout drapes were drawn. Mom slept soundly, curled into a ball, with the covers over her. William and I put dry clothes on, and I hung our suits over the spout in the bathtub.

I wrapped a towel around my hair like Mom wrapped hers after a bath. It made her seem glamorous, like an actress. The towel pulled my eyes tight toward my temples. My head throbbed. I felt small and dry. The real me was trapped beneath my lips and skin but ready to burst out any minute. I itched all over. I scratched, but I couldn't make it go away. Loaded with exhaustion, my lungs still pulsed with the memory of attempting to recapture lost air.

William curled up on the bed next to Mom. I landed on the bed with a jolt, laughing.

"Don't wake her up," he said. But I didn't care. I wanted to play by my own rules. Soon, it was dark out. I found some change in Mom's purse, which we used to buy candy and chips from the vending machine by the motel office. We watched the end of a movie, and William drifted off to sleep. I punched the Channel UP button on the remote until I came to a woman and man moaning together, naked. I lifted my head to make sure William's eyes were closed, and I lowered the volume to zero.

The man and woman kissed and touched and moved together as if they were one body. Where did the man end and the woman begin? They closed their eyes. I couldn't close mine, couldn't look away, afraid I'd miss something. Looking to Mom and to the TV, and to William and to the TV, I rested my finger on the Channel DOWN button, ready to press it if I got caught. Everything flashed fleshy gray-peach in the TV lightning. Being there with the man and woman doing sexy things made me feel dirty and curious at the same time like the time the liquor store clerk caught me flipping pages of *High Society*. I was losing myself in the taboo and a tingle from "down there."

In the morning, Mom put my hair in a ponytail. She pulled it so tight it seared my temples. "It hurts," I said, but she shook me still and combed the tail and braided it anyway. I leaned away, but then she smoothed my hair behind my ears and let her warm hand linger there for a moment. I cried but not enough that she noticed, which was for the best since I had secrets I needed to keep now that I had grown up a little while she slept.

In the car, Mom smoked with the window down, and the three of us remained silent. The events of the previous day put a sinking feeling in me. We drove all afternoon, and when the summer heat faded, giving way to dusk, my body shivered. We arrived in front of my grandparents' house.

"But Grampa doesn't want us," I said.

"Where else would you like us to go?" Mom said. It was a good question.

"What about back to Auntie Philys's?" William asked.

"I can't deal with her right now. She makes me so mad. I'll sort everything out with Grampa."

We grabbed our bags of stuff and dragged our bodies up the driveway. Mom unlatched the gate to the backyard and let the wide barn-style door swing fast against the brick wall that divided my grandparents' property from the neighbor's. The back door was unlocked, so we let ourselves in and went straight to the back of the house without announcing our arrival.

Mom wouldn't let us watch TV because that was the primary way the government brainwashed us, she said. I protested, and she shushed me. We sat in the stuffy room, staring at nothing. Then, she put her index finger in her mouth and pressed on her bottom back teeth.

"I think I have a cavity," she said. "Here." She pointed, and her mouth widened as she pressed. "And here." She pressed another molar. "I'm not going to the dentist. The last time I went was when this happened." William and I made eye contact. "They put radios in my teeth." Mom bit on her index finger as she pronounced the words. "So they can tell me to do things that make me look like a crazy person." She brought her wet finger out of her mouth and wiped it on her brown pants. "The voices talk constantly. They buzz all day." She brought her hands on either side of her head and held them there. "They won't stop."

"Let me see," I said. "Open your mouth and say, *Ahhhh*." When she did, I said, "I don't see anything but silver stuff. Besides, that's a really small radio to be in your *teeth*."

"They have their ways, Leslie."

Gramma poked her face into the room. "I thought I heard you," she said, shaking her head in a way that told me she was disappointed we had returned. She knew we had nowhere else to go. "We still plan to leave for the Sierras tomorrow," she said. "But I guess you guys can stay here while we're gone."

I almost asked if William and I could go with them, but I knew the answer would be no, so I didn't bother. The next day, they stocked the trailer and drove away as William and I waved goodbye.

Sitting in her bed, Mom doodled pretty flowers and swirly letters on her spiral-top notepad as if she didn't have a care in the world, but if everything was fine, then why was I so terrified to be alone with her?

chapter 4

1981

AGE 7

WHEN IT GOT DARK, THE THREE OF US PACED THE hall and rooms of the house. William shadowed Mom, tripping on her heels. Mom wrung her hands over and over as if she'd applied lotion that wouldn't absorb into her skin. She hunched over and tightened her closed lips. At one point, we settled in the den-bedroom. The harsh ceiling lights made Mom squint. She flipped the switch to *off* and turned on the credenza lamp. The bulb, through the soft plastic lampshade, gave off a dim yellow light.

William and I sat on the burgundy carpet, our backs to my couch-bed, and Mom sat on the edge of the burnt-orange velvet rocking chair. "It's my job as your Mom," she said, "to guide and protect you from all the evils of the world." I stared at her. "But I have one question," she said in a flat, hard tone that contrasted sharply with the quiet tone she'd used a moment before. "Which one of you did this?" She pointed at the credenza, which had three doors, and three knobs, which were covered with black scrunched up socks.

William and I shook our heads. Panic zoomed into my throat like electricity. When Mom accused me of something I hadn't done, or when she looked at me with furrowed brows and scowly eyes, I knew scary things stirred in her mind. She was all mixed up, but to her, everything was as clear and as real as the hand in front of her face.

"This." She pointed harder at the knobs. The socks looked like Grampa's—thin, ribbed men's dress socks.

I put my hand to my chest. "*I* didn't do it."

Mom raised one of her eyebrows. She was serious and unhappy with whichever one of us had put the socks there. She lowered the high eyebrow to meet the low one and tightened her closed mouth. Her face trembled. In the muted light, the recesses in her face emphasized her skeletal form. She sucked her cheeks in.

William sat on his knees as if to get a better view. "I didn't do it, either."

I reached for a sock, to see if holding it and unscrunching it might provide a clue to the mystery of how it got there.

"Don't, Leslie." Mom slapped my hand away. "One of you put these black socks here. One of you is lying. If *I* didn't put them there, and *you* didn't put them there, then *who did?*" This was a good question. Neither of us had left Mom's side. She kept us in her line of sight, and we were afraid to take our eyes off of her. She even waited in the bathroom when we peed.

"Shh." She pressed a finger to her lips. My eyes stung, and my breath caught in my throat. Mom shook her head, her coarse hair an unmoving cloud about her face. "They'll hear you."

How were socks stuck on the brass knobs of the credenza if nobody did it? I wrestled with every option in my mind. The socks had to be Grampa's. Could he have done it? But why would he? I grew cold, and shivers scrambled over my arms and under my ribs.

Mom pointed at us. "They programmed you like robots," she whispered. "That's why you don't remember doing it. They *brainwashed* you. And I don't know when—probably when you were at school. It's the only place they could get to you." Her whisper bloomed into a rumble. "And now you're lying, only you're *not* lying because you really *don't* remember. And now these socks are here to symbolize our torture."

She seemed scared, too, as if none of this made sense to her either. It was the end of summer. We hadn't been to school for over two months.

"They programmed us *that long* ago?" The thought struck me like thunder, waking me to the terrible possibility Mom was right. "I would remember putting socks there," I said. "And they *just* showed up tonight because I know they weren't on the knobs earlier. I would have seen them. At least I think I would have." I questioned my memory.

"It's all subliminal, Leslie," Mom poked her temple. "When you're older, you'll understand." She squinted and nodded like she was trying to teach me a valuable lesson.

"No, Mom," I said. "I swear I didn't do it. We've been with you the whole time. When *could* I do it?"

"Me, too." William crawled toward Mom and put his hand on her shaking knee. "I swear." He shook his head and then kissed one of her knees.

"Even if you don't remember it," Mom said, "I'm telling you, they had one of you do this. It's a message. They used a man's socks to say men are going to capture us. They used three socks to symbolize the three of us, *our* feet; they're going to hang us by our *feet*, upside down like bats—*black* socks symbolize *black* bats. This is only the beginning of our torture. They're going to rape us and ram us with logs."

Tears welled up. "Why?"

She pressed her finger against her lips again. "The whole place is bugged. They're listening to every word we say." She gripped one of the sock-covered knobs, slowly opened the cabinet door with a squeak, and took a sheet of paper from inside and crumpled it. "*Here.* Every time you want to talk, crumple this paper and talk in a low voice or whisper. That way, they won't be able to make out what you're saying." She crumpled and flattened the paper as she talked. She retrieved cellophane trash from her purse and crinkled it in her hand before giving it to me. "Leslie, use this. And William, use the paper. We can share it." She smoothed out the piece of paper over her knee and ripped it in two parts before crumpling each piece again. Her large, glassy eyes shone like small lakes.

Nothing made sense. I saw the socks on the credenza knobs with my own two eyes. So at least *some* of what Mom said was true. What if *all* of it was true? How could I ever be sure *I* was right and *she* was wrong? She was an adult. Didn't adults know more than kids about everything?

"Come on," she said. "I have a better idea." She shushed us again and took my brother by his pink hand out of the room. Cold overtook me. My teeth chattered. Grabbing William's free hand so I wouldn't be left behind in my room with the symbols of my rape and torture, I followed.

She took us to the kitchen. The light glowed above us, and the yellows of the linoleum and wallpaper were too bright after coming in from the dark hallway. I blinked hard. My eyes were drying out. Or maybe I was holding back tears. Rubbing my eyes made stars and fuzzy spots come into them. Mom stopped us in front of the mustard-colored oven. She turned the knob all the way. I got excited because I was so hungry I could have eaten the whole kitchen, including its printed wallpaper and dingy yellow-and-brown-patterned linoleum.

I crumpled my cellophane to ask her what she was going to cook for us.

Mom crumpled her paper. "Who wants to go first?" The kitchen ticked. My brother and I stood there, blinking at each other. Then Mom said, "Get on your knees and stick your heads in. It won't take long. You'll barely feel a thing." She'd said those words before. The memory of her sitting over me and strangling me felt more like a hammer than a thought.

I shook my head and backed away. "No!" I shouted. Snot gurgled in the back of my throat. Was she planning to cook us in the oven like the evil forest-witch in *Hansel and Gretel*? I might not have known what normal was, but this couldn't be it—our lives reduced to our own tragic fairy tale. Were other kids' moms talking about burning their heads off? William's hand slipped from mine. My eyes watered, and a terrible crying feeling rose in my chest like a storm. Everything blurred. I now hoped the government *was* listening— thought maybe there was a chance they would rescue us. But what if they took us away and hung us upside down like bats and tortured and raped us? It wasn't worth the risk.

Maybe it was time to call Auntie Philys. But I didn't know her phone number.

"I'll go," William said.

"No. Are you crazy?" I said.

"That's my good, sweet boy." Mom petted his golden hair.

"William, you can't," I said. "Don't you get it? If you put your head in there, you'll *die*. Then you'll be *dead*." I yanked on his arm and pulled him into the dark part of the kitchen where the dining table was. We hurried into the living room, which was pitch-black except for a thin light streaming in from the kitchen of death. There were two ways into and out of the kitchen, so I knew we'd have to be fast, or else Mom could capture us from the other direction.

We needed to *hide*.

William and I stepped inside Grampa's closet, trampling his shoes. I hoped for a "wrinkle in time" or a false door at the back of the closet—something mystical that would take us to another universe. If Gramma and Grampa were home, Mom would be forced to watch her actions, but with them gone, her paranoia sank its teeth into us.

William and I disturbed Grampa's shirts, pants, ties, and belts. I hushed the clanging hangers with my hands, and we squatted on Grampa's shoes with our backs to the cold wall. My body tightened; my breath got stuck in the space beneath my clavicles, making my shoulders and bones feel swollen and stiff. The sharp scent of shoe polish, leather, and mothballs made my nose tingle. I hoped Mom couldn't hear my heart pounding like a thousand drums. My jaw throbbed. I had no idea what she would do when she found us. Maybe she'd drag us to the oven by our hair, or maybe she'd squeeze us tight and shower us with kisses.

We waited. Why was everything so quiet, and why wasn't Mom booming after us or calling our names? Maybe she'd put her head in the oven and died. The thought made me woozy. I shook it away— had to focus on positive things, like waking to a new day where Mom didn't have murder on her mind.

William and I breathed in the dark with Grampa's wardrobe, waiting for a safe opportunity to exit the closet. I gave the door a slight push, and it groaned into the room. My eyes had adjusted to the darkness, and I could make out Gramma and Grampa's twin beds. William and I crept into the hall where light glowed from the kitchen. We tiptoed past Mom's room, the middle bedroom. I peeked in, hoping to find her sitting in her bed, or even standing behind the door, waiting to scare us. I needed proof she was alive. Friction from the carpet burned my feet as we shuffled to the kitchen.

She wasn't there; she hadn't put her head in the oven and died.

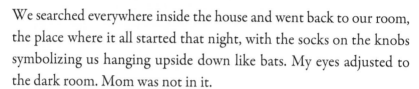

We searched everywhere inside the house and went back to our room, the place where it all started that night, with the socks on the knobs symbolizing us hanging upside down like bats. My eyes adjusted to the dark room. Mom was not in it.

"Where *is* she?" asked William.

Then I saw an orange glimmer pulsing through the open-weave curtains.

Mom's dark figure, more shadow than flesh and blood, was slumped in a chair on the back porch, smoking a cigarette. She smashed it into the ashtray on the table and stood up. Within seconds, the back door rattled, and she was inside the house again.

"Leslie. William." Her voice traveled from the kitchen to where William and I stood paralyzed. "Come here." She didn't sound angry or like she wanted to put our heads in the oven. "Mommy's been looking for you," she said. "Come out, come out, wherever you are." She giggled, and my fear flapped like a wounded bird.

William put his arms around me and buried his head in my armpit. As we were about to leave the room, a skeletal hand emerged from the hallway and flipped the light switch on. William and I jumped and cried out in alarm.

"There you are, my silly little ones." Mom giggled again as if we'd only been playing hide and seek. "We have to go outside," she said. "This whole place is bugged."

I steeled myself against the late summer chill. The night sky was dark, and the moon lit the yard in whites and grays. William was gray, too, his face and arms, teeth and hands. The tangerine tree in the center of the lawn next to where Gramma and Grampa kept their trailer was gray. How I wished their trailer was in its spot and they'd never left. How I wished they understood what we were going through so they could make it stop and keep us safe.

Mom came out a few moments later with a quilt Gramma had made. She held it up briefly and then brought it down in front of her legs.

"Body heat." William's voice cracked.

"That's right, my smart boy," Mom said. She locked us out of the house and slid the key inside her shirt, close to her armpit. "For safekeeping." She patted her chest and laughed. "Neither one of you are going to go digging inside my bra."

William and I followed her to the center of the cement in front of the garage. Like the rest of the house, the garage was painted seafoam green with white trim, but in the moonlight, it was colorless. Mom lay between the two of us and covered us with the quilt. It was cool against my skin, and I shivered every time Mom or William lifted the blanket with their movement.

"Here we are again," Mom said. "It's like we're camping. Fun, huh?"

There was nothing fun about lying on a cement seam. I imagined weeds growing into my back and trapped ants and centipedes burrowing into me with their pinching mouths and needling antennae. My scalp itched. I scratched it and sniffed my hand, which smelled like oil and bacon. When had I eaten bacon? When did Gramma last peel the fatty strips away from each other and lay them in the skillet? My eyelids drooped.

Mom pointed at the sky. "Can you see the man in the moon?"

I drowsily studied the moon. "I see it."

"It looks like a silvery seashell." Mom laughed. "Ha! A tongue-twister. Silvery seashell."

"Silvery seashell," William and I repeated. Mom gave us each a kiss on the cheek.

"I see a bunny rabbit." William pointed at the moon.

"You are so smart," Mom said. "I *do* see a bunny rabbit." She giggled her cigarette breath onto my face. "Can you see the rabbit, Leslie?"

I looked for the rabbit, but I could only make out the eyes and round *o* mouth of the man in the moon. "Yes." I burned in my lie even though it was a lie that didn't matter.

William said he, too, could see a man, one standing next to the bunny. I didn't know what he was talking about. My man was a face, a huge skull inside the sphere, with his mouth huge and ready to eat the sky. I wanted to sleep, but I was afraid to let everybody out of my sight.

The creepy crawlies came out of the ground, and Mom and William jabbered together in their private universe.

My eyelids fluttered. Sheep jumped over a fence and became bunnies hopping into ovens.

> *One sheep, two sheep, three sheep, four.*
> *Red sheep, blue sheep, close the door.*
> *One bunny, two, red bunny, blue.*
> *And all the cows fly over the moon.*
> *And someone, somewhere, silver spoon.*

Fluffy bunnies leaped over fences behind my eyelids. A spotted cow with his bell strung up on a star dangled there, his collar constricting his neck, and if somebody didn't help him, he was going to die.

The next morning, the sun shone bright and hot. Mom stood on her tiptoes at the brick wall. "Look at the neighbors mocking us. They have a tarp in their driveway. It's supposed to symbolize the three of us and how we slept in the yard with a blanket over us. Now, do you believe me when I tell you the government is watching our every move?"

William and I stepped onto the brick planter so we could peek over the wall. A blue tarp lay spread out on the ground in front of the neighbor's garage. Stray brown leaves stuck out here and there in a mess all around the tarp's edges.

Mom walked a direct line to the back door of Gramma and Grampa's house. She pulled the key out of her armpit, unlocked the door, and went inside, letting the screen slam shut.

"William," I said. "I think Mom might be telling the truth."

"I know." He blinked at me repeatedly, his long blond bangs catching in his eyelashes.

"The neighbors don't have any trees." I shuddered. "All they have is a swimming pool. Where did they get all those leaves?"

We dumped spoonfuls of sugar on our Corn Flakes and ate greedily, slurping until our bowls were empty. The events of the night before seemed like a bad dream. Mom hummed songs to herself and floated around the house like she'd gotten the best sleep of her life.

"You know we can't say anything," I said. "If Grampa finds out what happened, he'll kick us out again. Then where will we go? You don't want that, do you?"

"What are you little rascals talking about?" Mom walked toward the dining room table with a cigarette in one hand and her lighter in the other. "That's all I need. My own children telling secrets behind my back."

"If it's behind your back, wouldn't that be in front of your face?" I stared at my flakes.

"No, Mommy," William said. "No secrets. I love you."

She mussed his feathery hair. "I know you do. I just never know how much brainwashing they've done—how much they've programmed you to go against me."

"They haven't, Mommy." He swallowed. "I promise. I would tell you if they programmed me. It's like we told you last night. We didn't do anything. We swear."

"Oh, honey," Mom shook her head. "That's just it. You wouldn't know it if they programmed you. That's the whole point. You'd have no memory of it. You'd be acting according to their commands, like a robot." She booped him on the nose with her finger. "And you'd have no way of knowing what you were doing."

Mom sang "Que Sera, Sera" as she ran the vacuum over the living room carpet in preparation for Gramma and Grampa's return. When the truck pulled into the yard, I cried.

1981
AGE 8

ONE NIGHT, I DREAMED OF THE GIANT HAIR MONSTER from the Bugs Bunny cartoons, shaking its thick pelt that hid its eyes, nose, mouth, and skin. It rattled me forcefully, and right before it ate me, I woke up. The lights were on, and William was kneeling next to my bed.

My pink Barbie doll case stood upright, opened in a V in the middle of the room. Barbie and Skipper and their clothes and shoes and plastic purses were spilled out in a heap. William pointed to a sheet of lined notebook paper that sat on top of the case. He picked it up carefully as if it were made of brittle glass and held it toward me. I took it from him and got to my knees.

My Dearest Leslie and William,

By the time you read this, I will be gone. Trust me, please. This is the best way. I can't keep going. I can't protect you. I am sorry to leave you, my sweet darlings. Mommy loves you very much. You have each other. Always take care of each other. You are family.

I hope you know I've done my best to protect you from the evils of the world, but I'm not able to do it anymore. The deck is stacked against me. Against all of us. Don't trust strangers. Love each other. You're all you have.

I didn't want things to end this way. I have some advice for you, and you're smart, so maybe you'll be OK in the end. God, I hope so. When you grow up, buy guns. For protection. Don't ever have children. This isn't the kind of world to bring them into. Don't smoke. As you know, cigarettes cause cancer. I wouldn't have started if I knew that. But I was seventeen and you know it was a trick by the government to control people. Medicine controls people too, and doctors. Don't go to doctors or take medication. Don't take anything from anybody. They will want something from you even if they say they don't. Especially men. Don't trust them.

Mommy loves you very much. I'm sorry. Goodbye. I love you.

XOXOXOXO Hugs and Kisses Forever and Ever, Mommy

William's tears made roads down his pink cheeks. He sniffled and wiped his face on his arm.

"I think it means she's dead." My skin trembled, and my pulse bounced in my throat. I didn't know how to slow it. I turned the paper over as if I might find answers there.

"Let's make sure she's okay." William swallowed and his mouth clicked, like maybe he needed a drink of water.

Checking on Mom meant traveling silently down the dark hall to avoid waking Gramma and Grampa. Waking them meant showing them the truth about Mom and risking being put out on the streets. If we could only make sure she was safe, we could avoid troubling anybody else. I grabbed William's hand as I stood.

"No." He'd changed his mind. "I don't want to. She's dead." William licked away tears that fell onto his lips.

"I'll hold your hand. Come on. I can't go by myself." I was too scared to do anything alone. William thought we should wake Gramma and Grampa, but I didn't want to upset them, didn't want to make Grampa mad. William suggested that Mom would have taken the letter back if she were still alive. His intelligence amazed me sometimes.

I couldn't go back to bed without knowing the truth. Besides, if she were in the middle of a suicide, maybe I could stop her.

I returned the letter, which now felt cold and wet in my hand, to the doll case and squeezed William's hand.

We tiptoed into the dark dungeon of a hallway. My eyes failed to adjust. Was the floor there as it always had been? Or if we stepped forward, might we fall into a bottomless pit?

My foot was so pale it seemed to glow against the dark carpet.

"What is that?" William whispered, pointing to a blackish, silvery blob of a thing on the floor, right against the baseboard. Dread flushed through me, my teeth chattering over the metal taste that flooded my mouth. I swallowed a cry.

"Is that her head?" I whispered. "Oh my God." We moved so slowly, we might have been going backward, shrinking more and more as we moved, never to arrive at our destination. I don't know why I kept myself from screaming out—why I thought I should stay quiet at a time like this. If Mom *had* killed herself, she wouldn't have left her head in the hallway. Also, nothing would be right ever again. What worse harm would a scream do?

My eyes played tricks on me like other times when I saw shapes and shadows that made me think someone was sitting there waiting to get me. And when my eyes focused, I saw how silly I was.

William pulled on my hand with both of his. Hotness ran rings around my eyes and ears, and a thin, cold sweat formed between my skin and polyester nightgown.

We approached the blob, and I bent over slightly to get a better view. The blob had uneven edges, like maybe it was the back of Mom's head and she was facedown on the carpet, and her hair was all messy, making her head appear misshapen instead of rounded. As we got closer, I stuck my foot out and tapped the blob with my big toe. It was soft and crinkly, and it gave way, floating upward.

"It's a plastic bag," I whispered. I imagined her attempting to suffocate herself, gasping for the vanishing air as she sucked the bag into her mouth.

Next to the bag was the sash to her brown dress. How clearly I could see now. Had she planned to hang or strangle herself with the sash of her dress? She must have tried.

I was relieved we hadn't found Mom dead in the hallway. But was she dead in the middle bedroom only a few steps from where we stood? I pulled William gently into Mom's room. I was terrified, but I had to finish this thing I'd started. I couldn't turn back now and leave these knocking questions unanswered. The stale air smelled faintly of freshly ironed sheets, vacuumed carpet, and Mom's smoky, soap-scented skin.

When I pushed on the door, it became shiny from a spray of moonlight coursing in over the tops of the cafe curtains along the far wall. William pressed his lips into my shoulder. His wet breath left a cool spot each time he inhaled.

"Mom," I whispered. No answer. "Mom," I said again. I wanted her to hear me and be alive. I didn't want my grandparents to find the letter or the plastic bag or sash. I could see what seemed to be a body in the bed, but it might have been a heap of crumpled blankets and sheets or pillows put there in such a way to make it resemble a body. "Mom?" Leaning against the bed, I pushed the lump.

It moved.

"Mom?" William said. A groan rose from the pile, and Mom's dark face emerged from under the blankets.

"What?" she whispered. "Why are you up? Go back to bed."

How could she act as though everything was normal, as though she hadn't left a goodbye letter for us to find or a trail of weapons in the hallway?

"We thought you were dead." William climbed onto the bed.

"We read the letter." I tried to sound angry, but my voice quivered. She deserved my hardness—my hatred—for her cruel trick, but I was small and soft in my need for her love, so I climbed into bed next to her and laid my arm over her ribcage like I was the mom and she the baby I needed to protect.

In the morning, Mom, still wedged between William and me in the bed, told us not to tell Gramma and Grampa about the letter.

"There would be irreparable damage, Leslie. Do you want to be responsible for us being homeless?"

I didn't, so I kept my mouth shut. Mom made us bring her the letter, and like good children, we obeyed. I stuffed Barbie and Skipper and all their clothes in their pretty pink case and pretended nothing bad had happened in any of our houses.

Mom wasn't finished scaring us to death in the middle of the night.

A few weeks after we found the letter on my Barbie case, William woke me up, crying. "Mommy's bleeding," he said.

"You're having a bad dream," I told him. "Go back to sleep."

His tears were real, and he wouldn't leave my side. His hot hand pulled on me, and I got out of bed to make him feel better, to prove him wrong.

The familiar and frightening hallway seemed to shrink and grow at once. Uneven shadows created by a veiled light emanating from Mom's room made the walls wavy. So, William *had* been in there. With her. They did this often—shared special moments without me.

I pulled on his hand to let him know I wasn't ready to go into the room, in case he had told the truth.

William pushed the middle bedroom door open and blinked back at me like an alien beckoning me with slow, black eyes. His lips parted slightly, as if to say, *See? I told you.* He dropped my hand and walked to the far side of the bed, where he got on his knees and leaned into the mattress.

The carved wooden acorns on the bedposts gleamed. Mom sat upright, leaning against pillows, the ghost boat painting slightly crooked above her head. I lowered my eyes and forgot how to breathe.

I couldn't tell where the blood began, but it ended in smears and pools over her arms and legs and on the white sheets. Was she in pain? Why wasn't she crying? Didn't bleeding *always* hurt? Maybe she'd started her period and needed me to get her a maxi pad from the bathroom. The blankets and top sheet were scrunched over her feet and ankles, and Mom sat in her bra and underwear.

A knife lay on the bed as if it might have fallen from the ceiling.

An accident—that's all this was.

But when Mom ran the knife across her thigh and a stream of bright red bloomed over her skin, a flood of panic spread through me. No words came to my mouth, no movement to my body. My feet were glued to the scratchy carpet.

"Leslie." She shouted a whisper at me that shook me into motion. "Come here." I moved closer to the bed, where rust smells thickened the air. My nose tingled and burned. Mom pressed the knife to the old scars on her inner wrist. She slit the pale flesh. Blood streamed from it and dripped like slow wax over her thigh and onto the bed.

Her sunken eyes gaped. And she cut again.

"No. Mommy, no." Tears dropped onto the front of my night-gown. "What are you doing? Stop it."

"Shh." She winced. "Leslie." She said it like a sad song with no music in it. I didn't trust that she wouldn't cut me, so I stayed back. Too scared to take the knife, I continued to beg. If she loved me enough, wouldn't she do what I said?

"I'm getting Gramma," I said. Maybe that's what I had to do. It was the only way to end this. Maybe Gramma wouldn't even have to tell Grampa what happened, and it could be our secret. Or maybe, as if I could control Mom, I could promise Gramma it would never happen again.

William whimpered. He reached for Mom from the far side of the bed. "Please," he said.

Mom ignored him. Her eyes grew and shrank as she spoke, telling me to get the big knife from the kitchen. I shook my head. "I'm getting Gramma." But I was too afraid to leave, too afraid she might die while I wasn't looking.

So I didn't get Gramma. I glanced at the corner of the room, to the cushioned rocking chair with mustard-colored fabric printed with old-timey brown wagon wheels, barns, and horses. The fabric came down around the base of the chair like a skirt, almost to the floor. It blurred.

"Leslie," Mom hissed. "Do what I say."

"Mommy, please," William said. "Stop."

"I'm your mother, Leslie," Mom said, and she never looked less like my mom than she did in that moment. "Do what I say. *Get me the knife.*" The middle bedroom was a lake, and the bed was a boat. Mom was about to fall out of it and drown.

No answer was the right one. If I woke Gramma, Mom would hate me for sure. And if I got her the knife . . .

I tiptoed into the kitchen, careful not to make the linoleum creak. The semidarkness of early morning cast a brownish tint over the countertop. Trembling, I pulled the drawer out, wiggling it from its cubby. Dawn hovered in the distance; through the worn curtains over the sink, the sun waited to light the sky.

Searching with only my eyes, to stay as quiet as a thief, I found the big knife and lifted it from the drawer. Holding its weathered wooden handle, I reasoned I could disobey and make Mom mad, or I could give in and show her how good I was.

I walked the knife into the bedroom, and like a faithful servant, I laid it in Mom's hand.

I woke with a wet pillow and crusty eyes. Tired and sick, as if I'd rolled over from one nightmare to the next all night, I put my fingers to my tight face, wiped the corners of my eyes, and smashed the gritty white sleep between my fingers. William was still asleep.

I slid out of bed and walked down the hall, dragging my hand along the cool, dry wall.

I stopped fast. The reality of what I'd done kicked me in the gut. I'd *helped* Mom kill herself.

The door to her bedroom was open. I didn't want to go in there, but I had to see it for myself. Morning splashed its light into the room. All the bedsheets were gone, and Mom was gone, and the green and gold damask bedspread was wadded in a heap on the bed.

My stomach lurched. *She's dead. And I killed her.*

"Gramma?" I yelled out, crying. "Mom? Where's Mom?" Her body had to be *somewhere*. Rushing water echoed from the bathroom, where voices garbled. I couldn't *remember* Mom dying. Maybe it was all a bad dream. I peeked around the door to see who was in the bathtub. Gramma's back blocked my view. On her knees, she leaned over the tub's edge. Beyond her, in the tub, Mom sat, leaning toward her knees, with her head down, so I could only see her bird's nest hair and not her face. The dark water sloshed and swirled. Gramma brought the washcloth over Mom's shoulders, back, and arms, squeezing the water out as she rinsed Mom's body.

Why was Gramma washing Mom's dead body?

"Mom?" I said, thinking she could still be alive. Water gushed from the faucet. "Gramma?"

Gramma turned, lips pressed shut. Her glasses had slid to the tip of her nose. Beads of sweat lined her forehead. Mom's body didn't fall. Her head turned just the tiniest bit, and I saw the side of her face, the tip of her nose, the flesh of her lips.

Gramma didn't even look me in the eyes before slamming the door in my face. I ran to my room and fell onto my bed, burying my face in my pillow. Sadness and relief stung in that strange mix of hot and cold that made me think I'd never know the difference between the two.

William turned in his bed and opened his red eyes. Had he cried all through the night?

"She's alive," I said.

Gramma entered our room minutes later. "Your mother's had an accident," she said, wiping her hands on her pant legs as if hoping to erase the memory of things touched. "When Grampa gets home, we'll figure out some things. I just don't know what's going to happen."

Grampa came home from his work trip on schedule. He didn't want to interact with Mom. He was strong and stern in my eyes, and his voice deepened when he said, "Keep her out of my sight." His gruffness made me stay out of his way, too. He kept a strict house. But that didn't mean he knew everything that went on under his roof.

And the next morning, Mom was gone.

At the breakfast table, William and I asked where she was. Gramma wouldn't talk about her. All Grampa said was, "Your Mom is in the hospital. We'll give this a try and see how it goes." I chewed my Raisin Bran, and the raisins stuck between my teeth like glue. I thought I might pull a muscle, working to free them with my tongue. Grampa left the table, his cereal bowl in hand. He rinsed it, dried his hands, and disappeared into the living room to finish reading the newspaper.

Eyes watching the flakes drown in my bowl, I said to William, "I found you on the floor this morning. Do you remember?"

"Yeah. I was running away," William said.

That night, Grampa rolled my long hair into pink sponge curlers because I told him I wanted it to be pretty. My hair belonged only to me, and if my hair was pretty, maybe everything else would be less ugly. Maybe my sadness wouldn't be so loud, and maybe the memories of Mom and the illness that made her think and do violent things wouldn't scream and beg to be let loose in my head.

He unrolled the curlers the next morning, sitting on a chair in the kitchen under the yellow light. My hair bounced, and it was as if the curls had made every ounce of me lighter. I went to school like all the pretty girls did, and I tried to be like them, those girls with smiles built into their lips and happiness streaming under their skin.

When I lay my head on my pillow that night, an irregular lump pressed into the base of my skull. Grampa had missed a curler.

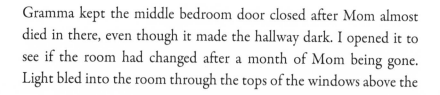

Gramma kept the middle bedroom door closed after Mom almost died in there, even though it made the hallway dark. I opened it to see if the room had changed after a month of Mom being gone. Light bled into the room through the tops of the windows above the thin, white cotton curtains, and it glimmered in the vanity mirror above the polished oak dresser. Gramma had put the same green and gold damask bedspread back on the bed. She must have gotten all the blood out. Gramma's ironed sheets and pillowcases—the ones she made pretty with embroidered scalloped edges and flowers—gave the room a slightly fresher scent.

But a vague odor of rust and tin also floated in the air like unsettled dust, knotting my stomach. Blood smell lingered like cigarette smoke; it seeped into things and people. The room and I shared blood memory. Neither of us forgot what happened in there. I smelled Mom, too—a faint fusion of her skin and hair and cigarettes. I inhaled, desperately needing to separate her from her blood.

Would she ever come back for us? Was she still my mom if I couldn't recall the shade of blue in her eyes or whether her frosty lipstick was more orangish or silvery pink?

From under the wagon wheel-patterned chair, something caught my eye. I lowered to my knees and put my cheek to the carpet. I pulled out a dry bottle with a label that read "POPOV VODKA." My hand also found an ax with a nicked and dirty handle. It had a speckled steel blade, curved and rough like it had axed a million things.

Had Mom planned to hack us to pieces as we slept?

I brought the items to Gramma who stood with her belly against the sink, washing dishes. She sighed and shook her head. She never spoke her secrets, but something changed in her eyes and mouth—a drawn down, silent type of hollowing out that made my breath shorten. It was like I had *her* eyes and mouth in *my* heart.

She took the items from me and left the kitchen through the back door. I followed her. I wanted to talk about the bottle and the ax and about how I hoped Mom would never come back, but I didn't know how to start. Gramma lifted the round lid off the metal garbage can and forced the bottle down deep. She stuck the ax far back in the tool pile behind the garage where Mom once found a wildcat that bit her in the hand so hard she bled.

chapter 6

1982

AGE 8

WILLIAM WAS CLIMBING THE BIRCH TREE IN MY grandparents' front yard, and I was in the upside-down part of a cartwheel, when Mom drove up to the curb. She didn't care that her car kissed the curb backward, on the wrong side of the street. She never cared about rules.

The window on our side was rolled all the way down, and she leaned toward us. "Kids, get in the car. Hurry." She had a white bandage wrapped around her wrist when she put her arm out to pull the lock up. Her other hand rested on the steering wheel. A bandage cuffed the wrist of that arm, too. It had only been a couple of months since she tried to kill herself in the middle bedroom. Nobody had talked about it, and now, here she was, arriving as if nothing ugly or bloody had happened.

I thought about the white lines across her wrists. I somehow knew she'd cut her wrists, and I believed her when she said the scars were from before I was born. This made me feel better, like maybe it wasn't my fault she wanted to die. Something else had made her feel like killing herself. But that was then. I couldn't shake the idea that if she loved William and me enough, she'd never, ever want to leave us by leaving the world.

William jumped out of the tree and ran to the car.

"Don't," I said to him. "Stay back." I backed toward the house. "You can't be here," I shouted at Mom. "Gramma *said.*"

"Just get in the car, now." Mom said it like she was in a big hurry. I knew she wanted to drive away with us before Gramma and Grampa could stop her.

"I'm getting Gramma." I ran to the door, but Gramma already stood there with her hands on her hips, and Grampa walked up right behind her. They darted out onto the grass. The screen door banged shut.

"Go on, Roberta." Gramma put her arm out and flicked her wrist as if shooing a fly. "Get out of here. We've had enough. Stop harassing us. You can't have them. You're not *well.*"

I beamed at Gramma, feeling secure in her ability to protect us. *That's right,* I wanted to say to Mom. *You can't have us.* Mom scowled before giving up and speeding off, using the neighbor's driveway to turn around.

"Come on, kids," Grampa said. "Get inside. We're done for the day." He went into the house first, and then Gramma, followed by William and me. The sky was blue, and all the dirty, flowery smells of spring rose into the air. It had been such a perfect day for playing outside.

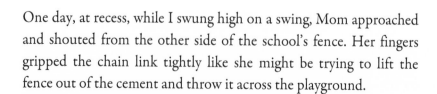

One day, at recess, while I swung high on a swing, Mom approached and shouted from the other side of the school's fence. Her fingers gripped the chain link tightly like she might be trying to lift the fence out of the cement and throw it across the playground.

"Leslie," she said. "Come out here. We're going." Her voice rushed from her mouth in a strained, harsh, and deep sound, like maybe she didn't mean for it to come out that way. She wore over-sized sunglasses and an orange and pink paisley scarf over her hair. She'd always stood out as the most stylish person in our family. And even when she was trying to steal me, she was beautiful.

I scraped my shoes along the dirt to slow myself and hopped out of the swing. Standing on the safe side of the fence, I glared at her. The way her scarf blew in the breeze made me want to run to her.

"Leslie, it's time to go." Her voice sounded normal this time. "Come around and get in the car. Hurry."

"No." I shook my head to show I meant it. "I'm getting my teacher." I turned away.

"Do what I say, Leslie. It's very important that you listen to me. We have to go."

I turned toward her again. William was sitting in the passenger's seat, which made me think I should join him. I relaxed. Then, I ran around to the skinny gap in the fence by the office and squeezed through. A bag of Fritos and a cold Pepsi greeted me when I slid into the back seat. We drove and drove for what seemed like hours. My stomach turned sweet-and-salty-sick.

When the sky darkened, I said, "What are we doing? Where are we going?" Big rigs roared past us, their headlights beaming through the chilled twilight.

"Vegas," Mom said. "But first, Apple Valley. It's where Sherry lives. You remember my girlfriend Sherry, don't you? She used to live down the street from Auntie Philys."

We exited the highway. Tumbleweeds bounced across the asphalt, and even though the windows were rolled up, a musky, earthy scent streamed into the car. Turning into a barren neighborhood with flat-roofed single-story houses, Mom eased her foot off the gas pedal and read address numbers.

"Here we are." Mom pulled into a gravel driveway.

At the front door, Mom peeled the doormat from the ground to get a key. We tip-toed through the cool, dark house. Mom switched on the kitchen lights. They buzzed.

"Be quiet inside." Mom waved her hand around as if to make sure William and I knew she meant inside the *whole* house.

In the backyard, a giant trampoline sat in the middle of a grassy area. Mom didn't stop us from climbing onto it. We alternated our jumps and tried to get in sync. I bounced and laughed until my breathing heaved, my legs ached, and so much darkness descended I could barely see where the edge of the trampoline stopped and the grass below began.

"When are we going home?" I said once we'd reentered the house. "Gramma and Grampa must be wondering where we are."

"Aren't you glad you're with me and we're reunited? Mommy's missed you so much." She leaned against the kitchen counter, smoking a cigarette, and came closer to hug William and me at the same time.

William and I said we were hungry, so Mom searched the kitchen cupboards one at a time until she found bread and peanut butter. She pulled a jar of strawberry jelly from the fridge and a knife out of one of the drawers. The glint of the steel reminded me of Gramma's knives. My stomach turned.

"Peanut butter sandwiches, it is." Mom untied the bag of bread. Her cigarette dangled from her lips, and the ash grew long like one of those snake fireworks that squirms on the asphalt.

"Mom," I said, "your ashes are gonna fall into my sandwich."

"Here." She held the knife out and pushed the bread, jelly, and peanut butter along the counter toward me. "Make it yourself, then."

I ran my finger over the knife's shallow, serrated edge, feeling good that it was in my hand instead of in Mom's. I made sandwiches for the three of us. William and I stood in the kitchen as we ate. Mom squinted through cigarette smoke. She never touched her food. We left the ingredients on the counter, and I put the knife in the sink.

"What now?" I said.

"Nothing," Mom said, tapping her fingers on the counter. "We wait."

"For what?" William asked, peanut butter clinging to his lips.

"For tomorrow, when it's safe to get back out on the road."

Sherry never came home.

Mom stared at the dark television screen. She must have been focused on the glare and slices of light and movement we created. She closed the drapes, and we sat there in Sherry's living room, saying nothing while the kitchen lights buzzed unevenly into the night.

Hours passed, and Mom said it was time to go.

"But it's not morning." I sat up on the soft couch where I'd been hoping to sleep. William slept in a recliner by the window.

Mom stared at me. "Leslie . . ." Her voice seemed to come up through her from the ground when she said my name. William jolted awake.

"Can't you for once just stop going against every single thing, and do what I say?" Mom lit a cigarette. I didn't want to get spanked, so I shut up. Mostly, Mom didn't hurt us, but the possibility of it hung over me always, like a rain cloud, heavy and ready to burst.

She'd snapped leather belts at us and whipped us with wooden spoons. Once, after I'd talked back, she grated a bar of Ivory soap on my teeth, hitting me in the mouth so forcefully my lip bled.

And then there were those other times I tried to forget.

Mom glared at me, puffed on her cigarette, and crossed her arms. She cocked her wrist to hold the cigarette away from herself a bit.

The air outside was dry and wet at the same time, as if summer and winter were battling for climate control. And that earthy scent came back strong, begging for my attention with its full, wooden spice that I hadn't smelled before this trip. It was a gloomy, warm aroma that made me long for rain.

William asked, "Are we going to Gramma's?" Hope glimmered in his voice. We believed Mom when she said we'd be at Gramma and Grampa's soon.

"We have to keep driving so the Communists don't find us." Mom's head bobbed and shook as she spoke. "We've been over this before. See all those bright headlights approaching? They never stop. Those are semi-trucks. Big rigs. They are sending a message from the government that they're after us, so we better keep running."

"They're *just* trucks, Mom." I was and wasn't sure they were *just* trucks, but I didn't know why she would lie about such a thing, so I watched those trucks intently as they came up behind us and as they drove toward us on the other side of the highway. I could only relax after each one passed when I was sure it wasn't going to ram into us.

"Don't be a brat, Leslie." Mom smashed her cigarette in the metal tray below the radio. "They are just trucks, but with Communists behind the wheel." She rambled on. "They hide behind all these machines and medical procedures and political agendas. And the trucks are their way of telling us they're going to ram into us to stun us, make us unconscious before they rape us and hang us by our feet. We are their puppets, and they're using us for their gain. William knows, don't you, my sweet boy?" Mom faced him and smiled. William nodded to show he knew. "But we're smarter than that, aren't we?" Mom patted his left leg with her right hand and then punched the lighter knob in the dash. A ring of orange glowed, and when it popped, she removed it and brought it to the unsmoked cigarette in her mouth. As she set the cigarette's tip on fire, it sizzled. New smoke burst from it, burning my lungs.

Stomach growling and eyelids drooping, I moaned, "I'm hungry." I was terrified, but I was also starving. "When are we going to eat?"

"You just had a sandwich," Mom said.

"But that was forever ago." I threw my back against my seat, again and again, finding comfort in the rhythm.

We pulled into a Stater Bros. grocery store parking lot and walked inside to use the restroom. Then, in the aisles, I cradled a bag of Oreos. William asked Mom to get Mother's Animal Circus Cookies from the top shelf. I wandered off on my own without realizing it and spotted a miniature baby doll in a sky-blue polyester dress on a low shelf. She had a beanie body and plastic arms, legs, and head, with a wisp of painted-on hair. I picked her up. A helpless baby, she fit in the palm of my hand.

"Put her back." Mom pointed at the aisle behind me. I ignored her and carried the baby around while Mom pulled a six-pack of Pepsi off the shelf before pondering the produce section. At checkout, I laid my baby on the conveyor belt.

"I told you to put that back." Settling her eyes on the cashier as if sharing a private moment of sympathy with her, Mom said, "Kids," and shook her head. Then she said, "No," with meanness in her voice. I expected her to look me right in the eye, but she avoided me, laughed unevenly, and handed the cashier some money. And I got my baby doll. In the car, I ate Oreos and caressed my hairless doll. I examined her more closely every time a car passed, letting flashes of light in. She seemed so sweet, her face frozen in smooth, mute happiness. I couldn't get over how small she was. And how perfect. And how mine.

"Leslie, wake up." Mom's fuzzy voice reverberated in my head. I felt dizzy. My nose itched with chill. I rubbed my hands on my thighs and then sat on them for warmth. The car wasn't moving. At some point, while I slept, Mom had pulled off the road and parked in a deserted lot. Evenly spaced halogen lights glowed hazy yellow. Lines marked where cars should be parked, but ours was the only one. And it was just like Mom to ignore the rules and park sideways across two spots.

She faced forward and spoke to the windshield more than to us. "This is important. Listen carefully, both of you. You must take these." Mom turned in her seat and held two white pills in her palm.

My baby—where was she? I felt all over the seat and in the cracks. Then I put my hand under Mom's seat as far as I could.

"Leslie, pay attention. It's just something to help you stay awake." She dropped the pills into my open hand. She popped the tab on a can of Pepsi, and it made a crisp hiss.

I shook my head. "I don't want to. I don't want to take any pills." I didn't trust her. If I took pills from her, I might fall asleep and never wake up.

"Leslie, *take* them, dammit."

"Did William take them? *William*, did you take them?" Were they teaming up to kill me?

"Yeah," he said. "I took the same thing, and I'm fine, see?"

I believed him, and I trusted him, but I still was *not* going to take any pills. I pretended to put them in my mouth and then took a gulp of Pepsi. I lowered my hand and dropped the pills onto the floor of the back seat, hoping they would make it all the way under William's seat so Mom wouldn't find out I'd lied. She clapped once and pressed her palms together. Then, she made me lift my tongue to show her my empty mouth in the dark.

"Here's what's going to happen." She sounded the most serious and clear she had all day. Her eyes shone like gems in the rearview mirror. "We are going to stay here in this parking lot."

Where *were* we? Would anyone hear me if I screamed?

"And I'm going to get out of the car," she continued, "and lay down with my head in front of one of the tires. And one of you is going to drive. Right over my head. Which one of you wants to do it?" Her question had a strange lilt in it, as if we'd all agreed it was an honor to be chosen to kill her. Mom looked at William and then turned around to look at me for real instead of in the rearview mirror.

"No way," I said. "Neither one of us are going to do it. We don't even know *how* to drive."

"I'll lay down right in front of the tire," Mom said, "and all you have to do is step on the gas. It'll be quick and easy." She said it so matter-of-factly, as if asking us to kill her were the most common and natural thing in the world.

"But you'll *die.*" The words wobbled through a bubble of snot at the back of my tongue. "What'll happen to us if you're dead?"

Silence took over for a minute, and the windows fogged up. And so much heaviness swelled, I was about to come apart at the seams like an overstuffed pillow.

Then, William said, "*I'll* do it."

My entire body pounded with ache. "No, just stop it. Stop it. Stop agreeing with her." I sobbed, wishing I knew where my baby doll was, wishing she could protect me. But she couldn't. She was nothing but a stupid doll with a stupid plastic face and a stupid beanie body in a stupid blue dress.

"Who knows?" Mom said. "Maybe they'll go easier on you with me gone."

"It's okay," William said. He sighed as if he were giving up.

"No." I shook my head. Could my brain be loose in there? It was all stuffy and throbby. "William, stop it." The words hooked in my throat. "Mom, *nobody* is going to drive over *anybody's* head."

Then *she* sighed and said, "Okay."

It was that simple—as if I had only confessed there were no more Oreos in the bag.

"I have another idea," Mom blurted. "I could strangle you two, and that way you won't have to suffer *any* torture. And then I'll find a way to kill myself afterwards, without you trying to argue me out of it. Who wants to go first?"

"Stop it. You're scaring me," I said. "You can't strangle me." I knew she could if she wanted to. That one night on Auntie Philys's couch, she must have seen something in my eyes that made her stop. But here in the car, making decisions in the dark, she wouldn't be able to see anything more than a flicker. If she decided to kill me, once and for all, there would be no way to stop her.

"I'll go." William's voice wavered.

"That's my good boy." Mom gave William's knee a hand-hug.

"Shut up!" I yelled. "God, why do you always have to go along with everything she says? Stop it. Nobody is going to get strangled. Everybody, just shut up." Tears rushed out, and sickness filled my stomach. I was going to throw up, or explode, or die from trying to make everybody stop saying crazy things.

Mom tapped a rhythm on the steering wheel. "If you won't cooperate," she said sternly, "there's only one thing left to do."

"What's that?" William asked. How could he be so calm? Maybe he *had* been brainwashed to do permanent damage.

"Drive us into a tree."

I grabbed the sides of her seat and shook it violently. "Let us out."

She laughed like she'd just told the funniest joke in the universe, and she turned the key in the ignition. I tensed, waiting for another word about trees or strangling or driving over heads. An emptiness came over me. Something was missing...

I'd forgotten about my baby doll. I knew she couldn't help me, but I needed to find her. I regretted thinking she was stupid. What had she ever done to me? She was a sweet, innocent baby doll. Blind in the darkness, I checked between the seams again, to see if she'd gotten stuck, and I ran my fingers over the floor mats. I patted the floor under William's seat again, but my hand found only the discarded pills. Then I checked under Mom's seat. Relieved to feel my baby's polyester body, I clutched her tightly. I wiped her on my pant leg and held her to my cheek. She smelled like cigarette ashes and dirty car stuff, but I kissed her tiny plastic face anyway. I could've fit her whole head in my mouth if I wanted to.

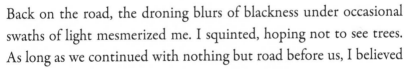

Back on the road, the droning blurs of blackness under occasional swaths of light mesmerized me. I squinted, hoping not to see trees. As long as we continued with nothing but road before us, I believed Mom would forget about her plans to kill and die.

At some point, I drifted off to sleep and dreamed:

William and I climb into the front seat of the car. William sits on a phone book because he needs a boost to see over the steering wheel. His short legs can't reach the pedals, but the car moves steadily along as if magic is driving us. We stop in an intersection somewhere, and the lights throb and streak in the night—all reds, whites, greens, and blues like a kaleidoscope blur.

"Where's Mom?" William asks.

"We drove over her head, remember?" Cars race toward us. Horns blare. "Drive!" I yell.

The other cars disappear. The city spins around us, and I grow dizzy, fall away from myself, and sink like a crumb into the seat crack. The car becomes magic again and drives us to Gramma and Grampa's.

"Where's your mother?" Gramma asks. Grampa is dusting his car with a chamois to make it shine.

We don't want to admit we killed her, so we shake our heads and say, "We don't know."

The next morning when I awoke, William was asleep in the passenger seat.

Mom's head was down, and her arm shook, so I scooted and leaned toward her, to peer over her shoulder. She wrote in her unlined notepad, with her bony hand, in red ink along the edges in all directions, in cursive here, printing there, all lowercase for several lines, and all uppercase letters for certain words. Her hand moved like a machine, gliding and writing, filling the pages with words. Some of the all-uppercase words said, "Democracy," "Murderers," "Puppets," "Manipulate," "Government," and "Communism."

"We've got to warn people," she said. "Tell them to watch out, you know, so they can at least be prepared for what's coming. We are *all* puppets, and the government is the puppet *master*, directing our every move." She unlocked her door, which woke William, and handed us stacks of flyers. She must have written them over many hours, maybe all through the night in the dark, or under streetlights, while William and I slept. "Help me." Mom got out and pulled her seat forward to let me out of the back, and William hurried around the front of the car.

As people walked from their cars to McDonald's, Mom held out the flimsy pages. She was so calm and convincing that she might have been offering coupons for free ice cream. As more people approached, she warmed up her voice, shouting, "The government is evil. You're all pawns in a Communist scheme." Mom stepped in front of a woman holding hands with a small child. The woman tried to avoid Mom, but Mom wouldn't let her pass. "Listen," Mom said. "Communism will destroy America. Don't be fooled. Protect your children!"

The woman jogged in an arc to get away. Some took Mom's flyers and then let them fall to the ground like trash. The aroma of fried potatoes wafted from the building. Zings and pings zapped inside my gut. As I handed out flyers that warned people about the government, Mom's stories about the government became my stories, my lies.

Mom shouted as she read one of her flyers: "Buy guns. Save the USA now. Russia, the drug capital of the world, is killing our children and America by using drugs as their weapons to slowly torture and destroy, manipulate, and control America. The government wears a mask of democracy." She waved the flyers above her head.

After the crowd cleared, Mom told us to get into the car. She tossed her flyers onto the driver's seat before shutting the door. I still had most of mine, too. William had given most of his away. He possessed an innocence that drew people in. He said nothing, and people willingly received his flyers. Mom leaned over the hood of the car, reaching like she was going to wash it. She had a can of spray paint in her hand. Her baggy clothes hung away from her frame, and her entire body moved as she made big, spraying sweeps on the hood. Then she moved to the door panels and sprayed something there, and finally, she ambled around to the trunk. I turned to watch her through the rear window as she released black aerosol onto the car's metallic red surface.

Then, she got into the car, and we drove away. She mumbled. Concerned, scared, and wild-looking, her eyes flashed in the rear-view. Then they widened and narrowed in a way that made them seem empty inside.

We stopped at a Burger King. I hung back and walked around the car to see what she'd sprayed. In black paint, the doors said, "WE HAVE NO HOME," and the hood said, "RUSSIA MURDERS." The trunk: "COMMUNISM RULES AMERICA." Everything was in capital letters, like shouted curses.

In the small, urine-scented bathroom, we cleaned our armpits with wet paper towels. On the way out, the high menu mocked me. Sliding into the back seat, I shivered, and pins pricked my hungry stomach. I picked up my baby doll and pressed her face against my cheek.

Later that day, as the sky darkened and we got back on the highway, Mom talked about Communism some more and about the government's ploy to slowly torture and kill Americans. With each big rig that sped past us, I shrank, wondering which one was going to ram into us.

Then, circling lights and sirens closed in behind us, and we pulled over to the side of the road. Mom checked the rear and side-view mirrors.

A police officer approached and asked for Mom's license and registration. He took them and left for a while, and the lights flashed at us through the rear window.

"Just be quiet and don't say a word." Mom's hands gripped the steering wheel. My teeth chattered.

When he returned, the officer said, "I'm going to need you to step out of the car, Ma'am. Don't make any sudden movements. Keep your hands where I can see them and get out slowly." The officer opened the door and stood back while Mom got out. He walked her to his car. A series of words ran together too far away for me to decipher.

I wiped the wet fog off the rear window. After putting Mom in the back seat of his car, the officer talked into the radio on his shoulder.

Another police car arrived, and the new officer rolled up our car window and took the keys from the ignition before escorting William and me to his car, which reeked of old sweat. A black wire cage separated us from the front seats. Mom and the other policeman hadn't left yet, and here we were, driving off with a stranger. Where was he taking us? Where were they going to take Mom? Were they going to rape us and hang us by our feet?

I wished I'd listened to Mom, wished I'd been able to draw comfort from her before being hauled off. I wanted to be back in our car with her. Nobody knew where we were, and I had no way of getting to safety. I said a silent prayer asking God to please help us. I slid one palm under William's tensed hand and reached for my baby doll with my free hand, but she wasn't there. I'd left her behind. I swallowed my misfortune and sat straight. This was not the time to let myself be destroyed.

The officer placed William and me in a small room with windows looking into the police station where uniformed men and women rushed about. A wall clock ticked, and fluorescent lights buzzed.

"I'm going to leave you here, the officer said, but everything's okay. Your grandparents are on their way."

Gramma and Grampa were going to be so mad having to come

and get us when we knew we shouldn't have gotten into the car with Mom. Before I thought to ask the cop where Mom was, he'd exited the room and shut the door with a click. William and I sat on a frigid metal table. Our feet didn't touch the floor, so we swung our legs.

"You go forward," William said, watching my legs as if timing their rhythm. "And I'll go back. We'll swing our feet opposite of each other."

I shivered as I waited, and my eyelids drooped. My back and jaw tightened like I was a ball of seized up muscle. Adrenaline and curiosity kept me awake. I watched the bustling station through the dusty window blinds.

I put my finger against the glass when I saw Gramma and Grampa talking to the officer. William sidled up next to me, leaning toward the window. Gramma's voice came to me muffled, but I made out her words: "Thanks again for finding them," she said.

Grampa had the police issue an APB, or else they might never have found us.

Grampa said Mom was in jail, so we would be safe.

Back home in my grandparents' kitchen, we were allowed to eat sugar cereal, which Grampa usually forbade, as a snack. We sat at the table with only one light on. I ate Waffelos, the sharp maple bits cutting the roof of my mouth. I didn't care. I ate fast, slurping the milk, letting it dribble down my chin. Gramma didn't correct me. Manners were unimportant at a time like this.

Once in bed with the lights out, I was too restless to sleep. I couldn't stop thinking about the things Mom said and about what she painted on the car. Sleep seemed a million miles away from me now. Like most other things I'd wanted recently, it eluded me. I stared at the bedroom ceiling in the dark and asked if William was scared Mom would come for us again. He said he was, and his answer saddened me, but it also made me feel less lonesome.

chapter 7

1982

AGE 8

A KNOCK SOUNDED ON THE SLIDING GLASS DOOR of our bedroom. A familiar voice called my name, and when I pulled the curtains aside, Mom stood there in the dark with her big, wild hair and fire glowing from the tip of her cigarette. She demanded I let her in.

I shook my head and contracted the muscles in my chest, letting the solidness of my ribcage be my armor.

"I am your mother, Leslie. Do what I say."

The night she tried to kill herself with knives came rushing back to me. I had obeyed her then and regretted my actions. She hit the glass with the palm of her hand, and it shook like an earthquake. I jumped. I couldn't stand her being mad at me. I rushed to the kitchen and unlocked the back door, but if she wanted in, she would have to turn the knob herself. I ran back to bed and hid under the covers. I held on tight. If she was going to take me, the sheets and pillows and blankets were coming, too. They provided another layer of protection, even if only in my mind. I planned out a kicking and screaming routine to alert Gramma and Grampa if I had to, for help.

William lay asleep, oblivious to things that went bump in the night. Or maybe he slept shallowly like I did, eyes closed but body bracing for disturbance, for capture, for death.

From what I assumed was the kitchen, a loud thump rang out in an echo. I imagined Mom hitting the counter with the heel of her hand. Whispers sizzled, falling glass tinkled, and a small chirp followed. I couldn't make out the words as Mom's voice rose, but Gramma whispered something inaudible next. More thumps thumped before a slamming door ended it all.

In the morning, Mom was nowhere in the house, but the ashtray on the back porch held two cigarette butts.

"Your mother's trying to get you back," Gramma said. "I don't know what we're going to do if we can't keep her from harassing us here."

I didn't want Mom to come back. Life rolled along more smoothly without her.

"Can we see her?" William asked, which just about ruined the moment.

"I refuse to let her step foot in this house," Grampa said. "She has no business spreading lies to you guys. It's not right. She's not right in the head." Gramma pointed out that Mom had a right to see us because she was our mother. I pinched a cry at the back of my throat.

William manipulated a Rubik's Cube, eyes down, concentration working like mad as if by solving the puzzle he could put Mom and our lives back in order.

Gramma answered the phone, and someone on the other end said something that made her voice shake.

I tugged on the sleeve of her homemade blouse, the one with the top hats pattern that made me think a hundred fancy men had lost their hats and Gramma's blouse had found them.

"Your mother's been in an accident," she said and hugged my brother William and me at the same time.

We asked if Mom was okay, and Gramma said yes but refused to share details. She was the keeper of hats *and* secrets.

Then, I overheard her telling Grampa that Mom had shot herself.

I imagined what it must've been like for Mom the night she crashed.

She's alone with voices raging in her head and a gun sitting in her lap. She holds it like a baby, her pale wrists shiny in the flickering light and the revolver glimmering like black licorice. Her eyes shift from mirror to mirror to mirror, to the road, where truck head-lights blind her. She thinks the Communists are coming to get her. The glossy windshield turns tail lights into blurred halos.

Then an explosion cracks, and the car careens into the concrete median like a pinball in a machine. Mom's head hits the steering wheel with the force of an arrow shot from an automatic bow. Her knees slam into the base of the steering column, and scrapes, gashes, and bruises paint a dark sunset over her skin. The gun fires into her gut, opening a bloody wound. The car is totaled, and she blacks out.

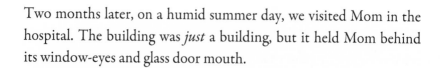

Two months later, on a humid summer day, we visited Mom in the hospital. The building was *just* a building, but it held Mom behind its window-eyes and glass door mouth.

In the parking lot, I pulled back, slipped my hand from Grampa's. I didn't want to go in. William followed Gramma. He *always* followed so easily. *I* always fought. Even when I tried to be good, I couldn't help being difficult.

Grampa said, "Come on, now," and kept his arm out toward me, and I was supposed to take it as if I didn't hate Mom for being sick and for getting into a car accident and ending up in this place. As if I didn't hate my grandparents for dragging me to see her, my constant reminder of fear and unpredictability. I wanted to avoid her and love her at the same time, but nothing *I* wanted was possible.

The slow rise in the elevator made my stomach drop. When the doors opened, Gramma gently pushed me out.

Patients in hospital gowns groaned and moaned like animals. The odor of wet cardboard and urine laced the air. Everyone was free to roam like it was one big human zoo. I looked for Mom, but I hoped I wouldn't see her. I didn't know what to say.

Grampa had kicked her out months before the accident. Now, she was more like a stranger than a mother.

Something was wrong with her. I just didn't fully understand what. Still, I knew she wasn't a drooling, moaning, brainless lunatic. Did she belong here with *these people?* She'd only crashed her car and shot herself. Then again, when she was with William and me, Mom had done many dangerous things. Maybe *I* wasn't the best judge of where she belonged.

I was going to throw up. I clutched my stomach. My body was proving to me the truth about fear and how it made me hungry and sick at the same time, made me wish I was anywhere else but here.

My nose was good at remembering the things I tried to forget. There she was, standing at the far end of the wing, and even though she wasn't bleeding this time, the tinny smell of blood filled my nose.

My insides burned. Was I on fire? I could go up in flames and nobody would notice until it was too late.

A wide-eyed man stumbled toward me, licking his lips over and over again as if I were a delicious treat for him to devour. Another man barked at the wall, and a human kitty *meow!* answered him from somewhere in the distance.

Mom smiled at me from the doorway of a room, a hospital gown hanging to her knees over a pair of sweatpants. She squinted. Her eyes were smaller than I'd remembered.

"Hi, my babies," she said. "I love, love, love you so much." She held her arms out toward us like a monster.

"I love you, too," I said, but the word "love" felt fake on my tongue, empty and sour, hollow, like we'd only just created it.

"I love you, too," someone said. It sounded full and real. William. It was the first noise he'd made since we exited the car. I'd almost forgotten about him.

"Mommy wishes she could be with you all the time." She hugged William and me again. "But they won't let me leave. And they electro-shocked me." As I pulled away from her, she put her hands on her temples. "It was awful. Come here." She moved to the bed and patted the spot next to her.

William snuggled into the space under her arm. If she wanted to be with us so badly, why did she keep doing things to separate us? She missed William's seventh birthday because she tried to kill herself that one night with a knife, and now, she was probably going to miss me turning nine.

Mom leaned back against the pillow. "Thanks for bringing them," she said without looking at Gramma and Grampa. "And *about* the accident..." She glanced at me and then at William. "I wasn't even going *that* fast."

Grampa said Mom's name and Gramma shook her head, which

meant they didn't want her to talk about the bad stuff.

"They are *my* children," Mom said.

Gramma said, "I know . . ." Mistakes, pain, and truth lay under Gramma's tongue, or maybe even deep in her throat. She ignored the subject and sent it away with a prolonged sigh like she always did.

Mom hugged us again. Then she placed my hand under her gown, along her rib cage, to the exact spot a bullet had ripped a hole in her side. It stretched on like a thin, already calloused rope built into her skin. Mom guided my fingers back and forth over the crusty scab as if she intended to teach me about the nature of woundedness.

Touching her scar like that made me think of Aladdin's lamp, and how, when you rub it, a genie slips out in a puff of smoke to grant wishes. I pulled away, but she wouldn't let go of me. She wanted more. She *always* wanted more. She squeezed my hand, and my knuckles shifted under the weight of her grasp.

"It's healing fast," she said. "I'm not even sure what happened, exactly. I didn't *mean* to pull the trigger." Her jaw shook, and she reached up to steady it. "It's the medication. It does this to me. And I can't have my cigarettes here. It's driving me crazy."

"You weren't on your medication when you crashed," Grampa said, still in the doorway like he expected the frame would protect him if the building crumbled. "You've got to take it, Roberta." He shook his head once and ticked his tongue.

"The gun wasn't even mine," Mom said. "You *have* to believe me."

"Roberta, now," Grampa said, "let's not discuss it in front of the kids. They've been through enough."

My grandparents thought they were shielding us from harm. They didn't know half of what William and I had experienced when we were alone with Mom.

We had secrets, too. *We* had protected *Gramma and Grampa* from the truth.

"I just want you to know," Mom said, "I was holding it for a friend, keeping it safe so it wouldn't get stolen in that place I was staying in."

Grampa said Mom's name again.

Mom readjusted her position on the bed as if getting comfortable with the idea of shutting up. She used her arms to boost herself, grimacing.

It was possible *she'd* stolen the gun. With Mom, truth and lies ran together in the same pack, often blending into each other to create a single mixed-blooded beast. If I was supposed to believe her about the gun, wasn't I also supposed to believe the other stories she told, like how we were better off dead than captured by spies and hung by our feet like bats in a dungeon awaiting our torture? None of those things had happened, so maybe the gun story wasn't real, either.

Was I *supposed* to believe her when she said she loved me?

Grampa said it was time to leave, and Gramma stepped toward the door.

"But you only just got here," Mom said.

"Gramma turned toward her and said, "It's been a good visit." Her cheeks were wet. "We'll call."

"*Please* come back soon?" Mom made William and me promise not to forget her. She hugged us and wiped her eyes.

The oxygen had been sucked out of the hallway, or maybe I'd forgotten how to exist. Once in the elevator, I faced the doors, and as they closed, Mom stood outside her room, watching us and waving. I was so mad at her, but I still needed her to love me. I waved, but the lip-licking man blocked my view of her. The elevator shook on its descent, reminding me of Mom's shakiness. How could I forget her? She was *everywhere*.

I didn't know the difference between how I felt and how I

should have felt. Maybe without Mom, William and I could be normal. *With* her, the only things that seemed possible were fear and my need to make her keep loving me. Maybe I didn't even love *her* anymore. I didn't know. At least, if she was in the hospital, I wouldn't have to worry she might kidnap us. I wouldn't have to fight so hard to stay alive.

But was I betraying her by wanting her to stay locked up while I was free?

My stomach growled. I imagined it was a machine, grinding its gears and eating itself. I thought about the scar on Mom's magic lamp belly. I'd rubbed it enough to bring a genie, but a genie never came.

Mom moved into an independent living center when she was released from the hospital. She had a roommate and no privacy, and she ate meals in the dining hall. She sank dollar bills into the outdoor vending machine for cigarettes and Pepsi. She used the pay phone on the stucco wall to call us on Sundays. William and I visited her a couple of times, but mostly Gramma picked up Mom and brought her to us. Free to come and go as she pleased, Mom sometimes arrived unannounced, and without an invitation, having walked the three and a half miles from Bell Gardens to my grandparents' house in Downey.

By the end of July 1982, Mom had improved considerably, and she made more promises to Gramma and Grampa about taking her medicine and staying on track. And when she crossed her heart and hoped to die as a show of how serious she was about keeping William and me in school, Gramma and Grampa softened.

We all went to the courthouse, where our immediate futures

were to be decided. The judge asked Mom about the car accident.

"I didn't mean to crash. I guess I forgot to take my medication." She seemed focused on him, and remorseful, as if she'd read books about how important it is to look the judge in the eyes and act like you mean it when you tell him what he wants to hear. The judge raised his brows and then cast his eyes over some paperwork in front of him. I wondered if he knew Mom had been jailed for kidnapping us before. Records showed some of what had happened, but I doubted the judge knew the whole truth. William, Mom, and I were the only ones who knew everything.

Mom continued, "I might have had my hand on the gun just a little, to hold it so it wouldn't get out of control and go off accidentally." A nervous laugh escaped her throat. "I was just holding it against my stomach."

When the judge regarded me, a shock of nervousness blasted through me. I thought he was going to ask me something, but he looked at Mom again and said William and I belonged with her. Grampa knitted his eyebrows together in that look of dissatisfaction he often got when things didn't go the way he thought they should. It was the same expression of disapproval he gave the television when Fernando Valenzuela threw a bad pitch. I sometimes felt bad for him because he married Gramma and inherited her five kids as a result.

The judge gave us back to Mom.

For almost a year, William and I had lived alone with our grandparents. Getting our mom back was like a present and a punishment at the same time.

"Do you love your mommy?" she asked.

I never wanted her to be heartbroken, and I'd learned that when somebody tells you they love you, you're supposed to say it back, so I had to say *yes*, and it dropped out of my mouth like it was the only word I knew.

chapter 8

July 1982
AGE 8

ON OUR REUNION DAY, MOM PULLED UP TO THE CURB in front of Gramma and Grampa's in a car I'd never seen, a white station wagon with brown paneled sides. Gramma and Grampa waved goodbye from the front door as William and I threw our things and ourselves into the car.

"Hello, my babies." Mom patted William's leg and blew me a kiss. She drove us away without another word until we stopped next to a two-story building. Sunlight sparkled through the bean trees lining the uneven sidewalk. Mom stabbed her cigarette into the car ashtray and grabbed her purse. At the doorstep, my trash bag of things slipped out of my hands like a wet fish. I felt so out of place. We didn't belong anywhere.

"Welcome. I'm Jerry," said a man walking toward us, hands out to take our things. "Good to meet you, kids." His stomach jiggled like the belly of a mall Santa, and his tight, greasy afro shone salt and pepper. "Your room is upstairs." With his chin, he indicated the general direction of the second-story window.

Once in the room, Mom said, "We're *all* going to sleep in here?"

Jerry gave Mom and us the bed and said we'd get our bunk beds out of storage and put them against the wall, which he patted with his big hand. He would sleep on the couch.

Mom let her purse slide off her shoulder onto the bed. She tightened her lips and raised her eyebrows. She didn't have any makeup on, so her blotchy, pale, freckled skin dulled in the shadowy light. Jerry kissed Mom's cheek, which made me sad. Mom had a whole life I knew nothing about. Instead of being my mom, she had been gone, meeting strangers, getting Jerry as a boyfriend. The stairs creaked as he went down, down, down.

When I met Tony, a man who shared the downstairs room with Jerry's son, he was eating a peach over the sink. "I'm on a fruit diet. Gotta stay lean for summer," he said between slurps. He held two more peaches in his left hand. I eyed the dripping peach and Tony, who was tall, muscular, and tan. And shirtless. Tony held the fruit out to me, and I averted my eyes.

Tony agreed to drive us to the community pool one day. Mom, William, and I slid into the cab seat of his red pickup. His short spiky hair and goatee glistened in the light of the afternoon sun, and his thin T-shirt clung to his chest. He asked Mom questions about our situation, and Mom answered in clips of information.

"What do you do, again?" Mom looked at Tony.

"Optometry school. That's how I met Jerry's son, Mitch, and he mentioned early on that he and his dad were looking for someone to help with expenses." He touched his hair.

"You should marry my mom," I blurted out. He smiled, staring straight ahead.

Mom shouted my name and then laughed nervously, apologized to Tony for my behavior, and reached over William's legs to slap me on my bare thigh. "Don't say things like that."

"It's all right." Tony laughed and winked at me. My face burned. When I looked at Mom for approval, her eyes narrowed. She said I needed to mind my manners. I wanted to tell her *she* had bad manners and that it wasn't polite to tie a sock around my neck while I was sleeping. That it was rude to talk about killing us and to stab herself in front of us.

As we arrived, William craned his neck toward the dashboard and pointed at the *Community Center Pool Open* sign.

In the pool, I stayed close to Tony, hanging on him and begging for attention. I told him to throw me. He lifted me out of the water and threw me into the deep end. I somersaulted, aiming to impress him with my mermaid skills, but I flailed like a drowning seal.

"Watch me," I yelled and then plugged my nose with one hand and flung myself into three or four clunky somersault turns before coming up for air. I flopped to the tiled wall, pushing off with my feet, to make myself into a missile, diving backward. I arched my body and violently pushed the water forward to rotate myself. After I gulped air upon emerging, I said, "Watch *this*." My face plunged into the water. And when I came back up, I said, "You should marry my mom. That way, you'd be my dad."

He laughed and swam away, smiling. I dog-paddled after him. Mom stood close to the wall, submerged from the boobs down. Her midsection and legs were wavy and white, distorted by the water. She demanded I go to her. She held William at the five-feet mark on the wall, resting her hand on his forearm. William held the side of the pool and pedaled his legs underwater.

Angry, Mom pulled me toward her and William. "You're embarrassing yourself." She squeezed my elbow for emphasis. "You're embarrassing *me*. Leave Tony alone." I sighed and rolled my eyes again to let her know how annoying *she* was being, and I turned back toward Tony and the deep. When I lifted my head from swimming, I scanned the pool and paddled to the edge. Panic shot through me at the thought that he'd left me. When I spotted him climbing the high-dive ladder, I relaxed. His red swim trunks and bronzed wet skin glimmered like gemstones.

At the top, Tony sauntered to the edge of the baby-blue diving board and bounced, allowing a slight bend in his knees. He soared above the board in a vertical leap. For a moment I lost him to the blinding sun, but I found him again. He dove smooth and fast, and in a splash and a suck, the water swallowed him up.

William and I rinsed off the chlorine at the showers, located outside behind a tiled, curved part of the building. A man entered while we shook and danced in the cold water. He pushed the silver button to turn on his shower and dropped his navy-blue swim trunks to the ground. I stared. It was something I had never seen before on a real live person that wasn't my little brother. It hung there like a helpless, purplish, veiny snakehead, making me sick to my stomach.

William yanked on my hand to pull me away from the showers, away from the naked man, but I resisted, entranced, by the dangling thing, floppy, fleshy, and shaking like it might come detached at any moment. The naked bodies I had watched in the motel room, the off-limits magazine I had once flipped through at a corner store— these things existed, yet I knew they were supposed to be hidden and private. I shuffled my feet and followed William with my body, but my eyes remained with the man until we turned the corner.

Mom and Tony were sitting in the waiting area. William pointed to the showers and asked them if they'd seen the naked man. Then he tattled on me for staring at the man's crotch. My stomach turned.

Mom charged toward the shower area, her macramé bag bouncing against her butt with each step.

"It's no big deal, really," Tony called out to her. "People do it all the time."

She turned toward him. "It's public indecency. It's inappropriate. Disgusting." When she didn't find the naked man, probably due to the fact that he was now clothed, Mom came back, scowled at us and then at Tony, and told him to take us home. This concerned me because, if she stayed angry with Tony, she for sure wouldn't want to marry him.

In the truck, Tony beat his hands on the steering wheel to the metal music pouring from the speakers. I stole glances at his lap. His crotch shook with the jolt of the ride. I slid away from him and leaned my head on William's shoulder. I felt as if I'd done something naughty—something nasty and unacceptable that would disappoint everyone if they knew—and a sickness rolled in the pit of my stomach. Was something wrong with me? Why was I so focused on things nobody talked about? Why was I so in love with Tony?

When we arrived at Jerry's, Mom told Jerry about the naked man, and he laughed. "If a man wants to go home in dry shorts, what's he gonna do?" He waited, staring at Mom's face.

Mom stormed off, stomping up the stairs like Godzilla, shaking the floors and the banister as she went. When she slammed the bedroom door, the living room and kitchen windows rattled. She didn't come out for the rest of the night. And when William and I went to bed, I expected her to lecture us about decency. The room was dark, and she didn't stir when I climbed into bed next to her. I needed her to caress my hair, but she was already asleep.

Summer 1982

AGE 8

JERRY, MITCH, AND TONY HELPED MOM MOVE SOME
of our belongings out of storage. It was good to have our bunk beds
again, despite the fact that I felt warm and safe sleeping next to
Mom. With the bunks and Jerry's queen-sized bed in the same
room, there was barely space to walk between them. Jerry had been
sleeping on the couch, but once we got our bunk beds, he slept in the
big bed with Mom and wore only his underwear and snored like the
motor of Grampa's boat.

Sometimes, before Jerry came in, William and I crawled into bed
with Mom, and we cuddled. Little else mattered in those moments
when the three of us clung together as tightly woven as a rug; we shut
the world out, and nothing, not even a bad thought, wriggled its way
in.

William and I made friends with Sarah and Emily, who lived across
the street, and their parents were never home. We watched *Stripes*

even though it was rated R and we knew we weren't supposed to watch it. We sang and danced to music in their living room, and when The Human League's "Don't You Want Me?" came on, I jumped up and down and announced it was my favorite song.

One afternoon, the sisters invited us to go swimming in their Doughboy, an above-ground pool, with no adults or lifeguard present.

William shot down the stairs and through the door of Jerry's apartment, shouting, "Last one there's a rotten egg!"

I adjusted the straps of my bathing suit, which I'd almost outgrown, and trotted down the carpeted steps after him, but as I reached the bottom step, Mitch, Jerry's twenty-two-year-old son, stepped in front of me. His dirty blond hair, oily skin, and thick, wire-rimmed glasses repulsed me. He always tried to make me laugh with stupid jokes.

How do you drown a blonde? What's black and white and read all over? Why did the chicken cross the road? He paid too much attention to me in general. Mitch stood at the bottom of the stairs, his eyes strange and small behind his glasses. He spread his legs wide, gripped the banister with his right hand, and slapped his left hand against the wall, trapping me. I yelled for William to wait for me, but Mitch stepped into me and sighed, and his warm breath blasted my face.

"Tell me what happened at the pool the other day." He grinned.

"Nothing. We went swimming." I avoided eye contact.

"That's not what Tony said."

He wanted me to tell him about the naked man. I moved down one step, and he leaned closer still, blocking me again with his body.

"Okay, you can go," he said. "But first, you have to give me a kiss." He tapped his scruffy cheek with his finger. His sausage breakfast breath lingered between us. He looked at my mouth. He opened his arms wide to hug me as if he thought I'd willingly give myself to him.

I shook my head no, but he persisted and asked for "one quick peck," promising it would be "our little secret." I resisted and shifted, attempting to escape. He told me not to be a baby and that I could trust him because he was studying to be an optometrist.

I hesitated. I didn't want to kiss him, but I also didn't see the harm in a quick peck on the cheek, if, after that, he would let me go. I held the banister with both hands and turned my body to the side. His eyes flashed. I closed my eyes and leaned toward him to kiss his rough, ugly face. But his cheek didn't feel like a cheek.

I looked. He was kissing me back with an open, full mouth. I pulled back. He stared straight at me, smirking and tapping his fingers on the banister.

I wiped the lingering wetness of his mouth on the back of my hand. I shoved him and rushed past him, feeling stupid as I burst out of the house.

In Emily and Sarah's backyard, William and I climbed a ladder to enter the pool. Sarah ran her palms over her wet, blonde hair. I couldn't touch the bottom and keep my head above water, so I knew it was deep, and it frightened and excited me at the same time. William let go of the wobbly ladder and sank. He coughed and flailed his arms like he was drowning.

"He can't swim?" Sarah asked.

"He can," I said.

"Good, 'cause I don't want to have to babysit anybody." Emily's hazel eyes widened as she spoke. She had a large gap between her two front teeth, which made everything she said hilarious to me. Her frizzy dark brown mane added to her cartoonish appearance. I wouldn't have believed she and Sarah were sisters if I'd seen them on the street.

By now, William had calmed, but he held on to the steel rim with both hands. "It's like a big bathtub." He smiled, but his body shivered.

In a sing-song voice, Emily said, "You're afraid of the water, you're afraid of the water." She snickered and pointed at him.

William tried to act brave, but he and I both knew waves will always try to swallow you by making *you* swallow *them*. Ever since that day at Seal Beach, I dreaded the ocean but still loved water—as long as I could see the bottom.

Emily tested William by flailing her arms about and throwing her body back, making waves roll over the sides of the pool. Sarah put her hands out in front of her as if to steady the swells. I splashed Emily in the face and immediately apologized, taking the sincerity out of my voice. She blew water out of her nose and shook her head violently before splashing me back. I knew I deserved it.

"Have you heard the legend about the twins?" Sarah asked. We all stopped fast. William's teeth chattered.

"You're cold?" Emily said, and her tongue darted between her tooth gap. "God, can't take you anywhere. Just *kidding*." She flopped back again into the water. The swell lifted us and let us down gently.

"That's what Dad always tells *her* when we go somewhere." Sarah pointed her thumb at her sister. "She's a complainer."

"He wasn't complaining," I said, feeling the need to defend my brother from this bully.

"Yeah, but you look like you're about to," Emily said. "Ha!" She splashed us again, and her sister shouted for her to stop.

"Anyways, as I was saying about the twins—" Sarah wiped water from her forehead and eyelashes. "You know that lake at the Wilderness Park in Downey?" William and I nodded. Our grandparents lived about a mile from the park, and we had played on the huge jungle gym and visited the wildlife museum there, where they had a stuffed, cross-eyed bobcat with a crooked mouth. "A few years ago," Sarah continued, "there was this crazy lady who took her twin sons there at night and drowned them."

Emily chimed in. "Yeah. When they dragged the lake, they pulled up these two boys, identical twins, and their faces were pale blue and their eyes all glassy like blind people. It was a huge scandal. Everybody knew about it. Now the mom is in the nuthouse."

"Wild, huh?" said Sarah.

Emily said. "Wild things happen at the Wilderness Park. Ha!"

I drifted to the memory of the ghost boat painting that hung above Mom's bed at Gramma and Grampa's, drifted to the memory of Mom sitting in bloody bathwater and to the memory of her gone, a ghost.

"Is this a made-up story?" I said. "You're just trying to freak us out."

"Honest to God, swear on my life, it's true," Sarah said. And I believed her because I wanted to. I needed to believe William and I weren't the only ones with a scary mom. So, there *were* moms out there who'd successfully killed their children.

"Mom tried to kill me," I said, turning water over in my hands. My fingerprints had begun their transition into prunes.

"Leslie, don't." William shook his head. Tears formed in his eyes.

I wanted to disregard William's warning, wanted somebody other than him to know what I'd been through. But I stopped myself out of guilt.

Emily yelled and splashed water in my face, accusing me of making up stories and promising she wasn't gullible enough to believe something so obviously untrue.

William's face said he was relieved, but we both knew what Mom was capable of. There was no relief in that.

Sarah continued the story about the drowned twins. "Now, they say that if you're ever swimming and feel something brush past your legs, it's the twins. Your instincts will tell you to kick and swim and get out because you'll be scared of what's below you. The twins will think *you* are their mother and that you're leaving them. They will climb you like a ladder to save themselves, and you will drown from their weight."

I knew it was true that drowning people climbed others to save themselves, because that's what William had done to me that day at the motel.

Something brushed against my leg. I screamed. Sarah and Emily screamed. William screamed. I rushed to the ladder. William scrambled behind me to get out of the pool.

"Emily, staaaahhhp!" Sarah shouted at her sister and rolled her eyes. "God, you're annoying."

Then the sisters got out of the pool, too, and we all sat cross-legged in a warm, weedy mud puddle in what Sarah said was their duck pond.

"Where are the ducks if it's a *duck pond?*" William asked. He lay back, dipping his back and head into the slimy, scummy water.

Emily scrunched her face up. "I can't believe you did that. You just stuck your head in duck-shit water. That is so gross."

"We're all sitting in it anyways." William lifted his head. "What's the difference?"

I was proud of him for defending his actions on his own. Maybe he *didn't* need me to protect him.

"It's disgusting. Now you're a *shit* head!" Emily said, pointing and laughing. William stood and marched to the house. Failing to notice the shut screen door, he plowed into it nose first, which caused him to stumble back. He didn't look at us, not even when Emily shouted again, "Shit head. Proved me right." He opened the screen and entered the kitchen. He called my name, but I stayed outside, scowling at the girls. Gap-toothed Emily, eyes shut and snout in the air, reminded me of a wet rat.

I scooped a quick handful of shit water into her mouth as she laughed.

"Better to be a shit head than a shit mouth!" I said and followed William through the house and across the street to Jerry's.

When September came, I was supposed to be in the third grade, but I didn't go to school.

William and I did attend José's eighth birthday party. Mom walked us the forty steps or so to the rear townhouse in the duplex courtyard, where José lived with his parents. A frizzy-haired woman welcomed us. I zeroed in on José immediately, crossing the room to the kitchen. A man standing next to the open freezer handed William and me paper bowls of chocolate ice cream.

William and I wished José a happy birthday. His mouth a mess of smeared chocolate, he skipped to the living room to talk to a man who rubbed his head, mussing his grease-black hair. William and I stood in the dim kitchen, spooning ice cream into our mouths. In the living room, people talked loudly over the movie playing on the television: *American Werewolf in London*. I sat on the tweed couch, and William sat on the floor next to my legs, his back against the couch.

Excitement and shame stirred in me.

The movie was intriguing and confusing. What did it mean if such scenes drew me in? Mom said the naked man at the pool was disgusting. I found him fascinating, but did that mean I was disgusting, too?

The werewolf burst out of the man under the full moon, and the creature's hunger raged in him. He howled and prowled and ripped people's throats out with his bloody mouth in a foresty midnight. My ice cream turned to soup. Even it was disgusting. The room grew hot and hazy with people and cigarette smoke.

The sharp music and the cracking of the man's bones on the TV blended with party noise until competing chaos engulfed the entire room. My stomach turned. People laughed at the scary movie. But when the man who got bit transformed into a werewolf, shedding his clothes and becoming naked in the forest, my face burned. The werewolf's glowing eyes and beastly body reminded me that things aren't always what they seem. I squinted, zooming in on the details of his private parts. The TV was too small, the scene too short as the camera panned away from the naked man to something less interesting.

The tweed couch made the backs of my legs itchy. I looked at William, who looked at me, and when our eyes met, I looked away. I wanted to belong to somebody and to feel like I was theirs and they were mine. But these werewolves and party people shrank me, made me feel ashamed and invisible.

Back at Jerry's, the quiet apartment made my hot ears pulse. I wanted Mom to stroke my hair and cool my sickness. I wanted her to sing about how I was her only sunshine, so I would forget about blood-thirsty werewolves and naked men.

I climbed the stairs before William and turned the knob of the bedroom door. Mom slept soundly, a slight smile resting on her lips, and Jerry lay next to her, snoring.

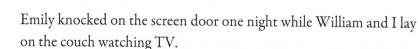

Emily knocked on the screen door one night while William and I lay on the couch watching TV.

"Psst! Hey, you guys. Come out here." She shushed us, putting her finger to her lips. Emily smiled, so I figured she wasn't holding a grudge about the shit water. William and I followed her to the side of the building where her sister waited. The four of us crept across the cement, past the big dumpsters, and through the dark courtyard behind Jerry's duplex. No moon hung in the sky, and streetlights were too far away to illuminate our path. We might as well have been in the middle of a dense forest. We stalked, hunched slightly, arms linked like we were about to square dance or do the can-can. The crisp night air tickled the fuzz on my arms and legs, sending a nervous shiver into my skin and bones. Emily and Sarah led us to the gravel patch in front of José's apartment.

Emily scooped up some gravel. Lights flickered and cast bluish shadows behind the drawn curtains. William, Sarah, and Emily's faces glowed as my eyes adjusted to the night.

"I think they're watching TV," I whispered.

Sarah scooped up a handful of pebbles. She and Emily stepped away from the picture window and tossed one pebble at a time onto the roof and at the window. We scattered and ran like hell to the front of Jerry's. We heaved quietly and then laughed maniacally in each other's faces.

"Let's do it again!" I said.

"What if they catch us?" William said.

Emily said, through the black space between her two front teeth, "We won't get caught. Come on!"

Before we reached the trash dumpster between Jerry's and José's apartments, I stopped. "Oh my God, you guys." The words quivered in my throat. "I think I see someone." My upper back ached with the thrill of our recklessness. I contracted my core and chest, hunching over and shrinking back simultaneously.

Sarah said it was my imagination. She let go of my arm and moved forward a bit, slower this time. Emily squeezed my arm and whispered that she didn't see anything.

"Right there, behind the dumpster," I said.

Why were my eyes better than everybody else's? Was I hallucinating? Were my eyes playing tricks on me? Mom saw things and heard voices. Was this how it started? I imagined a werewolf rising up on two powerful legs before attacking us and snapping us in half, ripping out our guts, and tossing our bodies over the rooftops. I knew werewolves were fake, but my imagination built the feral beast anyway. I dug my fingers into Sarah's arm.

I pointed. Sarah slapped my arm. "Just be quiet and wait." Older than all of us, she had the final word. We waited.

Then, a black figure popped out from behind the trash, snapped on a flashlight, and aimed it in our faces.

"What are you punks up to?" A clear voice boomed at us—José's father. "Get out of here before I call the cops. Go on. Go home."

We screamed, ran, and crouched against the side of Emily and Sarah's house as wheaty grass and damp dirt smells lifted from the earth.

Mom called out for William and me. We ran across the street, gasping.

"I saw a werewolf," I said. "I was the only one."

William spoiled the story and confessed that it was really only José's dad.

Mom didn't laugh. "You need to stop running amok around the whole neighborhood *just asking* the Communists to capture you." Her words made me sink into that deep, dark place that swallows hope whole. "Go to bed, now," Mom yelled and pointed to the stairs. William protested, but she shut him up. "Now." Her voice rose and face tightened. If William couldn't settle her, nothing could. For much of the summer, Mom hadn't talked about the government or torture. Now, though, summer was over, and Mom's paranoia was back.

chapter 10

September 1982
AGE 8

ONE LATE AFTERNOON, WILLIAM AND I LAY ON THE couch, our heads at opposite ends. Mom watched television, one leg over the other, letting her toe-ring sandal dangle from her foot. She had poured herself a glass of white wine, and she filed her stubby nails with an emery board. William and I giggled at each other because our feet and legs touched. Mom told us to go upstairs so she could watch television without interruption. We climbed the stairs, making faces at each other, moving our mouths and eyes to mimic Mom. Stifled laughter escaped from our throats.

It was four in the afternoon. A creepy, soft light streamed in from behind the closed curtains, making everything a hazy blue-gray. William rolled onto the cave-like bottom bunk, and I climbed onto the top. My mattress vibrated. "Did you feel that? Was it an earthquake?"

"I didn't feel anything," William said. "You're imagining things."

My mattress lifted from its frame. "William, it's you. Knock it off." But he insisted he wasn't doing anything but lying there. Then he snickered, and my mattress lifted again, higher. I dropped my head down to scold him. "Leave me alone," I yelled. He continued kicking me up and letting me fall. "You're going to make me fall, and you're gonna get crushed."

He blew out a shrill laugh. So, I called for Mom. She'd put a stop to this mattress-lifting madness.

"Be quiet!" Her yell reverberated through the walls.

Then, on its way back into the frame, my mattress missed the edge, and the bottom end tilted, falling into William's bunk. I slid into the wall. My shoulder thumped as it hit. I screamed.

Mom pounded up the stairs. "I told you to be quiet." She clenched her teeth, yanked me off the bed by my ponytail, and dragged me into the hallway. Cupping her other hand, she smacked my face, and my nose stung and tears streamed from my eyes. I put my hand to my nose, half in shock and half in hope of easing the pain. I pulled my hand away to find a smear of blood in my palm. Still holding on to a fistful of my hair, Mom turned me toward the bathroom. "Stand up." She crushed my forearm in her grip. Then she took her ratting comb from the counter and struck my bare legs with it too many times to count. I crumbled. She jerked me around like a cotton-stuffed doll. She put the comb down and hit my face, grabbed the comb again and swatted my legs.

Then, everything stopped, and it was as if the universe needed a moment to breathe. We both stood before the bathroom mirror, examining the mess she'd made. My head throbbed. I tried to focus on my wet, swollen eyes and blotchy face. I was a blur. My nose burned and twitched. My stomach and lungs turned to mush. Mom's eyes in the mirror seemed to search for something far away; she didn't see me, didn't see that I'd almost drowned beneath her hand. Blood gushed out of my swollen nose. I snorted it back in. Tasting of metal and unnatural things, my spit and phlegm lined the back of my mouth.

Mom held a wad of toilet paper to my face. I blew my nose hard. It throbbed harder. Blood spurted out of my nose in streaks, in globs mixed with snot, and it seeped into the white paper. I kept blowing. And bleeding.

"Stop blowing," she said. "You're making it worse." Mom dabbed the bloody slashes on my legs with a wad of toilet paper.

"I have to," I said, between gasps. I blew again. It felt good—to be so ugly and to make her feel guilty—to make her see how much blood she'd brought.

"Just hold the paper there and put your head back." She pressed the toilet paper into my nose and pushed on my forehead to tilt me back, forcing the blood to hide, to flow down my throat instead of out of my face.

"I'm suffocating. I have to blow it. I'm choking."

"Now, just calm down. You're not dying." She spun the toilet paper roll and gathered another wad to put against my face. I inhaled, but my lungs were too thick to catch and hold enough air. As Mom pulled the ponytail holder out of my hair, I resisted her. My scalp screamed and burned. I rubbed my head. Mom slapped my hand away and used the blood-tipped ratting comb to detangle my long, brown hair. When the blood from my nose finally stopped, Mom ran a washcloth under a stream of water and wiped my hideous, red face and neck with it. Intent on reviving me, she transformed into Mom, and the werewolf in her died.

But the damage had been done.

A friend of Jerry's came to town one night with his two small daughters. Jerry said the girls could sleep in our bunk beds.

I had already tucked into the covers on the big bed when William entered the room and pointed at the naked girl asleep on the bottom bunk with her legs spread, mouth agape. Like a frog, she lay there, ready to catch a fly.

Mom said, "The government brainwashed this man to bring his girls here and let them sleep in your beds naked. It symbolizes your rape." She flew down the stairs and returned with Jerry.

In the doorway, Jerry said, "I helped *you*, didn't I? What would you have me do? Leave them out in the cold?"

Mom folded her arms and stood at the threshold. "Get them covered up, and get them out."

The girls' father raced into the bedroom, shaking, his shoulder-length hair a matted mess. He apologized a thousand times, and I felt bad for him. The man scooped the frog girl off the bottom bunk. She stayed asleep. His eyes watered.

Jerry stood at the foot of the big bed, where William and I lay waiting for the room and air to clear so no angry mom or naked strangers would keep us awake. I was glad it was them and not us having to go back out on the streets—I knew how the cold night, with its lonely smells, wet air, and unanswered questions crawled under your skin and stayed there forever.

"They don't have to leave, right, Mom?" My throat pulsed.

"Yeah, we'll just turn over and keep our eyes closed, like this." William shifted forcefully, turning away from the door and all the people. "Promise."

The man returned in a few seconds and took his other daughter off the top bunk. He explained that it wouldn't have been right to put them in someone else's bed with dirty underpants on. His scraggly beard glistened in the lamplight. Jerry stared at Mom, hands on his hips, with eyes that said he couldn't believe her.

"Have a heart, Roberta," Jerry said.

Mom smoothed the sheets on William's bunk and then mine. "I can't afford to. Not when my kids' safety is in jeopardy."

I climbed up. The cold sheets surprised me. I scooted all the way to the wall and put my nose against it to avoid lying where the naked girl had been. When the lights went out, Mom's and Jerry's voices whispered in the hallway. I prayed for nothing bad to happen to anyone and for sleep to take away the rotten feeling gnawing at my stomach like a rat.

Soon after that, Mom cooked scrambled eggs for breakfast while singing one of her favorite songs, "Que Sera, Sera." *Whatever will be, will be.* But then Jerry smothered them with ketchup. Mom calmly set her coffee mug on the table and glared at him. "If you don't like my eggs, you *sonofabitch*, then don't eat them, but you smother 'em with ketchup? I've never been so insulted in my life."

Jerry shook his head. "Your mother's crazy, you know that?"

It did seem to be the pattern, so I didn't argue.

We left Jerry's that day, and my dreams of Mom marrying Tony and us being a happy family were crushed. It was back to the streets, back to being so tired I could scream, and back to the unpredictability that came with Mom's way of thinking. At least it also meant Mom wouldn't be marrying Jerry. And for that, I was glad.

Worried about us being on the streets, Gramma and Grampa co-signed on an apartment in Bellflower, only ten minutes from their house.

Mom promised to take her medication and keep us in school. Our two-bedroom place sat far back in a small complex with a swimming pool on Cornuta Avenue, a street whose name reminded me of *Corn Nuts.* On the day we moved into the apartment, Grampa and Auntie Philys's boyfriend carried pieces of the bunk and Mom's headboard from the truck. Many of our things had been in storage. It felt familiar and safe to have them back. We were starting fresh but not from nothing.

I unpacked the roller skates Auntie Philys had given me for Christmas. They were white with a red stripe, red laces, and a red rubber stopper. Gramma had cut my hair in a shag, and when I caught a glimpse of myself in the windows of the parked cars, I looked good, a bit older, and maybe even pretty. Smiling revealed my small, wide-spaced teeth. I closed my mouth quickly and practiced making a straight smile without parting my lips.

I skated in a small circle next to the truck on the passenger's side as Gramma climbed into the driver's seat. She put the truck in gear and stepped on the gas. But instead of backing up, she crashed right through the building.

People rushed out of their apartments, shouting and putting their hands over their mouths and on their foreheads. A man and woman exited through the broken part of the building, shouting profanities at Gramma as if she had intended to drive the truck into their living room. Grampa ran out from the back of the building, where the pool and the other apartments were, and he squeezed between the bits of broken building and the truck to get Gramma. He led her out by the elbow with so much tenderness, I had to tighten my lips over my teeth so I wouldn't cry.

Gramma said she was okay, just embarrassed.

Mom appeared and demanded that William and I go to her. I roller-skated to her, and William rushed after me.

Mom held us so we'd stay facing her. "I can't believe this. It's just like the government to do something like this." She shook her head. Her blue eyes flashed.

"At least nobody got hurt," Grampa said. "Just a bruised ego, ain't that right?" He observed Gramma with his big brown eyes.

She shook her head and giggled in a way that meant something other than laughter. "I could've sworn it was in reverse," she repeated.

"Leslie." Mom jerked me to make me look at her. "Come here, both of you." She pulled William and me farther from the crash scene, back by the laundry room, twenty feet away. "They brainwashed Gramma to make her drive into the building. It's a sign they're going to ram us with trucks."

Heat spread into my face. "It was an accident, though. I saw it happen."

"Leslie, you have to trust me. Get inside." Mom motioned for me to skate past her. She held William's hand and led him back to the apartment. Mom was supposed to be taking her medicine, so why did she say such horrifying things? I felt bad for Gramma and embarrassed for us all. The precrash me would have lurked around and made new friends, but the post-crash me stayed hidden. Mom said it was safer to stay in the apartment, which made sense and eased my nervousness.

Auntie Philys stayed with us that night, and we played Monopoly at the dining room table. Even though she blew on the dice for good luck, nobody won, and we left the game out, fake paper money, dice, cards, metal pieces, and plastic houses scattered about as if uprooted by a board game tornado.

After the shame of the crash died down, William and I spent what remained of the warm weekends swimming in the pool, and we made friends with the other kids in the complex. It seemed we might make it as a normal family. Mom took her medication. She made us wait thirty minutes after eating before getting back into the pool so we wouldn't get cramps and drown.

Mom baked peanut butter cookies with fork marks in them and

brought them to the door on a plate, bending down in her brown terrycloth romper that tied at the back of her neck. Her frosted, orangey nail polish shimmered in the shady afternoon light.

"Come and get 'em while they're fresh," she called out. All of the kids ran from the pool to our door. I ate a cookie with pride. I grabbed another cookie, idolizing Mom. Her eyes smiled as the cookies disappeared, and she seemed magically cured and healthy. I would have given up all the cookies in the world to keep her that way.

chapter 11

Autumn 1982
AGE 9

THE WEEK BEFORE THANKSGIVING, THERE WAS A knock at the door. A stranger stood there holding a grocery bag. We'd signed up to receive a free Thanksgiving basket from Goodwill. Mom set the bag on the kitchen table. She unpacked the contents: canned green beans, pumpkin, and cranberry sauce, a box of Stove Top stuffing, a small Butterball turkey, and a gift certificate to the Goodwill store.

"We're broke." Mom put the cans in the cupboard. "But at least we won't starve. I do have this." She held a wrinkled blue Food Stamp. I reached for it. Mom whisked it away. "It's not worth getting tortured," she said and ripped it to pieces. "But this—" she fanned herself with the Goodwill certificate, "we'll use." It meant she'd already inspected the certificate for bad symbols.

At the Goodwill store, Mom said William and I could get one item each. Sliding every hanger, delicately caressing its article, seeking the softest garment, and hoping to find something perfect, I was a real person in the real world, *shopping*. I came across a pair of pink

Jordache five-pocket pants. I'd never owned designer brands before except for a pair of Vans I requested for my seventh birthday, and those had been a mistake. Their brown and yellow tropical print was ugly and embarrassing, so I refused to wear them.

Goodwill had no dressing room, but when I held the pants against my body, they hit the floor at my heels. Most other pants only went to my ankles. I tossed them on the checkout counter. They were going to make me feel pretty and fashionable, something I'd dreamed about since I first rubbed crayon over paper to create stylish looks with Fashion Plates as a six-year-old.

In the second grade, I once wore a black-and-white-striped tube top. Standing at the curb, waiting for the light to change, a dirt-smudged blonde girl who was an older daycare mate of mine yanked on the front of my top, exposing my nipples. She let out a goony laugh, and I would have punched her in the nose if I hadn't needed my hands in a hurry to pull up my top. I never wore it again.

Mom wore floral scarves, wrap dresses, and bell-bottom jeans. She applied makeup with precision, lining her eyes with black liquid and gluing on a full set of false lashes. Her sense of style made me yearn for my own. And now, with this one pair of pants, I would finally have another chance at fashion. I wore the pants to school the next Monday. I felt special in my brand-new-to-me pants even though they required a hearty tug every now and then to keep them up. I preferred loose to tight because tight clothes restricted my boy-chasing abilities during recess. But the baggy crotch swished back and forth when I walked, rubbing a rash onto my inner thighs.

Once home from school, still proud of my pink pants, I rushed into the bathroom to inspect myself. Without switching on the light, I studied my face first, adjusting my smile to hide my teeth and raising my eyebrows slightly in hopes of permanently making my eyes bigger and creating more space between my eye and brow.

Standing on my tiptoes, I turned to each side, modeling my pants in the vanity mirror above the sink. I'd never had a full-length mirror—never wanted one until then. The pants were too perfect—the best pair of pants I'd ever owned. I wore them into the evening, and when it was time to change into my nightgown, I handled my Jordache pants delicately, smoothing the material as I folded.

And that's when I saw it. I brought the pants closer to my face to inspect them, dragged them into the bathroom, and held them to the light to determine if I'd only seen a shadow. It was true. My perfect pants had a continuous, jagged, yellowed stain of somebody else's pee just below the crotch and across both legs. The pink color of the pants had faded along the stain.

Why me? Why my pants? How could Goodwill sell me *pee* pants? I should have noticed. *Mom* should have. And now that I knew it was there, I could not unsee the pee.

Mom wouldn't let me get something else to replace my ruined pants. I cried and carried on, but she wouldn't budge. "There is no money for more pants. Every dollar we can spend goes toward food."

I threw the pee pants on the floor and stomped on them. "I hate you," I screamed at her.

She flipped the pages of *Better Homes and Gardens* and never looked up.

William often tried to get my attention. One night, he called my name from the front door. Annoyed, I walked into the living room, where he held the door open as he leaned his head outside.

"It's raining," he said. He knew rain was one of my favorite things. It always put a fresh, clean feeling in me, and something about the smell of wet earth made me imagine that everything bad had been washed away to make room for the good. I should have heard the drops falling to the ground or gently kissing the windows. When he made room for me, I stepped into the doorway and leaned outside to check.

And when I did, he slammed the door. But the fingers of my left hand were in the jamb, immediately below the hinge. I screamed and tried to pull my hand out, but it wouldn't come. It seemed I was stuck there for eternity, and when Mom finally opened the door and saw my bleeding hand, she screamed, "Oh, God, Oh, God" so many times, it made me think maybe God did exist and maybe He would help me. I brought my left hand to my face. The ring and middle fingers swelled. The middle finger had turned purplish-white with an outline of blood under the nail and at the distal knuckle where the wooden door had almost severed the tip.

Mom put her hand under my elbow to lift my hand higher. She said to William, "How could you?" as if he'd *planned* to chop my fingers off. Her lowered eyebrows made her look concerned and gravely disappointed at the same time. William's downcast eyes told me how regretful he was. He refused to leave my side. His wet, remorseful face sparkled in the yellow haze of the porch light.

"Didn't you see my arm up and my fingers in the door?" I shouted, making myself even more the center of attention than I already was. There existed a darkness in me, a selfishness that didn't care about putting others down if it meant raising myself up.

Mom shushed me. "You've already awakened the whole goddamned neighborhood with your screaming." She held me—at the elbow, then by the shoulder, and then at the back of my head as if cradling me like that might make the pain go away.

When the paramedics arrived, I was holding a wet towel filled with ice cubes around my middle finger. The cubes were like rocks grating my wound; the cold shot a thousand bee stings into my hand. "It's cut off," I said. "I'm not going to have a finger." I kept checking it to see if the tip had fallen off.

Mom placed the towel on my wound. The weight of her hand over the towel, over the ice, over my finger made me sicker, made everything hurt worse, made me scream more. The neighbors stood around me like a cult about to initiate me into their inner circle.

The paramedics told everyone to give them some room. They wore perfectly crisp, white uniforms. I wanted to sink into them, my own personal clouds. Mom told William to get inside the apartment, and only when he lifted from me did I realize he had been leaning against me, his head on the back of my shoulder, sobbing in short bursts. Mom stroked my hair.

In the ER, the fluorescent lighting only made my dying finger more hideous. My hand shook uncontrollably. I held it out over a cold metal tray for a man in dark scrubs to examine. He gripped my hand and squeezed and prodded my middle finger like a laboratory experiment. The pain zinged like fire in my stomach and my ribs and even down into my private parts. I wanted to scream, to yank my hand away, to run.

"You're not dying," he said. "Calm down. We'll need to stitch it up, or we can leave it as is and put it in a splint." I made him leave it alone. "Okay, Okay, Jesus. It can't hurt that bad."

But it did. I wanted the paramedics in cloud clothes to come back. He cleaned my wound and wriggled a metal splint lined with blue foam over my finger.

A nurse guided me to the waiting room, where Auntie Philys, Mom, and William were. William sat with me in the back seat of Auntie Philys's car as she drove us all home. "I'm sorry, I'm sorry," he said with his round face a moon next to me in the dark.

At school the next day, the darkening sky held the promise of rain. My finger throbbed, and my throat still had leftover crying in it. At the uneven bars at recess, Shawn Coley laughed and pointed at me, teasing that I'd flipped someone off so they broke my finger. I gave him the bird with my good hand. He laughed and shot his middle fingers like guns, alternating them in the air and making blast noises.

My finger pulsed like it had a caged beast in it. At lunch, I sprinted along the inside of the fenced schoolyard, chasing Derek's brown body through the grass until he turned around to chase me. The goal was to chase or be chased, not to catch or be caught.

In the classroom, I finished math worksheets first and filled empty time by helping classmates make sense of fractions. And when Mrs. Carver told us to picture something beautiful and describe it on paper, I wrote a few lines about a purple, puffed-up bird, small on its branch and as round as a ball. It reminded me of my aching middle finger. Birds and wounds both twitched. But unlike my finger, the fat, fake bird made me smile.

chapter 12

1983

AGE 9

WILLIAM AND I SAT AT OUR KITCHEN TABLE EATING Cheerios when a tall man in black, with brown scraggly hair and a scruffy beard, appeared at our kitchen window. He stared at us and then sauntered away. William and I screamed.

Mom rushed out of her room. "What on God's earth?" When we told her what we saw, she asked, "What is he doing back there?" She held back the thin, white curtains. "He must be a government spy." She approached us where we stood at the threshold between the kitchen and the living room. "What were you doing?" Her eyes shrank. "Where did he come from? How did he know we were here? Where did he go?"

William and I shrugged.

"That's *it*." She lit a cigarette and blew smoke at the ceiling. "If they think they can send their spies to scare us and get away with it, they've got another thing coming." She tightened the sash of her robe and marched out of the apartment, her hair a mess. In the kitchen, I stood on my tiptoes and leaned toward the window over the sink, looking as far into the yard as I could, seeing nothing but tall grass.

When Mom stomped back in a few minutes later, she kicked off her slippers and ranted, saying the apartment manager was in on it. "Told me to keep the curtains closed and mind my own business," Mom said and then mumbled a bunch of words I couldn't hear.

Milk dribbled down my chin, so I wiped it away with the back of my hand. "He didn't try to get in or say anything to us."

She removed another Marlboro from its pack and held it between her fingers. "He was spying on us"—she jabbed the cigarette at me— "and got caught." Mom struck a match, lit the cigarette, and took a puff. "Damn Communists," she whispered as she blew smoke over our heads. "Don't open the curtains or the door." Mom tugged the navy curtains tighter to close the gap. Her eyes shifted in the smoky haze. The cigarette burned brightly as it disintegrated. She extinguished it in the ashtray on the table and went into her room, slamming the door behind her. She exited again and took William and me by our hands.

She pulled us into the bathroom, pointed to the floor beside the toilet, and told us to sit. The three of us huddled together, waiting. "Be quiet," Mom said, lifting her head as if to hear the silence better. "They can't know we're here."

There was a knock at the front door.

I jumped. Panic pulsed in my throat.

"It's *them*," Mom said. "Either that, or it's the big bad wolf and he'll huff and he'll puff and he'll blow our house down." A hushed, staccato laugh floated from her mouth. I suppressed a cry that made the back of my throat burn.

I studied Mom's face. "I thought they weren't after us anymore." I placed my palm on the cool porcelain toilet bowl.

Mom pulled my hand away. "You always fight me, and you need

to stop." She stood up. "Remember to leave the curtains closed and door locked at all times."

We stayed quiet the rest of the day, and the dim apartment grew stale with unanswered questions. William and I sprinkled cinnamon and sugar on buttered toast for a snack, and we made sloppy peanut butter and strawberry jelly sandwiches for lunch. To pass the time we played Yahtzee, using our hands instead of the cup to shake the dice quietly onto the carpet. Mom remained in her room with the door closed.

For dinner, William boiled a bag of spaghetti. We ate in silence, the noodles slapping against our chins, until I was so full I wanted to throw up.

Later that night, Mom rushed out of her room, asking us if we could hear what she heard. She smoothed her hair and pinned it on either side with combs. "It's been going on for hours," she said. Back and forth, into the bedroom and out, into the kitchen and out, she paced before leaning toward the window over the kitchen sink.

Before she'd asked, I hadn't heard anything uncommon.

"It's a semi-truck." Mom hurried into her room, knelt on her bed, put her elbows on the headboard, and looked out the window. "I'm *not* crazy. Can you hear it?" William and I climbed up on either side of Mom to catch a glimpse through the window. "It's a sign. They're revving their engines. Remember when we moved in?" She scratched her head. "And Gramma rammed the truck into the front of the building?"

Of course I remembered. The shock and embarrassment of that day had stayed with me. My memory and my body always remembered the bad things.

"Well, that was the government sending us a message. Symbolic for how they are going to ram trucks into us. Semis. They programmed her to crash into the building." She shifted her eyes, got off the bed, and paced the carpet.

I put one hand on my hip and looked back at her. "That was an *accident.*" I couldn't believe we were back to this idea that semis were going to ram into us.

"Leslie, they have programmed you to go against me. You just don't know it. And it's my job to protect you—to protect all of us. Stop *fighting* me." She put her hand on the wall and knelt on the bed again, saying to no one in particular, "Probably doesn't even know he's brainwashed." She held the curtains back. A light shone in a distant garage. "Can you see it? The garage? The men standing there?" She didn't turn her head from the window. William stood to get a better view. The source—a dim, warm light—glowed from inside an open garage. "Don't let them see you." She pulled on William to make him get lower.

"I wanna see," William said, standing again, shaking the bed. He peeked over the edge of the headboard.

"Can you see that man? The one with the ponytail?" Mom pointed. "He must be in charge. He keeps looking back here and smiling like he knows we see him. My *God.* Leslie, William, turn away." Mom put her hands over William's and my eyes. We fell into each other on the bed. "Now he's pissing on the ground while he's staring straight at us. Disgusting *pig.* They're pissing on us like dogs marking their territory."

I did think it was strange that someone would rev an engine all day and for that man to smile at us and then pee on the ground next to his garage.

"We can't stay here," Mom said, finally. "We're not fools. They can ram into this apartment all they want, but when they do, we won't be in it." The engine rattled. It seemed to get louder and softer, growling and roaring, ramping up and dying down. I imagined it like a matchbox truck that gained more speed every time you charged its wheels by pulling it backward against the floor. When you finally freed it from your hands, it would zoom out of your grip and eventually crash into whatever got in its way.

Then the noise seemed so loud, I couldn't believe it. I covered my ears. Mom led us out of the dark apartment into the night, where faint, yellowy lights guided us to the laundry room next to the dumpsters. We could still hear the engine. I looked back at our apartment, half-expecting a huge semi-truck to bust through it and land in the pool like the Kool-Aid man. We stood at first, William and I leaning into Mom to hold us up and keep us warm. After a while, I sat on the pebbled stairs and put my head on my folded arms over my knees.

Mom held me by the shoulders, commanding me to stay awake. Her jaw shook, which made me think she was very cold. She was right. We had to be alert and ready to go when they came for us. Unless she was wrong. I didn't know anymore which was which. But I was so sleepy. Being forced to stay awake made me even sleepier. I wished I had toothpicks so I could use them to hold my eyes open like Tom in the *Tom and Jerry* cartoons. I poked my closed eyelids with my fingers. My head bobbed to the side. All I wanted was a soft place to sleep.

Mom pushed my shoulder, which jolted me awake. She said she wished she had some caffeine pills. I knew she meant like the pills she tried to give me the night she wanted William and me to drive over her head.

The dumpster stink was getting to me—the laundry room, too—with its disturbing mix of clean and filth. Rotten oranges, spoiled meat scraps, and sour milk cartons snuffed out the good smells. I tried to recall the scent of Mom's smoky skin or Gramma's rosy face cream, but those comforts were as lost to me as sleep. As it got later, or *earlier*, the sweet fragrance of jasmine filled the air. It made my nose tingle as if I were about to sneeze.

And all night long, the engine revved. I couldn't avoid the thought that every strange, unlikely thing Mom had said might be true. In the window of the small laundry room, my ghost-face took on strange features. My cheekbones stuck out, and my hair hung in strings. I tried to see my freckles. My eyeballs were glassy black in the skeleton of my face. Maybe facelessness was better. If I *couldn't* see myself, I didn't have to *see* myself.

I hated that morning. I hated the revving engine. Hated being so tired I wanted to die, so tired and so angry at Mom for not letting me sleep, for saying such terrifying things.

"Can't we go back in now?" I said. "I think the truck would have smashed through the apartment by now if it was going to." Mom sat on the pebbled stairs, and William sat next to her and put his head on her lap. The lights snapped off with a hiss as daylight moved in. I considered the possibility that a truck could get to us more easily by the laundry room since it was adjacent to a parking lot where cars fit.

"Do you hear that?" Mom said. "Oh, isn't this just the icing on the cake." She cocked her head toward the trees lining the other side of the wall. "Now the government is telling us we are cuckoo. Over and over just like the engine. They will not give up until they get us or at least until they drive me insane. They're watching us, mocking us, waiting for us to make a mistake. And that's when they'll strike."

The birds *were* saying, "Cuckoo." Why now, unless Mom was right and the government *did* send these birds to mock us? They cooed like broken records, but nothing twittered in the trees. I studied the trees to search for the birds. Mom put her hands over her ears.

And then, it seemed, all the trees on the street sang and cooed and shook and moved in a flurry of noise. A flock of birds blasted out of a tree across the street.

"Mom, I'm scared." William stood from the stairs. Mom hugged him and said we had to leave. The coos kept cooing and the revs kept revving, and as the apartment complex awakened, the mockingbirds quieted, the engines died, and we went back inside to collect some belongings.

Mom rushed to gather some items from her room. She shoved her writing tablet and a bar of Ivory soap into her purse. She dropped a pen, and when I bent over to pick it up, I glimpsed a big piece of poster board under her bed. It was a drawing Mom made of two boys with blond hair standing next to a house with some birds and a large yellow sun in the sky. And there was a tree and some grass and flowers. The boys held hands. At the top of the poster, Mom had written the word "TWINS."

They both resembled William. She hadn't drawn me, but she had drawn *two* of him. My heart ticked. She stripped her pillowcase off the pillow and stuffed clothes into it.

"That's what your twin brothers would look like today," she said. "If they hadn't been stolen from me. Come on."

I thought about the story of the twins who were drowned by their mother in the Wilderness Lake. But never had Mom mentioned that William and I had twin brothers. "Go get your stuff," she said. I grabbed some of my coloring books and crayons and my teddy bear, Jellybean.

We walked through the parking lot and down the street to an unfamiliar place. "You know we can't go to Gramma and Grampa's," Mom said. "So don't even ask." Would this be my life forever, on and off the streets, with Mom improving for short periods only to unravel again, worse every time?

chapter 13

1983

AGE 9

AFTER SEVERAL DAYS WALKING STREETS AND SLEEPING in parks, we returned to the apartment. But that didn't mean Mom was going to allow us to return to school.

"But we've been going all year, and nothing bad has happened." I shrugged my shoulders. She gave me the side-eye, and I knew why. The government sending engines to rev all night and cuckoo birds to coo all morning hardly counted as "nothing bad." Mom lit into me about how school brainwashed William and me and why couldn't we be like most kids who would be ecstatic about getting to stay home and play games all day. Then she added the most convincing argument of all; we had a pool to swim in. She followed it up by reminding us it was her job to protect us.

A couple of weeks later, someone knocked on our door.

"Go to your room," Mom said. "It's probably spies."

William and I hung back and listened.

Through the door, a man's voice said, "I'm a social worker assigned to your family. We received a report of truancy."

"Open the door, Ma'am," another voice said. Mom, groggy-eyed, braless, and disheveled, opened the door with the chain still hooked. I came back into the living room. Through the gap, I saw a police officer with his hand on his belt. He said he had orders to remove William and me from the home.

"Like Hell you will," Mom said and closed the door, but the cop pushed through the door anyway. "Fucking communists," Mom said, heaving all her energy against the door. She was no match for the officer, who pushed back.

"Unlatch the chain," he said. "Or I will break it."

Mom grabbed my wrist. I slid from her, backing into the room, and my arm pulsed with the memory of her grip. William leaned into me and held my hand. We stumbled together.

Mom told us to go to our room. William and I were huddled on the top bunk against the wall when a strange man entered the room. He handed us each a brown paper shopping bag and said to put some clothes in them. I pulled an outfit and a change of underwear from our dresser, and William gathered jeans and a T-shirt. The man led us into the living room, to where Mom and the cop stood. Mom mussed our hair and hugged and kissed us.

Once we'd stepped outside, Mom said, "Where are you taking them?"

The social worker handed Mom a piece of paper. "Here's the information we have at this time. You'll be notified of the court date." The cop and social worker walked us along the fence to the parking lot. Our apartment door slammed shut. I looked back to see Mom's face in the front window, half-maniacal with fluffed-out auburn hair and sad eyes. She pressed her fingers to the glass.

I choked out a few sobs in the police car but was too anxious to ask questions. William held my hand and looked at me with eyes that said *everything will be okay.*

The social worker took us to a foster home in Compton, California. The Burnses were a quiet, black couple, and their home was a cold, quiet place with wet-smelling walls, a sunken living room, and creaky bedroom floors. William and I collapsed into a lime-green bean bag in front of the television. I wanted to be back with Mom or at Auntie's with the scent of her Jean Naté bubble bath and Dawn dish soap—or at Gramma and Grampa's, where the aroma of bacon wafted from their warm kitchen and lingered in the hallway for days.

Being with strangers was the scariest thing of all because strangers don't know you. They don't know where you come from or what you've been through. Their smells are new and strong enough to wipe out all the smells you ever loved—all the smells that make you feel safe.

At the Burnses' I slept in a separate bedroom from William. I'd never slept so far away from him—we'd always shared a bedroom. The dusty wood floors squeaked when I walked, and the distance from the door to my bed felt like forever. My feet didn't belong there. My body didn't belong there. And as the floor cried its warped song, I heard a frightening truth in its discord. Mom, William, and I were falling apart for real, and there was nothing I could do about it.

In the morning, William and I talked, wondering how we would all get back together again. It made me think of Humpty Dumpty, and his big egg face was *my* face, and he lay on the ground with a cracked head, so *I* lay on the ground with a cracked head. If not even all the King's men could put *Humpty* back together again . . . I knew what that meant for me.

I wanted to go home, but I didn't even know where home was anymore. We had lived together at the Corn Nuts apartment for almost nine months. Was *that* apartment home? Was Mom going to live there now, by herself, sleeping all day with piles of laundry and dirty dishes surrounding her like mini explosions? Or would she end up in jail again? Was she back on the streets, hurrying along on foot, searching for us, trying to get us back? It was possible William and I had only made things more difficult for her. And now, with us gone, she could be free to live without the burden of us. I hoped Mom was safe. I imagined her at Gramma and Grampa's, sleeping soundly in her old bed beneath the ghost boat painting.

Was *that* home?

And at Auntie Philys's, where Auntie smoked cigarettes and we drank Pepsi and played video games in her bedroom? Was *that* home?

I was blatantly sullen the first few days as I kept my arms crossed and mouth silent. And nobody asked why. It seemed nobody cared. Or maybe they assumed I had plenty of good reasons to cry and the best thing to do was leave me to it.

At least Mrs. Burns was nice. She asked us if we wanted triple-decker sandwiches.

William, without understanding what he was getting himself into, said, "*Yes, please.*"

She made him a peanut butter and green mint jelly sandwich, which *sounded* good but in reality smelled like VapoRub. William took a bite and made a sour face. His eyes said, *Help me.* Maybe he thought I would eat the sandwich for him or push it off the table. I did nothing, and he choked the whole thing down.

We traveled with Mr. and Mrs. Burns to their relatives' house in a junkyard neighborhood in a long, skinny mobile home with a partition between the living space and a set of bunk beds. Beyond this space, there was a small kitchen, a bedroom, and a bathroom.

Jammy, a girl about my age who wanted to play cards, led me up a rickety ladder to the top bunk. She taught me how to play *Crazy Eights*. It was a fast game, unlike the evening, which seemed to move in slow motion. The adults' voices mumbled below; the kids' high-pitched voices squealed and laughed; the television blared.

As I was getting the hang of the game, Jammy sat on her knees and leaned her tightly braided head into my face to see if I was playing right. She pressed her fist into the bed, but my left hand with the smashed finger was there, still wrapped in its original gauze. Something crunched and cracked, and pain shot from my middle finger all the way to my elbow.

I pulled my hand away from her as soon as she lifted her knuckles. My hot, dizzy head swirled. She had no idea what she had done, and I was not at home, so I did not tell her—I did not scream or yell. I was not free to cry. I was only free to say nothing—to act like everything was fine even when I knew everything was so *not* fine that I almost wanted to die. I swallowed the feeling because I didn't have the courage to let it flow. That would have meant complaining and interrupting strange adults in order to get what I needed.

I hadn't peeked at my finger since the night of the accident. I was terrified to look now. Instead, I looked at William, who sat in a chair next to a black woman we didn't know. His eyes were on the television, which lit up his face with its million flashes. I cradled my left hand and sucked up the pain.

Pretty soon, the kids were bored, so we all left to go walking around the neighborhood in the dark. There were about six of us. The others skipped and laughed and talked, the older kids poking each other and whispering together in front of the rest of the pack.

We passed crooked chain-link fences, lopsided couches, and old tires in dry, weedy yards. Dogs barked and whimpered and howled from all directions in the distance.

William and I stayed close to each other. We didn't know these people. We didn't belong on these streets in this unknown town on this chilly night. My finger throbbed. I squeezed my palm and wrist with my other hand to make it stop. I was certain the tip of my middle finger was about to explode, and nobody knew or cared. Part of me wanted to squeeze my finger and snap it off, releasing streams of blood and pus, giving me something obvious to cry about.

Back in the trailer house, in the bathroom, I studied the splint and gauze around my finger. I knew something was wrong. It felt different—scratchy on top. But if I removed the gauze, I'd have no way of covering my finger again. The cotton had been on my finger so long it was a thin cast of matted fur. And I couldn't interrupt my foster mother in the middle of her conversation with a room full of people I didn't know to have her undo the fur and tell me the tip of my finger had fallen off.

In the car on the way back to the Burnses', I told William, "I think something bad happened to my finger."

William stared at my hand in the dark. "I'm sorry," he said. I knew he meant he was sorry for slamming the door on my hand. It comforted me to know he cared. Through all of this, at least I had William.

When we got back to the foster home, I told Mrs. Burns about my finger. She sat me at the kitchen table where William and I had eaten weird new food hours before. The rest of the house was quiet and dark; the only light was the one hovering above us, a cold, white light. Mrs. Burns pushed her glasses up, along the bridge of her nose. It made me think of Gramma and how her glasses always slid to the tip of her nose when she got sweaty while ironing pillowcases, plucking weeds from the garden, or cooking a hot meal over the stove.

I was afraid my finger had come off inside the gauze. I brought my shaking hand onto the table. Mrs. Burns gently tugged at the bandage. Queasiness rolled through me from head to knees. When the bandage came away from my finger, it fell to the table.

"Ew! Get that filthy thing off the table." Mrs. Burns picked it up by an edge between the tips of her thumb and index finger and threw it in the trash. I was amazed to see I had a whole finger and also an attached fingernail.

"I heard it crunch," I said. To get a better view of my finger, I put my face close to it. Mrs. Burns turned my finger from side to side, and it throbbed in her grip. She didn't know me—or what my nail looked like before. It had grown back different, narrower and bumpy on the surface. Like a lizard, regenerating its lopped off tail, my body had made a new, imperfect nail to replace the old.

Too timid to ask to see the bandage—and the gross old nail hiding inside it—too insecure to retrieve it from the trash, I followed Mrs. Burns's lead. I wanted to hold it in my hand, peel the sticky parts away from each other, turn the thing inside out. I wanted to see the blood and gunk that was left behind from my nail being torn off.

But Mrs. Burns had said it was a *gross thing*, and the house was cold and dark, and it wasn't *my* house. So, I remained silent and let my dirty bandage and my old, dead nail go out with the garbage.

Mrs. Burns was tall and thin like Mom. She had rules like a mom is supposed to. She was doing her job. But she didn't caress my hair. She didn't hug me goodnight, or tuck me in, or check for the boogeyman under the bed and in the closet. I supposed she might have done those things if I'd asked. But it was impossible to ask for what I wanted in a stranger's house. And Mrs. Burns closed the door all the way at night, which frightened me because it made everything so dark, and I worried I'd be trapped inside if someone came to hurt me.

Was William already asleep? What if I got into bed with him? I pulled the cold comforter to my chin and kept all of my limbs under it so the monsters wouldn't get me. I tried to stay awake so I would see trouble coming. I wondered how Mom was doing without us. Eventually, my eyelids got so droopy, I had to close them. The boogeyman never came, but I knew he was out there somewhere.

We were a part of this new and strange family for three weeks, waiting for our court hearing where a judge would decide if Mom was competent enough to take care of us. The day of our court hearing, Mrs. Burns drove us in her shiny, frog-green Cadillac to the courthouse. William sat in the back, and I sat in the front passenger seat next to Mrs. Burns. Between us was an *Ebony* magazine with a picture of Michael Jackson and E.T. on the cover.

Not even a year earlier, with allowance I'd saved while living with Gramma and Grampa, I bought my first cassette tape: Michael Jackson's *Thriller*. I listened to the album so many times, "Billie Jean" had a warped spot. But no matter how many times I heard "Thriller," Vincent Price's voice scared me into fast-forwarding past the song. Even so, while the tape whirred in the deck, his deep voice resonated in my head, and monsters conspired to murder me. He had me convinced that, eyes open or not, I would never be able to protect myself from something evil lurking in the dark.

The song made me think of all the things that can come after me, like policemen and Communists and Mom.

The magazine cover on the car seat next to me and Mrs. Burns reminded me of the time Mom, William, and I went to the movie theater to see *E.T.* We bought Reese's Pieces, popcorn, and Pepsi from the concessions counter. I identified with E.T. because he needed protection from those who sought to harm him. And E.T. and I both longed to go home.

"Ebony and Ivory" played on the car radio. This was us—me and Mrs. Burns. This was what this song was all about.

I also wanted it to be true that Mom, William, and I could live together in perfect harmony.

In the stuffy courtroom, William and I stood next to a social worker, a different person than the one who took us away. This was a woman who didn't tell us her name, but she wore a pretty red skirt and a matching blazer, and black cotton candy hair bloomed from her head.

Mom glided into the courtroom. We'd only been away for a few weeks, but she looked like a stranger. I hugged her like I meant it, but secretly, I hated her for being too sick to take care of us. It was almost summertime now, and because of that, the judge granted Mom custody of William and me. He held his hand out as if he were guiding us somewhere. "And, Ms. Newson, I assume you will be more responsible and take your prescribed medications? And in September, back to school they go."

"Yes, of course." Mom nodded her head so fast I expected her plastic hair combs to fall out. I wondered why the judge believed her. She'd made these promises before, and she'd always broken them. Wasn't anyone going to ask me what I thought? I didn't want to go back to the Burnses', but I was also afraid to live with Mom. Why couldn't the judge see me, gaze deep into my eyes, discover my soul, and know how terrifying life was with Mom?

My grandparents hadn't said anything this whole time, either, and nobody asked them what they thought. If Grampa had his way, he'd have requested that Mom be locked up or banished to a faraway land. Gramma would keep her in a cage like a bird so she couldn't fly away. Mom was nothing but trouble for them. Gramma's eyes showed sadness and exhaustion. Grampa's eyebrows seemed to grow closer together every time I looked at them.

It seemed to work in Mom's favor that she was capable enough to stand before the judge and rationally express her desire to do better. Keeping children from their mother was not what the court wanted, so this was "the best-case scenario," the judge said. And with my grandparents there to vouch for Mom—to show their support— we were able to prove we had somebody to help take care of us. This made the judge happy and convinced we would survive. The judge said he couldn't legally keep us from our mother since nobody was in danger. The system was "jam-packed anyway with kids who had no families at all," he said. "You are better off than a lot of kids." The judge looked at me as if I should've felt satisfied, but his comment made my head pound with guilt. I *knew* he didn't know the whole story. He stacked some papers together neatly and evened them out by tapping their bottom edges against the wooden desktop.

Could I have found the courage to tell the whole story, from the beginning, right there in the courthouse while this man sitting high on the bench stared at me? No, I could not. Nobody asked me anything, and it didn't occur to me to interrupt. The judge released us into Mom's custody on the condition that we maintain regular visits with our grandparents. Gramma agreed to stay with us in the apartment for a couple of weeks to make the transition easier.

Relieved yet terrified, I was still torn between loving and hating Mom. She hugged William and me, and as I hugged her back, I tensed to protect myself.

chapter 14

1983

AGE 9

THAT NIGHT, GRAMMA TOOK US BACK TO MOM'S at the Corn Nuts apartment. When we arrived, Mom stood in the kitchen, grilling onions and Steak-umm. The room was warm and dimly lit, like a tiny, fancy restaurant. Mom flipped food with a spatula like a beautiful chef. After dinner, we played Yahtzee. Mom giggled when she rolled five fives and clapped her hands as if to show how pleased she was, how together, and how well-adjusted. We laughed like a family, a real, normal family, and it was as if Mom had never gone crazy at all.

Mom's medicine seemed to be working again. She smiled more than she scowled. She didn't talk about the government or about how it had brainwashed William and me to go against her.

I colored for hours at a time, making drawings come to life, drawings of Disney princesses, fairytale creatures, and children from countries all around the world engaged in ceremonies and rituals of their cultures. These pictures sucked me in; they depicted cheerful, happy lives, and I, with my sixty-four-count box of crayons, could make their worlds even more alluring. And so, I was not Leslie. I was Cinderella, stepping out of my glass slipper as Prince Charming ran after me. I was Thumbelina, small enough to fit inside a flower bud in a magical garden. I was a South American girl with plaited hair guiding a calm, shiny horse through a field.

The real-world weather warmed up, which forecasted more swimming, laughter, brightness, and joy. But even meteorologists make mistakes, and on any given day, a storm could be brewing over the ocean of Mom's head, gaining speed and preparing to destroy.

When I returned to school, Mrs. Carver announced I had won the district poetry contest for my bird poem. Her arm flab shook as she handed me a certificate of thick white paper with a lacy blue border. "First Place" was embossed on a large, golden seal. She had entered it in the competition without my knowledge.

I had never won anything. Everyone hollered and applauded because I had created something good, and it made my pain seem insignificant.

I didn't tell Mom about the poem or about winning the contest. She'd already started sleeping during the day again and into the evening. She was like a ghost, leaving her cigarette smell in all the places she'd been while William and I were at school and staying absent from our lives when we returned. I had a whole life outside, away from her, too busy chasing boys around the schoolyard and seeing how fast I was, too concerned with being Mrs. Carver's teacher's pet. School was my freedom, but home was a dark, lonely place where dishes piled up in the kitchen sink and broken promises littered our lives. I believed Mom had good intentions because she sorted the laundry for the wash. But then she left the laundry basket upside-down on the brown chair, like a plastic jail cell for all of our dirty clothes.

Some people think everything happens for a reason, as if things break so they can be fixed. But it was foolish to think this way. Not everything broken can be mended.

I found a single blue pill on the floor next to Mom's bed one afternoon, so William and I stuck our hands between the mattress and box spring, and we discovered a sea of pills. I'd sensed Mom was spiraling again, but now, I knew we were headed for serious trouble. How many days had it been since Mom had swallowed her medication? And did it mean Mom had stopped doing other things she was supposed to do like pay the electric bill? The rent?

We got evicted, and even though Gramma had been checking in on us often, we were able to leave the apartment without her knowing. Mom didn't want to explain herself and see sorrow and disappointment in Gramma's eyes, so we took off, once again roaming streets on foot.

In a Sav-On drugstore, we pretended to shop, so we could be "customers" and use the restroom. My stomach was a balloon, crampy, bloated, and constipated, and then the urge to explode was so strong, so immediate, I couldn't move. Scowling, mumbling, and fidgeting, Mom might have been warding off the evil voices, but she also might have been scheming new ways to murder us or kill herself. I shifted from one foot to the other, crossing my legs, tightening everything to keep from letting go right there in the magazine aisle.

In the restroom, we used our underwear as washcloths before dumping it in the bathroom trash can. I'd tossed my last pair, so Mom pulled a white T-shirt between my legs and safety-pinned each side at my hip bones. She dressed me in her coral wrap dress. It hung on me like a muumuu, but at least it hid my bulky T-shirt diaper.

The next day, we hung around in a park and sat on a rotting picnic bench until late afternoon when hunger overtook us. We walked to a corner store and bought Doritos, Pepsi, and overripe bananas. Sitting on the curb, we gulped our snacks. Then, William and I begged Mom for money to play Joust to cure our boredom.

After Mom studied a few bills, holding them close to her face, reading and analyzing the serial numbers, she said, "I need glasses." She squinted, stretching her arm out and bringing the money in close again. "I can barely read these."

I sighed, and I became like Gramma, frustrated, annoyed, and disappointed all at once. William and I never should have made fun of her. She'd only tried her best to deal with Mom and us. I wished she was with us. I would never make fun of her again.

I exchanged the dollar Mom eventually handed over for quarters inside the musty store. William and I played doubles, riding our flying ostriches, jousting, bopping ostriches on the head to get them to drop their eggs so we could scoop them up. It was a game of recovering what was lost. One trap to avoid was the lava pit. When we failed, a giant, lava troll emerged to pull us into a red, fiery death.

Mom remained seated on the curb outside, her chest against her knees. We pleaded for her to watch how good we jousted, but she ignored us, smoking and staring into the void as if it had the answers she sought. Once all the "safe" money was gone, we strolled to the park across the street.

Twilight settled in the sky, but plenty of daylight covered the sand, swing set, and chipped green picnic tables. The prickly dry grass reminded me of a hamster's cage floor. Scattered straw stuck to my ankles through holes in the afghan when I sat on it cross-legged. I wondered if hamsters itched, annoyed by their environment. All they had was a tiny cage, a few bits of food, a waterspout, and a wheel they spun for eternity. I wanted to stop being tired and trapped and start living life again with a stable home, school, and friends. I ran to the swings to get a bit of freedom and some distance from Mom. William followed.

I pumped my legs furiously. "Swing higher," I said to William. "I bet I can swing higher than you."

He lazed about, jerking the swing from side to side, not wanting to play my game, not caring about competition. My euphoric heart pumped in time with my legs. I was a machine, swinging so high the chain slackened and yanked me in quick jolts. At once, it seemed the sand below me was lava, and an evil hand might pull me into a sea of fire as I soared low over the pit. I swung lop-sided, in uneven jerks, nearly ramming into William.

Once I evened myself out, I ramped up again, flying so high I could have strung myself up. If I did a loop-de-loop, I'd never come back down. I stopped pumping. Since the ground was molten lava, I'd be stuck between the sky and the fire, and I'd hang there forever, upside down like a bat.

Swinging didn't seem so fun anymore. I slowed, pulling my hands down so the chain wouldn't catch my fingers when it twisted. I couldn't brake fast enough. Finally, I could drag my feet in the sand and let go of my wild thoughts. I threw myself out of the seat and galloped back to where Mom sat in the shade.

"You lost," William shouted at my back. "First one to stop loses, and you stopped. Loser."

"That wasn't the game." I held back tears. "You can't just start making new rules to a game you weren't even playing." I knew *I'd* made my own rules, but I didn't like it when William used my own tricks on me. William jumped off his swing and followed me to Mom, who wrote in her notebook in long, smooth strokes and short fast scratches. Was she writing messages like the ones on the pages we handed out to passersby at McDonald's?

I turned to William. "You be Tom, and I'll be Felicia. Those are our new names, and this is our new life." I motioned with my hands to imply the entire park lay before us like a wide-open field of freedom. William agreed, skipping around the blanket before settling on it cross-legged. Mom stopped writing and glared at me. I thought she squinted because the sun made her do it, but then a feeling passed inside me like a shadow, and I knew I'd said something wrong.

William lay back, with his face to the sky. Maybe he was dreaming of an escape like I was, my mind vibrating, ignoring Mom, and plotting a fantastical journey to another place. William flopped his arm over Mom's leg. Or maybe he'd already found peace by accepting things the way they were.

The trees fluttered in the thin breeze.

"*Leslie* is stupid, and *William* is dumb." I put my arms straight above me, pretending I could squeeze the sparkly trees and the sky far beyond. The remaining sunlight broke into a million flickering specks glowing through spaces between branches and leaves.

"Leslie," Mom whispered. "Don't ever say that. Your names are your names. Don't use those other names. They're bad. Do you hear me?" I squinted at her. She stared back, her face trembling, her lips tight.

"Why are they bad?" I said.

"What's wrong with *Tom?*" William sat up.

"Not you, too," Mom said. "The last thing I need is for *both* of you to challenge me. Believe me when I say they're bad."

I rolled my eyes. Bad was being homeless when we had an auntie and grandparents who lived in roofed places. Bad was gnawing on liquor store junk food when my stomach twisted and growled for a real meal.

I let Mom have the final word, but in secret, William became *Tom*, and I, *Felicia*.

"Tom and Felicia," I whispered. And in my imagination, we lived in a perfect world where nothing chased us, nobody scared us, and we never shivered or starved ever again.

We left the park for Auntie Philys's, and when the door opened, Mom told her, "It's only temporary. Promise." She crossed her heart.

"It better be." Auntie Philys dropped her shoulders, sighed, and let us in.

"I'll buy you a carton of cigs." Mom stuck her hand in her purse.

"With what?" Auntie Philys brought a Carlton menthol to her mouth and lit it. The fluid shook inside her clear blue lighter as a wisp of smoke hid her face and her olive-green eyes for a moment before she cleared the air with a puffy hand and pushed her wide-rimmed glasses up. "You don't have any money." Her short laugh was more of a sigh than a laugh. Auntie Philys wasn't making fun of Mom. She knew Mom was more likely to break a promise than keep it. Auntie, the younger of the two, and shorter and squatter, seemed to be the follower and Mom the leader, and she mostly gave in to her only sister, especially regarding situations that included William and me. She loved us more than anything—almost as much as she loved her cigarettes.

We lived in the front room of Auntie Philys's one-bedroom apartment for a couple of months. Though she tried her best to be quiet, Auntie Philys woke me every weekday when she crept into the kitchen and flicked on the light to make her lunch. At 4 a.m., she spread crunchy peanut butter and grape jelly on sliced French bread, and she filled her Thermos with milk. The metal swish and clang of her screwing on the Thermos lid told me she was ready for work. When it was my turn to sleep on the pool raft, I did my best to move in toward the rickety wooden coffee table to make a wider path for her from the kitchen to the front door. She looked at me, her frizzy brown hair hanging from the sides of her face like the uneven boughs of a willow tree. During the day, she glued lampshades, working to make things stick together, while Mom, William, and I tried not to fall apart. We haunted the apartment with our impatience, our tempered laughter, and our anticipation of Auntie's return.

One night, Mom woke me by shaking my shoulder. William, already awake, sat cross-legged on the deflated plastic raft. Tired of asking, tired of fighting, I rolled my blanket and put on my shoes. We walked down Clark Avenue like we'd done before, past the Pizza Hut, and past the school I attended for a couple of months in the second grade. Now, the idea of school at all seemed foreign. Fourth grade had ended, and so did my chance of having a normal Mom. Here we were again, out in the cold night, with nowhere to go. What did this mean for the rest of the summer, and was Mom going to put us back in school when the new year began like she promised the judge? Mom was bound by her own laws. Why did my grandparents and the judge believe her? Was it common for people to hand out second chances—and third and fourth chances?

We stopped in a park, in the darkest part, with no lights. I surveyed my surroundings, squinting to see what I could in the distant darkness. There seemed to be only grass, trees, and houses.

"Why did we have to leave Auntie Philys's?" William said, helping Mom lay the blanket on the wet grass.

"We were going to get kicked out anyway," Mom said and caressed William's hair. My aunt had received a letter from her landlord telling her we had to go because no kids were allowed to live in the apartments. Someone said William and I had scratched bad words into their car and "abused" them. William and I defended the truth and our integrity. Mom said she believed us because it was just like the government to lie about something like that and put us back on the streets where we were like sitting ducks. Thankfully, there was no shit water anywhere. I didn't ask her why she sometimes made us stay on the streets if it made us such targets.

Mom lit a cigarette.

The next morning, before sunrise, we walked, and my unchecked anger made my jaw tight and shaky. I thought about hiding behind a tree and running back to Auntie's house. But I was a coward. Wouldn't the government pick me up? Then I would really be alone, or worse, and it would be *my* fault. Robbed of sleep, my head and stomach swirled in nausea and delirium. My hands and legs jittered. That jasmine scent clung to the air again, and it was becoming the smell of my hunger, exhaustion, and dread. I craved its sweetness but hated it for the bitter memories it pulled from me.

Eventually, when the sun blazed directly overhead, we stopped at yet another liquor store for food. Sitting on a curb with weeds growing out of the crevices, we washed Fritos, bananas, and Peanut M&M's down with Pepsi. For days, we continued through the residential neighborhoods between Norwalk and Downey and over the San Gabriel Riverbed. Cars zoomed past us. All those strangers and their lives—and not one of them knew who we were. Nobody cared.

After hours of not talking, Mom said we would go back to Auntie Philys's and everything with her landlord and neighbors could be smoothed over. "We just have to stay indoors," she said, "and be quiet at all times."

Auntie Philys would take care of us this time, wouldn't she? I would tell her how scared and sad I was, and she would protect William and me. She'd *have* to. She wouldn't care about that letter of lies from her stupid landlord, and she wouldn't let us leave. She'd know we were good kids and had nowhere else to go. Then, she'd talk some sense into Mom and keep us off the streets for good.

I couldn't wait to get there. I would eat until I threw up. I would sleep on the couch forever, even if it *was* the couch I almost died on. And I would never go outside again. I stood to gather a blanket and my teddy bear, but Mom didn't get up. "Are we going?"

"In the morning, Leslie. Relax." She patted the ground next to her. I dropped the blanket and sat. Darkness fell, and creepy crawlies came out. Soon, we were the only ones in the park—the three of us and the bugs and the jasmine, that sickening night-blooming scent I couldn't forget.

A stranger in a cowboy hat, jeans, and a button-front shirt approached us. He spoke with a Hispanic accent and asked if we needed a place to stay. Then he rattled off questions without giving Mom a chance to answer.

Was he a Communist? Was he here to brainwash us or ram us with logs or take us away and hang us by our feet and rape and torture us? Mom blinked at him as if she didn't quite know what to say.

She pulled William and me closer to her and said to the man, "Thank you. We'll be fine." He persisted, explaining he had a trailer at his house and food and extra blankets. The man and his cowboy boots and hat turned toward the parking lot by the rusty merry-go-round. He got inside his truck and kept the headlights off. I couldn't see him from the glare cast onto his windshield by the streetlight above him.

Mom got up and motioned for us to collect our things. We followed her to the truck. She knocked on the glass, and the stranger leaned over and unlocked the door. William and I climbed in first. The man drove us away from the park, and I placed my hand on Mom's arm and focused on the red fringe dancing across the windshield like bangs. I patted my own greasy bangs to set them straight. The man's stubby hands gripped the steering wheel. How glossy they were, and how dark, too. *One, two, three* streaks of light. *Four, five, six.* Street sounds drowned out my thoughts. A clanging like that of cans, chains, and bones rose from the back of the truck's camper until we parked in front of a brick house on a quiet street.

"Wait here until I tell my wife who you are." The man slammed his door shut and jogged up the walkway. When he came back to the truck, we got out and followed him inside the house. A woman he said was his wife passed through the hall to the kitchen. She had a slight black mustache across her lip that glistened as she stood over the stove, scrambling eggs and heating flour tortillas. I ate fast, barely chewing. I coughed and choked; my eyes watered and I resumed chewing slowly like a normal person.

The TV was on when we entered the upstairs bedroom. *Poltergeist.* Mom took a shower first while William and I watched the movie. Skeletons were bobbing in the mud when Mom exited the bathroom with one towel wrapped around her body and another around her head. She sat on the toilet while I showered, and William sat on the fluffy, white bathroom rug. I was used to baths, so it was awkward standing there in a strange bathtub, letting water crawl down my body.

The man led us to his trailer parked on the street. The whole way down the stairs and out the door, I breathed in onions, and it made me feel so warm and cozy I wanted to cry. We got set up in the trailer with blankets and pillows. Mom tucked William and me into tight cocoons. Then, everything was quiet. My eyes couldn't sit still. They were closed but restless. Settling into sleep one layer at a time—first my skin, then my blood, then my bones—my body fell.

I woke to Mom's voice. Whispering at my face, she said, "Come on. Let's get out of here. They're watching."

I thought she meant the poltergeists. My blanket cocoon was so tight I couldn't sit up. The space in front of my face was dark and staticky. I moaned and kicked. I accidentally punched myself in the face when my hand finally broke loose.

After putting our shoes on, William and I followed Mom out of the trailer as quietly as ghosts without chains, and we walked and walked. Night became dawn and dawn, day. I kept thinking about being somebody else's daughter. Maybe my name *could* be Felicia. Girls named Felicia *never* had to wake up in the middle of the night and roam the streets for a million miles when all they wanted was sleep. If I collapsed on the sidewalk, I wouldn't care. I would sink into the earth like a skeleton and become invisible as everybody stepped over me, over me, over me . . .

chapter 15

1983–1984

AGE 9–10

THIS TIME, WHEN MOM SAID WE WERE GOING BACK to Auntie Philys's, she'd told the truth. When we arrived, I rushed to the rocking chair. My body ached as it lowered itself onto the cushion. I pumped my feet against the floor, rocking and hitting the stack of jumbo cardboard boxes behind me with a thump. In the kitchen, Mom untwisted a bag of sliced French bread.

Auntie Philys was at work, gluing lampshades, but she was also very much in the apartment. The menthol trail of her Carltons and the sudsy memory of her Jean Naté bubble bath tangled together in the air. And although the towels lay securely in their cupboard, their bouquet of detergent wafted into the hallway. My head swirled in fuzzy comfort and pulsed with hunger. The fluffy canary sang his broken song. Why couldn't I have been born a bird? I'd make sweet, smooth music and hop around in my simple wire cage . . .

Fearing Mom was about to yank us onto the streets again in a minute, I had to think fast. My aunt might sense that we'd been at her house. Maybe we'd leave crumbs on the counter, drop them along the sidewalk as we went, so she could find us. Or perhaps the rocking chair would still be rocking, and Auntie would know I'd been sitting there. She might come after us because she'd know we couldn't have gone far.

Mom opened the fridge and clutched the milk jug. I brought the peanut butter and jelly down from the cupboard. Mom made me a sandwich; I took it from her like I was taking back something she'd stolen from me. The bread stuck in my teeth. The sweet jelly and salty peanut butter melted together on my tongue and made the corners of my mouth sticky. We each popped the tab of an RC Cola. The cold sugar filled my mouth, and the carbonation burned so good. For a moment, that's the only thing that mattered, and I was at peace.

Other than our chewing and gulping, and the sizzle of carbonation, the room was silent. I went back to the chair. Rock, *thump,* rock, *thump.*

Things were different at my grandparents' house—everything had a place. Everything belonged but us. But here, there was no room for anything, *especially* us.

Mom slung her purse over her shoulder and raced to the door.

I didn't get up. "I'm not going." Hearing myself say the words aloud frightened me. Maybe I *did* have a choice in the matter—I could *refuse* to go back out on the streets.

Mom grabbed my wrist. Her wrist scars gleamed in the warm light. The truth of Mom's illness screamed. She'd cut herself over decade-old scars. If her illness had kept her prisoner for so many years, would it ever let her go?

All the destructive things she'd done, all the strange, frightening things she'd said—they knocked at my sense of logic. Going with Mom when I could stay behind suddenly seemed like the stupidest, scariest choice I could make. I pressed my feet into the floor. "No.

I'm not going, and you can't make me. William, you should stay, too. Stay with me, please." I stared into his eyes. Rebellion pounded in me but so did hope—hope that I might be able to change Mom's mind.

"No, I'm going with Mom," William said, grape jelly on his cheeks, flickering as he spoke.

"Fine, leave me here by myself." If I made him feel guilty, his conscience might wake up, and if he stayed, Mom would, too. I knew she would never leave both of us. She would never leave William. He was Mom's favorite, and she was his. While I knew it to be true, I needed to disprove it. So, there I was with my big mouth and my unrealistic demands, ruining everything. I was the outcast, fighting every step of the way.

"I'm waiting here for Auntie Philys." I folded my arms across my chest. "She'll take care of me." Mom clutched my other wrist, and I yanked both from her grip with one violent burst of force. She sighed and moved to the door. "Suit yourself, but I think you're about to be very disappointed." Mom and William and two trash bags of belongings left, and the door clicked shut behind them.

I pumped my feet against the floor, letting the rhythm distract me as I licked salty tears from my lips. Sitting on the pine bookshelf that held Auntie's glass menagerie, a fox with a white-tipped tail stared at me with dead eyes. With each pump of my legs, the chair clicked, and the storm of reality welled up in me higher and higher. Had I ever been this alone? I waited there for hours.

Then, the lock turned with a clack, and I shuddered.

It was Auntie Philys. She jumped at the sight of me. I must have startled her, sitting there so quietly, unexpectedly. Standing in the doorway with big eyes, she stared like she didn't believe I was real. She shut the door behind her and dropped her purse on the desk before approaching me. She asked where William and Mom were.

Maybe she thought something had happened and William and Mom were dead. She bent to hug me, and I stood to meet her, putting my arms around her.

"They're gone," I said. "I stayed here to wait for you." She let me go and backed away. A mass of frizzy hair surrounded her questioning face. I wanted to sink into her until I had no more tears, until I was all cleaned out and new again. Then she could be my mom, and we would live there happily ever after. She'd let me color in her thick Disney coloring book that was off-limits to people who couldn't color within the lines. She'd love me and tickle me, and I'd laugh until I forgot about everything that came before.

"I can't take you." She shook her head. "I have to work. I can't afford it." Gears in her eyes turned and stopped, getting stuck on every excuse not to take me.

"I'll be good. I promise. I'll stay out of your way. I'll be as quiet as a mouse, and I'll even do the dishes."

She disconnected from me and lit a cigarette.

That night, since my grandparents were out of town, Auntie Philys drove me to my aunt and uncle's in Yorba Linda, California.

My uncle Howard was Mom and Auntie's oldest brother. He and his wife owned a two-story home with a pool and plenty of room for a nine-year-old. My aunt Carrie answered the door and hugged me as I entered. She thanked Auntie Philys and told her they'd figure something out once my grandparents got home.

I'd already figured one thing out. Nobody wanted me.

I'd moved around a lot from apartment to apartment and street to street, but my uncle's huge house made me lonelier than ever. Being on the streets was exhausting and unpredictable, but at least Mom and William made it familiar. Now I was with relatives I'd barely spoken to. I cried myself to sleep into the pillow that smelled like the oils of a strange head.

The next day, my aunt and uncle left me with their youngest daughter, Jessica. Seventeen and pregnant, she babysat me by the pool. We talked about when her baby was due. I had a strong sense of wanting to be pregnant so I could have my own baby to take care of. If I were a mom, I'd be the best mom, and I'd never let my baby feel the way Mom and all these other people made me feel.

Jessica caressed her full, round tummy. "I'm naming her Julia." I thought back to how I'd wanted to be Felicia—a different girl with a different life. Julia wasn't even born yet, and even *she* had a place to go.

When I answered the knock at the door, Gramma and Grampa stood before me with drawn faces. I threw my arms around Gramma. There was so much I wanted to say, but my loneliness sealed my mouth.

They were like strangers to me now.

"You got your things?" Grampa said, all business. "Let's get back before dark." My Aunt Carrie offered a pat on my shoulder and a look of pity. Emptiness pressed into me, and even though my grandparents had come for me, I wondered what came next. Would I live with them? Would we search for Mom and William and bring them home, too? Relieved Gramma and Grampa didn't refuse to take me, I scooted to the middle of the back seat of the car like always because from that spot I could see the road. The radio was switched off, but I played Air Supply's "I'm All Out of Love" and Dolly Parton's "9 to 5" in my head so I'd be distracted by songs about other people's lives.

Mom had caused Gramma and Grampa so much trouble. The word Grampa used was "harassment," which I found funny since it's the same word Mom used to describe what the government and everybody else was doing to her. At my grandparents' house, I settled into the den where William and I had stayed over a year ago. I only had a bag of clothes, three cassette tapes, my little silver radio with cassette player, my teddy bear Jellybean, and my fairytale coloring book and pack of sixty-four crayons. They were part of me. Even more, they helped me escape outside things by allowing me to spiral deeper into myself.

Mom called one Sunday, and Gramma said into the kitchen phone, "She's here, Roberta. Stop worrying. I don't think that's a good idea." Gramma leaned against the desk chair in the kitchen nook. I waited with my arm out, but when she failed to hand me the phone, I inhaled a gulp of shame. I didn't want to talk to Mom, but I needed her to want me. The base dinged when Gramma placed the handset on it.

It made me wish I'd stood closer to Gramma to get a better sense of Mom's voice coming through the line. Her sound in my memory had already faded. I felt gross and guilty for not demanding to be reunited with William.

But I settled for it anyway.

The fifth grade had already started for the year, so once again, I was the new girl who knew no one. I entered Mr. Lee's class. His black, shoulder-length hair was so wispy it was as if feathered wings had sprouted from the sides of his face. Mr. Lee welcomed me, but I glanced around the room to find the cute boys. Some of the other kids were familiar to me, like maybe I knew them when I attended school there two years ago.

During my first class spelling bee, Mr. Lee made us all stand in a circle around the desks and face each other. He gave a word for a student to spell, and if the student spelled it wrong, he or she had to sit. My palms sweated, and my heart raced whenever the word got closer to me.

"Leopard," Mr. Lee said.

Marco, the cutest boy in the class with his shiny, curly black hair, who I definitely remembered, repeated the word and spelled it: "L-E-P-E-R-D."

"I'm sorry." Mr. Lee shook his head. Then the word went to Tanya, who misspelled it through the gap in her front teeth. She reminded me of Emily from when we lived with Jerry in Bell Gardens. The kid next to me, the shortest kid in the class, had stiff, straight orange hair, textured as if it had been painted with clear glue. He stood straighter and released his smile to say the word.

"L-E-P-P-A-R-D." His flat expression said he was serious.

Mr. Lee shook his head. He seemed so disappointed as if he thought their inability to spell might somehow be his fault. He combed his hand through one of his hair-wings. My heart sped up again as he indicated it was my turn, and now, almost everyone else sat in their spelling shame. The tallest one in the class, I loomed like a giant.

As I spelled the word correctly, Mr. Lee smiled as if I had restored his faith in humanity.

The kid with the glue-hair flashed his eyes at me. "How'd you know how to spell it?"

I didn't know how I knew.

Mr. Lee chose me to represent our school in the District Bee in February.

Lying in front of the brick fireplace on the brown and gold shag carpet in my grandparents' living room, propped on my elbows, I studied the words on my practice sheet.

"Tungsten," I said to Grampa, who sat in his cushioned chair, reading the newspaper. "What is *tungsten?*" He told me to look it up, so I did. The word would be harder *and* easier to remember because it wasn't the same kind of "tongue" as the one in my mouth. I would have to remember it for what it was—a hard, rare chemical element, known for its robustness and high melting point. "Tungsten." I tried to picture the word, but I couldn't *see* it like I could other words.

On the day of the spelling bee, Gramma drove me to the auditorium. "Time After Time" streamed from the car radio, and I sang along, imagining my voice in perfect harmony with Cyndi Lauper's. Gramma didn't cringe or tell me to shut up. It sounded pretty good to me, like when I sang in the cave of the bathtub and my voice transformed into a sound that was way better than my actual voice. I imagined what it would be like to love someone so much you'd write a song about them.

On stage, the bee proctor announced my first word: "harvest." It was so easy. I didn't think I heard him right. But it *was* right, so I pictured the letters in my mind, hovering over a field of wheat. I trembled, and my palms squished. As soon as my voice made a sound, I knew what I had done. I had rushed everything and started spelling the word out loud before I'd finished spelling it in my mind. I was on the "s" in my mind, so I started there, out loud, with the "s."

And I spelled "sharvest," which meant I was out on the first round.

chapter 16

1984
AGE 10

SOMETIMES IT SEEMED THAT WILLIAM AND MOM had died. Most of the time, I got by without thinking about them at all. Instead, my world held Marco, the cute, curly-haired Italian boy with chocolate eyes. My world contained Ryan, the best long jumper whom I tried to out-jump every day at recess, squatting and throwing my arms back to gain momentum before leaping from the grass as far away as possible from where I'd started. And I did beat him sometimes. But he kept jumping farther. So, I kept jumping, too.

My world included how strange and deep my voice boomed when we sang "This Land is Your Land" and the awkwardness of singing about where people belong when I belonged nowhere. My world centered on being the first one to finish my math worksheet and turn it in so everybody could see my speed and intelligence. The faster I went, the tighter things held together in my brain, because if they loosened and fell apart, everything else might fall apart, too. If I gave my brain a chance to slow down, all the things I didn't want to think about might creep back in. I was determined to be strong and special, like *tungsten*, and to construct a world where I beat everybody in everything, so I would never have to lose anything ever again.

One day, I raised my hand to answer one of Mr. Lee's questions. Tanya, who sat next to me, stared right into my armpit. I wore a shirt with short flutter-sleeves, and they slid up my shoulder when I raised my arm. Her eyes went wide; she blinked and then turned away. I snuck a glance at my armpit to discover what had fascinated her, and I gasped in shock at the collection of fine wispy black hairs growing there. They clung together softly like a tuft of rabbit fur. I stopped raising my hand when Mr. Lee asked questions.

How had I never noticed this clump of hair growing out of my body? Why hadn't anybody ever told me to check my armpits regularly because I might wake up one day and find them stuffed with hair? I supposed it shouldn't have mattered so much, especially since Tanya had a fuzzy mustache growing on her upper lip.

But it *did* matter.

We sang "America the Beautiful" that day. How could I think about America? All I could think about were my hairy armpits. And then I thought about how I couldn't remember if Mom had hair in her armpits. I didn't think so, but it had been so long since I'd seen her armpits, I couldn't be sure. I didn't know of any purple mountains or fruited plains. The America I knew was confusing. And I had hairy armpits, and everybody saw.

"I need help." I said to Gramma as I entered the house. Gramma dried her hands on the towel hanging over the oven door handle. "Just come here." I motioned for her to come with me into the bathroom. I flicked on the light, lifted one arm, and pointed. "What do I do?"

Gramma laughed and pulled a razor from the drawer. "Oh, it's just a little peach fuzz, that's all. You shave it." She held the pink handle and put the blade to her pit over her blouse.

"It'll cut me." I thought of Mom's wrist scars and of her bleeding in her bed. Tears blurred my eyes.

"Don't be silly. It's not going to cut you. Hold it like this and pull it down slowly over the hair." She didn't know the things I'd seen. Wouldn't she do it for me if she truly loved me? When she refused, I decided my desire to have the hair gone was greater than my fear of the razor. After Gramma left the bathroom, I dragged the razor over the hair in each pit. I was surprised at how easy and painless it was to remove the unwanted tufts.

I locked the bathroom door that night and took a bath. Had I ever seen Mom in the tub, shaving her legs innocently and *not* sitting in her own dirty blood-filth? I rubbed soap all over and, one leg at a time, pulled the razor, removing the fuzz. I paused, not sure what to expect. Would angels sing? Would bad thoughts of Mom and William disappear? Would I suddenly feel beautiful and mature, capable and strong?

I didn't bleed. I dried my body and then the razor and set it on the pink floral paper that lined the drawer. I couldn't erase the image of Mom in the tub. Maybe some things never leave. I went to bed wondering if I would someday become like Mom. Maybe being away from her and forgetting her was the way to become *me* and not *her*.

Tungsten, tungsten, tungsten. I repeated the word in my head until tightness no longer zinged the space between my shoulder blades, until I no longer felt as if I'd been snagged by a hook.

I lived at Gramma and Grampa's for five months. That was

enough time to believe I was better off without Mom. But I missed William—being without him was like living without a part of my heart.

Gramma and I had completed several rounds of doubles Solitaire at the dining room table. It was a game of silence and hope, but then Gramma said, "She called, you know" and unscrewed the cap of her favorite fuchsia nail polish. "Do you want to live with her again?"

I stared at her elegant fingers before judging my own. I used to chew my nails furiously until a classmate told me I probably had a baseball-sized clump of fingernails sitting in my stomach. From then on, I decided I would not be a nail biter. They were growing back nicely, even the one on my mangled middle finger that had replaced the dead nail. "No, I don't want to go back with her," I said. "Please don't make me." I'd finally learned to breathe again, but the thought of living with Mom again made my lungs too small to hold enough air.

Gramma casually painted her fingernails and blew on them. I cleaned the dirt from under my nails with my teeth.

Gramma shook her hands in front of her face to get the first coat of polish to dry faster. "She loves you. You know that." She blew on them again.

I stared at my newly clean nails. They were short but more attractive without the dirt. The sun bled through the curtains in the corner of the eating nook. A warm shiver crawled up my arms and spine. Mom was a threat to my routine and comfort. Gramma and Grampa didn't love me enough to let me stay with them forever. A sharp ache needled me between the shoulder blades.

Gramma capped the polish. I stared at the violets on the corner shelf. They'd thrived in the afternoon sun, delicate and deep purple, the color of a bruise. Gramma gently placed her palm on my arm and tried to help me put the pieces of my life back together. But she didn't know I'd learned to sleep lightly because Mom had a habit of listening to wild voices in her head—or her teeth—that told her to kill me. Gramma's ignorance made her seem a million miles away from me. I wanted to bring her down to my level, make her understand all of it, but I couldn't.

I picked up the bottle of nail polish. I shook it and whacked it against the palm of my hand. Painting nails, like coloring inside the lines, required extreme concentration. I held my hand steady as I applied a thin coat. I blew on my nails. Maybe things *could* be better. Was this the beginning of responsibility—my voice rising up to do the hard thing that also happened to be the right thing? Or was it best to shut up so I could focus on something else for a while and silence the restless wolf that howled in me?

When Grampa brought a duffel bag to my room, I was crying softly, which might have caused his lingering in the doorway, but he didn't say a word. I packed my belongings and sat on the *couch*—it would never again be my bed.

At the apartment, Grampa parked us in one of the spots facing away from the L-shaped building.

Gramma said. "We'll stay in the car until you get inside."

I exited, holding my bag like an offering of my belongings and myself to my mother's madness. The apartment door was open, and darkness loomed on the other side of the dirty screen. Another world lay in that darkness, a microcosm of unpredictability and fear where hope went to die. My stomach ached.

I turned back to the car; my grandparents faced forward, ignoring me.

The screen door creaked. I turned toward the sound and where Mom now stepped toward me, arms out, palms up.

One foot at a time, I moved toward her, William, and this new apartment that I knew held old things. This was a moving forward and backward at the same time. Her glossy eyes twinkled. I dropped my duffel to hug her, and tears came out of me so fast I couldn't catch them. Her hair cascaded down the front of her blouse, and it trapped my fallen tears. She smelled like cigarettes and Ivory bar soap, and it smelled so good I wanted to be bound there forever.

She pulled away and placed her hands on my shoulders. "My baby girl, my baby girl," she said, which softened me. But I still didn't trust her fully. How could I? And then the words I'd dreaded most of all blew lightly from her lips: "I love you." She sang, "You are my sunshine, my only sunshine" and sounded a partly wicked, partly genuine yet creepily quiet laugh.

"I know, me, too. I love you, too," I said, feeling dirty and ugly for saying words that tasted like lies, words I could not take back.

I couldn't make my feet move toward the door. But Mom pulled on my hand. "Wave goodbye to Gramma and Grampa," she said. "William, your sister's home," she called into the black hole apartment. "Come see your sister." I didn't want to go in, and I didn't want to face William after allowing a rift of time and distance to form between us. It was too late to run back to the car; Gramma and Grampa were already gone. *This* was my family. The only thing left to do was accept it.

Every morning, William risked losing teeth as he tried to wake me by cracking my toes. I kicked and flailed, but he held on tight, laughing in victory.

But he would never hurt anyone on purpose, so Mom's accusation that he'd been programmed to break the television antennae killed his spirit. Mom was the one who'd kept pestering him to position it precisely so, and he'd wanted to get it right.

Frowning, he moved the rabbit ears back and forth, across each other, to focus the picture. Static clogged the screen. He twisted the aluminum foil at the tips of the antennae like knobs as if he were tuning in to a far-away radio station.

Just then, Inspector Gadget had pulled one of his coat buttons and was now soaring into the sky.

"There," Mom said. "Oh, no. Wait. Stay there. Put your right leg up. Just like that."

William lifted his right leg like a dog about to take a pee on the television. When he realized the joke was on him, he lowered the antennae and gave up, dropping his arms to his sides.

"Put your hands right where they were," Mom said. William tried again, to make Mom happy, and Inspector Gadget evaded the M.A.D. agents. Mom laughed and, taking advantage of the opportunity to be in camaraderie with her, I laughed too. William had both arms out, one hand on each antenna. And the picture was perfect.

"How long do I have to stay like this?" he said. Then he lost his balance and snapped one metal rod from the plastic antennae base as he fell. Blocks of color flashed on the screen, and the picture went fuzzy. *Inspector Gadget* went dark.

"You *broke* it," Mom said, implying he'd done it purposely. William put the metal rod behind his back as if hiding it meant his mistake hadn't happened. He begged her to know he didn't mean to do it. But all she could hear was her own rage. She lunged at him like a storm and snatched the broken metal from his hand. She raised it as if she were about to strike him with it. "Do you know what you've done?"

William flinched and guarded his face with his arm.

Mom lowered the rod, and William's entire body seemed to sigh in relief. When she raised it again and pointed it at his face, he cowered. "This antenna represents your sister's private parts. See that? The shape of them?" She held the detached rod back in place and ran her finger over the V-shape to emphasize it. "Now, you've broken *her*. They programmed you to do this. It symbolizes men raping her and breaking her innocent girl parts."

William cried without tears. "I didn't mean to. I'm sorry." His eyes pained and remorseful, he said, "Leslie, I didn't break it on purpose. I swear."

"I know. It's okay." If I'd had a trench coat like Inspector Gadget's, I would have swept William up in it, so we could fly away together. I set my hand on his shoulder to comfort him while a secret satisfaction spread through me because Mom had stood up for me, defended me against everyone in that moment. It was like the time William slammed my fingers in the door. Her disapproval of him meant approval of, and love for, me. Mom sent William to bed, and I got to sit in the rocking chair. Without William in it, the living room was smaller and bigger at the same time, and spooky quiet. Intermittent static and blackness rolled over the TV screen.

Mom held her arms out to me, so I went to her and curled up on the couch. I rested my head on her lap, and she ran her fingers through my hair until I fell asleep.

chapter 17

1984
AGE 10

I'D BEEN AT MY EIGHTH SCHOOL, LORETTA LAMPTON Elementary, for only three weeks when Mom made me stop going. "If I've said it once," she said, "I've said it a million times, Leslie. It's where they brainwash you." I reached for the doorknob, determined to show her what would happen when she broke promises. Mom put her arms out, made herself bigger, as she blocked the door. So instead of going to school, William and I watched television with the drapes closed, and we didn't go outside until after school had let out for the day.

We needed to stretch our legs instead of suffocating in a small, dark apartment, so we crossed the street to play along the sidewalk in the sun.

I had wound pieces of Scotch tape around the tips of my fingers to give the appearance of long fingernails. Holding my hands out so I could admire them, I tapped the opaque fakes together lightly and enjoyed the plasticky *tuh tuh tuh*. I touched my face gingerly, imagining that someone might see me and think I was older and glamorous.

The electrical transformer hummed above us, and crows lined the phone wires. Cars whooshed in both directions in the distance, traveling Firestone Boulevard, the four-lane road with busy intersections to the east of us. I stroked William's pink cheek with my tape nails.

"Stop," he said and flinched. "Don't touch me." He hopped over crevices in the sidewalk.

"But look at my long nails. Aren't they elegant? Just like a grown-up?"

"No." He alternated feet. "Step on a crack, break your mama's back."

"But if you saw me," I said, "and didn't know me, would you think my nails were real?"

"No," William said, all business and black and white. "I'd think you had tape around your fingers."

I didn't believe him. The sun was bright and my imagination full. Warm winter and the dream of my independent, adult life swept me away from the reality of our bare cupboards. Except for some Lipton's tea, a box of condensed milk, and a bag of sugar, the cupboards were bare. Zapping pangs punched me in the gut, announcing my hunger. I clung to the hope that Mom would come out of her room like a clean and ready princess—Snow White, perhaps—shedding love and light on all creatures.

When she hated us, she ignored us. When she adored us, she invited us into her room where we crawled under the velvety brown bedspread dotted with cigarette burns. She sipped white wine and told us to catch her cigarette if she fell asleep because starting a fire would surely get us evicted.

I'd learned, on my first airplane ride when I was eight, when William and I traveled to Missouri for a family reunion with Gramma and Grampa, that when the oxygen masks drop, you secure your own before assisting others.

Still, William was the pragmatic one. We were hungry, so he suggested we get some food. His willingness to break Mom's rules surprised me, but if she was going to sleep all day, we would have to fend for ourselves. We walked to Lucky's supermarket, which was across the street from our apartment. The door fan blew on our hair as we entered through the automatic doors. We sauntered. *We do this all the time.* We pretended Mom was in the next aisle, deciding which can of vegetables would go better with steak.

"Get stuff you can hide," William said, too smart for an eight-year-old. We split up. I hit the produce section and made the bottom of my T-shirt into a hammock to hold three Granny Smith apples. I spotted a row of Scratch 'n' Sniff stickers hanging from a clip. They showed cartoon popcorn puffs with big eyes and red and white popcorn tubs smiling. Their buttery, salty scent broke through the plastic wrapper.

I slid the card of stickers down the front of my jeans. I figured I might as well since we were taking what we could. Stealing one thing made it easier to steal another. I strolled the candy aisle and clutched a king-sized package of Reese's Peanut Butter Cups. I slid them down my pants, too, and, doing my best to be smooth and natural, I strutted to the dairy aisle, where William pushed eggs, one by one, up his jacket sleeve. He pressed a gallon of milk against his chest and zipped his jacket over it.

Had anyone spotted us—maybe a worker or a shopper who might implicate us? A shopping cart squeaked by, and the woman pushing it stared at me. Did she know what we were up to? I knew stealing was wrong, but our hunger outweighed our ethics. Steal or starve. We had to try, didn't we? The refrigerated shelves hummed, and cold climbed into my bones. I hugged myself, teeth chattering like they did when we were homeless for many nights at a time.

As we turned to leave the refrigerated section, a police officer appeared, seized William by the arm, and asked what he had in his jacket.

"Nothing. Just some eggs," William said.

"And what's this?" The officer poked the hidden milk jug as if it were the Pillsbury Doughboy. The officer stared at my lumpy torso, my exposed belly button. "What are *you* hiding, Miss?" I wanted to make a run for it, but even if we dropped everything and ran, where would we go? We only lived across the street. This was *bad*. We were going to go to jail, and we deserved it. The woman with the shopping cart squeaked by, craning her neck and staring. Register scanners beeped.

"We're sorry," William offered. His eyelashes tugged at his straight, blond bangs when he blinked. I stood there with no words in my mouth. And now there'd be no food either. The policeman, manager, and I waited as William put the wet jug back on its shelf. It might've taken me all day to count the jugs and the cartons, pints, and quarts. Gallons and half-gallons and skinnier, smaller versions. This place was a milk palace. And they couldn't spare *one* jug?

What I should've said was, *Help us. Please save us from our Mom.* We'd been foolish. We'd drawn too much attention to ourselves and gotten caught. I sniffled.

"There's no need to cry about it." The policeman chuckled. "The manager says he's not going to press charges. If we let you go this time, do you promise never to do anything like this again?"

William nodded, and I said, "Yes, we promise." I stared at the buzzing shelves. I shivered. William pushed the eggs out of his jacket sleeves, setting each one back in their crate carefully, as if live chicks occupied the shells. There were so many eggs. But I guess, if I ignored all the cracked ones, there might not be as many good eggs as I'd hoped. The cop guided me to the produce section. I gave the officer one of my apples and put my hands under my shirt to push the other two onto the apple stand. They landed with a thud and rolled before settling in with the hundreds of other apples. He asked where we lived, and we told him the truth.

The manager folded his arms over his belly. "You two got lucky today. Get it? Lucky? The name of the store is *Lucky's*. Get it?" Nobody laughed. "Go on. Get out of here." He swatted the air with his hands.

The cop said, "You keep your promise, you hear?" William and I ran home, hungry and dejected but glad to be free from the clutches of the law. I pulled the Reese's out of my pants. I'd forgotten about the stickers. I slid them out and hid them under my pillow, delighted to have such a happy secret. I tore into the package of candy, and we ate it, the warm, melty chocolate covering our lips and fingers. We didn't disturb Mom. She'd locked herself away for days at a time in the past. It indicated her downward spiral. Still, William and I rested more easily when Mom tucked herself into her bed and left us alone.

William boiled water in the tea kettle and stood on a chair to get the box of Lipton's Tea from the cupboard. I scooped mayonnaise on iceberg lettuce, and we ate it as a salad. After rinsing the dishes, I became obsessed with cleaning. The place was a disaster. I closed all the cupboards, pushed in the kitchen chairs, and used wet toilet paper to clean the linoleum where crumbs, dirt, and hair congregated in their separate communities of filth. We didn't have much square footage, but everywhere I walked, hair, fuzz, dirt, and crumbs stuck to the bottoms of my feet. I brushed the gunk off with toilet paper and dumped it in the toilet. We didn't have a vacuum, so I crawled around, combing the carpet with the sides of my hands and picking up toenails, dried food particles, and other crumby things with my fingers. The baseboards were the worst, where all floor gunk and matted fur went to die.

William slouched in the wicker chair with one leg over the arm as he watched his heroes, the A-Team, save the day through the snowy, incomplete picture on the TV. The hanging lamp in the corner of the room cast shadows of furniture onto the walls. I couldn't sit around and watch static when I needed to be a human vacuum. My palms took on a charcoal-gray sheen, and they tingled and burned from the work, but I relished the pulsating sensation of my nerves firing because it meant I'd made our apartment less repulsive.

Mom wasn't the kind of crazy person you see on TV, or even anywhere close to the lunatics wandering around that hospital she stayed in after she shot herself during the car accident, but this was the scariest I'd seen her. Even the night she tried to kill herself with knives she didn't look this wild. Or the night she wanted to cook us in the oven. Or the night she wanted one of us to run over her head with the car. This was different from all those times. She sometimes laughed at nothing I could see. I knew the voices in her head spoke, making up stories, and that, to her, they weren't stories at all but demands and messages she had to obey.

"I cleaned the floor last night, Mommy."

Her hair was dark, reddish-brown, stiff, and messy like a nest. I half-expected birds to come flying out of it. She puffed on her cigarette quickly three times. Her nostrils flared, and cigarette smoke seeped from her mouth like fog. She muttered softly and scowled, widening and narrowing her eyes. She rocked in her chair, one foot on the thin carpet, the other pressing into the seat cushion, her knee in front of her face. In a daze, she stared at the far wall.

"Aren't you proud of me?" I said.

"M-hmm." But her eyes were empty.

It was time to leave again.

Mom combed her hair quickly, leaving it ratty underneath a smoothed outer layer. She put on a cotton blouse, dirty jeans, and her white leather sandals with the buckle at the ankle. Even in the cold, Mom wore sandals because she had a bunion on her right foot and she was allergic to rubber. She told us to dress warm. I shimmied into my olive-green turtleneck and purple corduroy pants that were too short.

Mom's dragon eyes glowed in the dim light. I moved toward the door, but Mom's short, jagged nails dug into my skin. I yanked away, but she held on tight, pulling me close to her. "We have to leave. I know you don't understand, but please trust me." There was nothing I could say or do to change Mom's mind and make her think clearly. And I was *not* going to stay behind this time. Sitting by myself in the creepy apartment would not bring me comfort. I'd end up back with Mom anyway, so what was the use?

We left the apartment with a pillowcase filled with some of our belongings, and we crossed the street to Lucky's. Traffic whirred in the near distance. Mom placed our pillowcase in the front basket of a shopping cart. I put my teddy bear next to it.

Mom told us to wait while she got some food and cigarettes, so William and I stood with our backs against the stucco building in the cold.

I zoned out and thought back to when I studied spelling words by the warm fire at Gramma and Grampa's. *Tungsten.* I sounded it out in my head, saw the letters strung together in the right order. *Tungsten, tungsten, tungsten.*

William blinked his long, white eyelashes at me. He raised himself up and down on his tiptoes. I was comforted by the thought that he already had what it took. He was strong.

"Do you know how to spell *tongue?*" I said. He spelled it right on the first try. Mom hadn't been gone five minutes when three older boys approached us, one on a bike, the other two on skateboards.

"What do we have here?" the tallest one—the one riding the bike—said. He seemed to be the one in charge. The other two eyed him, then each other, and laughed in quick bursts.

"We're waiting for our mom." I pressed into the wall, hoping it would swallow me.

He mimicked me in a high-pitched voice. Then he said, "Oh, two little babies waiting for mommy. How nice." The three of them laughed. The tall one got closer to us, leaning his face into mine. He had bad acne, and his breath reeked of rotting food. I turned my head and closed my eyes. He reached his hand toward me, but I slapped it away.

"Leave her alone," William yelled, coming off the wall a bit.

"Leave her alone," the tall boy repeated in a whiny voice. He cast his eyes over my body, steadying his slimy gaze on my crotch, then on my ankles. My pants were *too* short; I was *too* tall. I was certain the boys would've left me alone if I were pretty. But I was awkward and ugly, the kind of girl who had to wear too-short purple corduroys with an olive-green turtleneck, the kind of girl who had to wear pee pants from Goodwill. Where were the police when you *needed* them? The boy reached out again, this time grazing my chest with the backs of his fingers. His hangnail snagged. I pushed away his nasty hand.

"Stop it," I yelled.

"That's okay," he said. "I wouldn't want you, anyway. Your pussy's probably filled with *termites.*" The boys laughed again before riding away.

My stomach lurched, and heat spread upward through my face

as if to scald my scalp and set my hair on fire. I wiped my wet eyes on my sleeve, darkening the fabric.

"Are you okay?" William asked. "Don't listen to them. They're buttholes. They're gone now, anyways."

I hated those boys. I hated that they made me feel dirty and ashamed for standing against the wall. I hated that there was nothing I could do about any of it.

chapter 18

1984
AGE 10

MOM EXITED LUCKY'S AND DROPPED A BAG OF GRO-
ceries into the shopping cart with our belongings. We walked around
the streets of Norwalk all night. I kept my eyes peeled for the boys
who harassed us, so I could be prepared if they rode toward us. I
didn't dare say anything to Mom. Embarrassed to repeat what they'd
said, I also didn't want to give Mom any more reasons to start up
again about torture or about my private parts and what dangerous
men were going to do to them if we didn't get away from here.

"Where did you get money to buy groceries?" I asked. "Yesterday,
you said we didn't have any."

"Leslie. Stop being difficult." I concentrated on keeping tears
from falling out of my eyes. I clenched my fists, wanted to hit, fight, run.
But I weakened and followed Mom through the murky neighborhood.

We passed strip malls with neon signs and people smoking and
laughing outside bars. We stalked down alleys and culs-de-sac,
lightless streets and noisy intersections. Mostly, we avoided other
people.

"This way," Mom said, pointing to an alley darker than the one before it. "Let's turn down here." She checked behind us and stared down every street before we walked another stretch of cold asphalt and followed night-blooming jasmine and garbage stink into the night.

"Where are we going?" I asked.

The answer was always the same: "Away from them."

We walked. My legs ached. I turned my arches up to walk on the outsides of my feet, bruising the bones. I'd run out of uninjured foot area to tread on. I walked backward to alleviate the sting and throb.

I hugged my teddy bear to my chest as I dragged my feet. *Jellybean*. His name had come to me in a spark of creativity. It used to fit him perfectly even though he wasn't purple or pink or any other jellybean color. He had a potbelly. I thought *Jelly Belly*, Jelly*bean*. Or something like that. I fought to get Mom to buy me Jellybean. I'd thrown him on the conveyor with the ivory-and-fuchsia-striped shirt and stiff, oversized jeans I was getting as my new school outfit for the second grade. Mom pulled him off and shoved him at me to put him back. I persisted, crying and begging.

Except for my little silver radio and some coloring books, Jellybean was the only thing I had that was truly mine. Now, with his black eyes scratched up, and his polyester belly fur rubbed flat, his name seemed all wrong. I should have named him Warrior Bear. But I'd had no idea we would need so much strength.

I'd left my little silver radio in the apartment because Mom said we could be tracked through it since it was an electronic device.

For days, we pushed our shopping cart around residential neighborhoods between Norwalk and Downey and over the San Gabriel Riverbed. We ate Fig Newtons and apples and drank warm Pepsi. The sun got hot, burning my nose, cheeks, and the middle of my scalp where my hair was parted. I sweated through my turtleneck.

Mom held a blanket to shield me while I stood along a brick wall in an alley to change into a Mickey Mouse T-shirt. Cars zoomed past us. The sun beat down; for hours there was no protection, no trees, no parks, only cement, asphalt, cars, noise, and the three of us pushing our belongings in a stolen shopping cart.

Then, Mom said, "Leave the shopping cart," as if she'd only that moment received an urgent message from the voices in her head. We stood on a dead-end street with a freeway roaring in the background.

"It's all we have," I said. "Why do we need to leave it? I'll push it."

Mom sighed and furrowed her brow. Her lips tightened and parted again. "Why are you always fighting me? Why can't you be more like your brother and trust me? I am your mother. And when I say *leave* the shopping cart, I mean *leave* it. It's just *stuff*. Is all this stuff more important than our safety? Than our *lives?*"

I clung to the cart and dragged it behind me. She jerked me away from it with such force, I had no choice but to let go. I yanked my arm back. I was *not* leaving Jellybean. I pulled him by one of his cute fuzzy arms out of the seat of the cart where he'd been sitting like a good teddy bear.

"Goddammit, Leslie," Mom said, as she grabbed my bear and threw him in the big part of the cart. Then she seized my arm again. We were the same to her, Jellybean and I. She'd hurt us both, yanked us both the same, threw us around. I couldn't take it, couldn't stand it. I was going to die if I had to leave my bear.

"I hate you," I yelled. "Why are you making us do this?"

"Because I am your mother and the only one keeping us safe," she said. "Now stop your crying. It's time to be a big girl." She marched forward, pulling me along next to her. William's silence burned a hole in me. I wanted to shake his passiveness out of him. I needed him to back me up. When we approached the end of the street, I turned around and wiped my tears. A small man in ragged clothes had already claimed our belongings for himself.

Hours later, Mom slowed and bent toward me. "Do you know why we had to leave Jellybean?" The sun had baked salty tears into my face, forming a tight mask over my skin. I squinted and exaggerated the opening and closing of my mouth. Could I break through, crack my face, and explode into a million pieces? Mom pressed her hand into my shoulder. "They could've planted a bug in Jellybean, in his eyes, and they could've been tracking us and listening in on our conversations. I just couldn't risk it. We'll get you another teddy bear."

"I don't want another one. I want *Jellybean*." I refused to let her think she could soften me. How could I ever love her again?

At some point, we'd left Norwalk, and I didn't realize it until we passed a sign that said we were *entering* Norwalk. Trees in full bloom loomed over sidewalks and roofs. Houses in muted colors lined the streets. Everything started to look the same. Were we walking in circles? I was so thirsty, the back of my mouth clicked when I swallowed.

I was in the middle of thinking I might choke on my swollen tongue when we approached a dead cat—an orange and white tabby—mushed into the black, uneven asphalt. His body had been flattened entirely. It was as if someone had glued him there or intentionally stuck him in when paving the road. His legs and paws were splayed out like in a cartoon death.

It must have taken a few cars to make him that way—it had to be more than one—to run him practically into nothing.

I stared at this furry thing that *used* to be a cat. Maybe he'd belonged to someone who was now sad and missing him. I stared at his poor smashed kitty head. His eyeballs had popped out and pointed in different directions, making him seem both wild and surprised. And his jaw—it was unhinged *and* crushed. But his teeth were intact, and they sat outside his whiskered mouth, mangled and bent.

As we passed, I slowed. I wanted to study him, get right down on my hands and knees and absorb every detail. But Mom, who was getting good at bruising my arm, forced me to keep up. A blurry, gaseous haze buzzed over the kitty, and the smell was worse than the halitosis of the boy who harassed us outside of Lucky's. I wanted to know the kitty like I'd wanted to know my dead fingernail in its gauze bandage when my foster mom threw it in the trash. I tried to understand his life and his death and hoped never to forget the sight of him because somehow, memorizing images was the only way to keep them and to prove what I'd seen was real.

I hung back and slowed before turning back to roadkill kitty. I thought I should apologize as if it might somehow convince him he didn't deserve to die like that. He deserved to have someone take care of him, love him, and keep him safe. The streets were no place for such small, sweet, helpless creatures.

"Stop looking at that." Disgust spilled out of Mom's voice, but I couldn't tell if it was because of the kitty carcass or because of my obsession with it. I looked back anyway as she pulled me forward. It seemed I was always looking back. Eventually, the kitty was too far behind me, and it hurt my neck to keep caring about him. So I gave up.

For several days, we belonged to the streets again, sleeping in parks all night and walking around all day. My back ached and refused to relax no matter what I did to stretch and move the muscles. After sundown one day, a chill came in from the sky, and I shuddered. But I recognized that we had circled back around to our apartment, so I sighed with relief. Mom unlocked the door and let us in.

I ran to my room to check on my belongings. My little silver radio sat right where I'd left it on the dresser. I regretted taking Jellybean with me. If I'd left him in the apartment, I'd still have him.

In the living room, William said, "Are we staying?" He'd been uncharacteristically quiet for days. Had he been swallowing his feelings, too? Mom looked at the ceiling corners as if she might find answers in them. I relaxed my shoulders. The ache in my back eased; however, the walls seemed darker, closer. The three of us blinked at each other. There wasn't much to say. I imagined we were practicing being dead. I fell asleep on the couch without a blanket to protect me. Dead people didn't need protection.

One day in May, there was a knock at the door. I jumped. Mom cracked the door the teensiest bit and poked her face into the slit. William stood directly behind Mom, his hands on her back.

The voice on the other side was faint. "We're just doing a standard welfare check. Please open the door." Mom slammed the door and locked it. Banging on the door started up, louder and faster this time, and with something other than a hand, it seemed.

"Ma'am," another male voice said. "Are your kids in school? Did you know it was against the law to keep them home? Open the door. We just need to make sure the kids are okay." Mom followed instructions, and a gray-haired police officer stood back while a bald-headed officer put his foot on the threshold and pushed the door in.

"I'm their mother," Mom said. "You can't have them."

The cop shouldered his way inside and held out his hand. "There's no need to be afraid."

Mom looked at me. "Don't trust them." Her voice was hushed, and she shook her head. She stepped back, almost as if to say *I know they need to take you,* almost as if to concede.

The police hadn't tortured us before or raped or rammed us with logs. The policeman at Lucky's had let us go. The last *two times* police had taken William and me, we ended up somewhere else, but not in the dungeon of horror Mom had led us to believe it would be.

Mom cried, "They're my children. You can't just come in here and take them from me." She shook. A fire-like glimmer—a mix of sadness and madness—came into her eyes.

A foggy, heavy-headedness swept over me. I held back, remained secure in the safety of Mom's adamancy that the police leave us alone. Willingly, happily going toward the police meant I was a traitor. If I betrayed Mom now, what did it say about me? Still, I believed almost anything would be better than staying with Mom. "You're all Communists," Mom screamed. "Goddamn Communists." Her voice rattled. "You don't belong here, and now you want to take my children?" She reached out for William and me. "I'll send them to school if that's what you want. But you can't have them."

A chill scrambled along my neck and arms. Her voice raged in *my* throat. Her anger and pain flooded *my* body. I wanted to stay, *and* I wanted to go. The gray-haired cop pulled me gently and led me outside, where I waited. He turned back to the apartment. Mom's wet face glistened in the flat, low light of the afternoon. William wrangled free of Mom's grasp. Mom pulled him back.

"Ma'am, he'll be okay." The gray-haired cop's confidence calmed me.

"Why would I fucking believe you?" Mom said. "Why can't you just leave us alone?"

"Ma'am? We'll have to take you into custody if you interfere.

Let's do this quietly, okay?" Baldy pulled William from the apartment, and William stumbled out like a rescue victim gaining clarity in the light of day.

William and I slid into the backseat of the police car, and the officers got in the front. I looked through the rear window, back at our corner apartment, expecting it to burst into flames. Mom was inside, and who knew what the voices in her head might make her do?

The police radio buzzed in a mix of static and voice. Bubbles of tears formed over my eyes, blurring everything—the blue sky above, the distant shivering trees, the beige stucco building, the cracked and weedy sidewalk. And then a crash broke the air. Glass blew out in a million pieces as the TV flew through the apartment window and onto the grass. The gray-blue curtains waved like flags after it. Mom stepped onto the stoop, blinking at us. Her lips quivered. As the gray-haired cop turned the key in the ignition, Mom rushed toward us, her face tilted up, holding her arms out as if to catch a falling sky.

The car pulled away from the curb in a swift, smooth motion.

I hadn't hugged Mom goodbye. Or given her one last kiss. Who knew when I would get to see her again? Or when I would get to smell her hair? Or feel her cool, dry fingers across my forehead. Hot and tight, my skin itched. Could I burn up right here in the back of the cop car, sitting on the sticky black seat behind a cage? I stared harder through the back window, determined to show Mom how sad I was to leave her.

Mom held her sorrowful face in her hands. Her body heaved.

Next to me, William cried without voice. His wet bangs stuck to his eyelashes. I squeezed his hand and faced forward as we left Mom standing there screaming.

The police drove William and me to the station and set us up in a room with a metal table and plastic chairs. After a few moments, the gray-haired cop returned with pillows. When I lay back, the icy table zinged my arms, and I felt like a patient about to have surgery, so I sat up and let my legs dangle to the floor. Fluorescent lights flickered in the ceiling. Twilight peeked in through the high window. The red hand on the round clock with the white face ticked along. The chilled room hummed and buzzed. Stale air blew in from the vent, and the blinds scraped against the window.

I couldn't get Mom out of my head—the image of her holding out her arms, mouthing something I couldn't hear. The people in the police station rushed about, creating an urgency I didn't understand. William and I had nothing to do but wait. An unfamiliar officer entered, holding Wendy's fast-food bags.

I nibbled at the bun, trying to eat without tasting the meat.

"How cold does it have to be to make people freeze to death?" I asked William. He didn't know. I rubbed my arms and stood from the icy table. I expected Gramma and Grampa to arrive and take us to their house like they did the time Mom kidnapped us. I shivered.

A woman I'd never seen opened the door, making the blinds dance like hanging bones against the glass. "I'm your caseworker," she said. "Miss Hyland. I'm going to take you someplace you can stay until we get things figured out."

In the car, Miss Hyland told us about MacLaren Hall. A children's center in El Monte, California, it would be our temporary home—a place where others like us stayed until social workers found foster placements for them or until parents improved enough to get their kids back.

"Don't be scared when you get there," she said. "It'll be a change from what you're used to."

William said, "Where's our mom?"

Miss Hyland glanced at the rearview mirror and at the dashboard. She tapped her fingers on the steering wheel and then gripped it fully with both hands. "They're taking care of her."

I thought this meant they'd taken her to jail again. Or maybe to another hospital like the one she stayed in after shooting herself. I didn't care, not like William did. I'd had enough of Mom, enough of her stories and of hunger and staying home from school. Mom broke *all* the rules. I was ready to be free of her. Still, I blamed myself for our separation. I should have made us go to school, should have been more responsible, should have stood up to Mom, forced her to keep us all safe and together. But I didn't do any of that. I had failed.

chapter 19

1984

AGE 10

MACLAREN HALL SEPARATED WILLIAM AND ME because we were not of the same gender. A man escorted William to the boys' dorms while a young woman took me to the girls' dorms in another wing of the property.

"If you're good and keep to yourself, do your chores, and don't cause trouble, you get credits to spend like money at 'the store.'" The woman swung her keys on a black lanyard. The discord of their metal clanking annoyed me, but I liked the sound of her words. I could excel in a place that administered steps like laws for me to obey. The woman unlocked the door to the dimly lit merchandise store to show me my potential. A blue and white tie-dyed hoodie that looked like sky and clouds hung on a rack against the wall. The tag said it cost "100 points." I knew I had to have it. I could also select candy, pens, stickers, or earrings, among other things.

In my assigned dorm, the woman handed me off like a baton to one of the night girls in charge, who led me to "the closet," a storage room with columns of shelves stacked to the ceiling. Each rack held a different type of clothing in various sizes. The night girl looked me over and grabbed a plain whitish T-shirt. I looked down at myself to see what she saw. She scanned a shelf for what she thought was my size before stopping and pulling a folded pair of pants off the top of the stack. The navy pants, equipped with a drawstring, were scratchy and thick to the touch. I shuddered as I dragged my palm across the material. Stacks of underwear lay at her eye level. She tossed me a pair—dingy white with pink, orange, and blue flowers. I cringed. I may have worn a T-shirt as a diaper in the aisles of Sav-On, but I thought I should draw a line at *used* underwear.

The night girl didn't ask questions, so I didn't give her answers. I didn't have words for strangers.

"Hmmm," she said, sizing up my chest. She passed over the bras and reached for a pair of socks before bending into the shoe shelves. She measured my foot with a metal apparatus and handed me a pair of yellowing slip-ons.

As she handed me items, I became a shelf, too.

She guided me to a small room that seemed more like a closet than "the closet."

"Change out of your clothes, into these things," she said, waving her hand over me like she might cast a spell. She stood outside the room while I removed my smelly clothes and raggedy tennis shoes and dressed in my "new" pajama outfit that smelled like dirty socks and graham crackers. "Fold your things and give 'em to me," she said. She placed my real clothes in a large, heavy-duty plastic bag with plastic handles that locked together. "Any jewelry or anything on you?" I shook my head.

She set the plastic bag on a desk in a windowed office adjacent to the room where I had changed and led me into the vast hall again.

The cement walls were painted white. Fluorescent lights lined the ceiling, flickering slightly and buzzing like distant bees. The white-gray floors shone in the harsh, cold light except in places streaked with black marks. The barely visible multi-colored flecks in the linoleum reminded me of confetti.

"It's past lights out," the girl said. I wondered how old she was. Was she an adult? Or was she still a kid, a teenager, doing a job for credits? Her brown skin was smooth like melting ice cream. I saw no one else in the hall, probably since it was past "lights out." Preoccupied with wearing shared clothes, I remembered the pee pants I'd carelessly chosen at Goodwill. I wanted my own clothes, not some rejects made dirty and dingy by other people's bodies. "Take whatever bed you want," the girl said. "You ain't got a roommate. Don't turn the light on. Get into bed. The bathroom's there." She pointed down the hall. "I'll be there." She pointed in the opposite direction, to a window that separated the hall from an office.

I climbed into bed and pulled the stiff sheet and a thin, rough cover-blanket to my chin. I wasn't dead yet. I needed protection, maybe now more than ever in this strange place. An emptiness dragged itself through my arms, legs, and gut, settling in my throat like a fluffy, choky bird. Voices of the night staff rose and fell. They spoke in misplaced whispers, laughing at jokes I couldn't hear.

My head the only part of me exposed, I reassured myself nobody would attack my face in the middle of the night. Still, terrified of what could happen while I slept, I decided to stay awake. I itched to close the door, but *rules are rules*. I held my eyes open for as long as I could, turning them toward the sliver of light as bright as day streaming in from the hall. That way, I would know if someone came for me.

I met Lupe while sweeping the hallway. She cleaned farther down, almost to where the building made an ell and branched off into another wing of rooms. She told me about the Honor Dorm: "I was there once before but got kicked out for fighting," she said. She swung her dark brown hair back, behind her shoulders. "Now, I almost have enough honor points to go back. It's with the older kids, and you get to do more stuff. Here it's like a prison. There's better clothes there. The staff gives you more privileges, and they watch you less."

She leaned her broom between her boobs and used both hands to tuck her hair behind her ears. Her jagged bangs hung over her eyes like icicles. Lupe's skin was darker than I'd seen on anybody who wasn't black. She walked with her boobs out like a rooster and with more confidence. I had always wanted brown eyes like hers. Lupe's laughter rang in loud raspy, bursts, unlike mine. I contained my laugh—and my voice—in a box inside my chest.

For our good behavior, Lupe and I received invitations to the annual fashion show held in the banquet room. We were taken to the closet for fancier clothes. The staff member handed me a floral dress with puffy sleeves and two ruffles around the base. A sash, made of the same navy floral, tied around my waist. It made me think of Mom's terrycloth dress with the sash William and I found in the hallway. It made me think of all the ways Mom might be trying to kill herself while William and I were away.

The dress stopped above my knees. I wouldn't have chosen it, but in a world of shared clothing, you took what you got. If I didn't take the dress, I'd be stuck with my thick, drawstring pants and a baggy T-shirt. The staff girl handed me a pair of beige flats that smelled vaguely of bacon. I winced, but bacon shoes were better than no shoes.

Lupe took a red sheath dress from a small stack of options, and I stared at it, wanting it.

Lupe's narrow hips in striking red entered my room.

"Ready?" she asked, eyeing me, the giant in an old-lady curtain dress. I thought she was suggesting I change my outfit. Lupe gripped my hand with her stubby fingers and led me to the banquet room, which housed several round tables covered in peach tablecloths. A runway extended from the stage into the center, dividing the round tables into a left and right side and reaching almost to the double doors under an EXIT sign. A gift of pastel Jordan Almonds marked each guest's table place. Scooping one up, I admired its tulle wrapping and white satin bow. A sachet of potpourri that smelled like old leaves, stale cinnamon, and pepper accompanied the almonds. It made me want to sneeze, so I pushed it toward the artificial floral arrangement in the center of the table.

The show began with the dimming of the track lighting and the emergence of a spot-lighted man from between the emerald-green velvet stage curtains. "Good Afternoon," he said. "I hope you enjoy the show."

Instrumental music flowed from ceiling speakers, and primary-colored lights swirled on the stage and catwalk, illuminating each model as she walked. Young girls, not much older than Lupe or me, flaunted glamorous dresses. Blush defined their cheekbones and kohl outlined their eyes. Lips of crimson or orange pouted and smiled. I slunk in my chair and crossed my arms. Lupe's smile and her smooth, unblemished skin glowed. I'd spent so much time hating my freckles and "beauty" marks. Auntie Philys said once that I had been so perfect as a baby that when my first freckle came in, she tried to scratch it off with her fingernail. She laughed, but secretly, I wished she had succeeded. Nothing had been said about the gaps between my teeth or my crooked smile. I still practiced making it smaller every time I looked in the mirror.

I loosened the ribbon on the bag of Jordan Almonds I'd hoped to save for later. *Eat me*, they said as if I were Alice in Wonderland. But they weren't magical. Eating them couldn't change me in any meaningful way. Their jagged edges and nutty taste comforted me. And because nut shards stuck in my teeth like coins in a slot, I wore out my tongue attempting to wrest them free.

When the show ended, we clapped.

Exhaustion throbbed in me. In a weak and unproductive attempt, I coughed. I was curious about why Lupe ended up at MacLaren. Nobody talked about these things.

"Can I have your almonds?" I said.

"Don't you want your sachet?" She pointed to it. I didn't want it; it was a disgusting packet of dead things. But I took it anyway.

Later, the bitter taste of almonds in my mouth made me want to eat more, so I popped Lupe's almonds in, one at a time, while lying on my back on my bed, which was stupid, given my tendency to choke on things. I challenged myself to eat them slowly and to swallow intentionally. They were strange—almost impossible to chew thoroughly, almost as if rubber or tar and needles and nails might appear on the ingredients list. They stuck and cut my throat. I harrumphed and ahemmed and quacked like a mad duck, pushing air through my mouth. Then I resumed eating, grinding every last almond. I wasn't even hungry. But chewing things and swallowing them calmed me.

The potpourri sachet was a different story. Its filthy spices tainted the air. Why did it smell so foul, like someone peed on a bunch of leaves, ground them between their palms and added a drop of armpit funk for good measure? I couldn't stop putting the bag to my nose and sniffing it, as if by doing so, I had the power to transform into something beautiful.

Soon the stench infiltrated my nostrils and clung to my hands. I sneezed uncontrollably before throwing the bag away. I retrieved it from the trash. I couldn't keep it, and I couldn't get rid of it. Someone had given it to me; it was mine.

chapter 20

1 9 8 4
AGE 10

THE WEATHER WARMED UP, AND THE JUNE SUN shone hot and white. Some of us were granted free time at the pool. Wearing a community one-piece bathing suit, I jumped into the water. Children like me filled the pool, children with nowhere else to go and who wondered what came next.

Lupe wore a red bikini, and her evenly tanned body shimmered. My suit boasted thin horizontal stripes. It gaped where my boobs were supposed to be, and because of my long torso, the straps repeatedly snapped off my shoulders. I hunched like an overgrown vulture.

We raced each other the length of the pool, testing each other's lung capacity. Underwater, how my suit fit didn't matter anymore. I became a mermaid. I should have been born a fish instead of a girl. Fish didn't have to worry about things like the size of their tails or the shimmer of their scales. They swam freely and kissed the water and wore iridescence that flickered like jewels when the light hit them right.

We raced from one end of the pool to the other, and as she passed me, Lupe took an underwater swipe at me. We both came up for air at opposite sides of the pool before diving under again to finish the race. This time, on her way past me, she twisted my nipple between her fingers.

I shot to the surface, instantly sickened, like I'd done something wrong, something nasty. Coughing and gasping for air, I searched for Lupe. I submerged myself again, hoping to avoid her and swim past her on my way to the ladder. She torpedoed toward me, but I was not fast enough to evade her. She reached for me again, and I put my hands over my boobs, but this time, she jabbed her middle finger into my private parts. She swam away to the opposite end. Though I doubted she could hear me, I yelled toward her anyway.

"What are you doing?" I plucked at the crotch of my suit to un-wedge it.

"What?" she yelled.

"Why'd you do that?" I said as she came closer.

"Do what?" she said and laughed before disappearing again beneath the surface.

I lost her in the colorful crowd as I scanned the pool, hoping no one saw what she'd done to me, because I was embarrassed. I thought I must have done something to make her touch me like that.

Almost three weeks had passed at MacLaren, and I hadn't yet seen William. I'd put thoughts of him and Mom out of my mind, so the sight of him jolted me. He seemed at once oddly familiar and strangely distant. Another face in a sea of faces, another body in a pool of bodies, he bobbed with the movement of the water.

Seeing him was like seeing someone from long ago, someone I

almost didn't recognize as real but who I might have seen on TV or in a dream.

A slow smile emerged, and he said, "Hi. I miss you."

"Hi," I said, aiming for genuineness. I didn't hug him because I'd already forced myself to believe I didn't know him or need him. Guilt made me throw myself into a handstand and hold it as long as I could. When I came up, William was there, and he came into focus as if I were seeing him for the first time.

"Did you hear me?" His mouth hung open as if the question had sucked the spirit out of him. "I *miss* you," he said again. His lower half wavered below the water, making him seem smaller than he was. Instead of giving him a hug, instead of asking him to take a break from the pool to have a chat on the warm cement, I did mermaid things. I asked him if he wanted to see me do a backflip. I did a backflip. When I rose again, William asked how I was and if I'd talked to Mom. I said no but that I was having fun. When I asked him if he was having a good time, he shook his head. His blue eyes reflected the chlorinated water, and they searched my face for something I couldn't give him.

I vaulted into another backflip, turning my scales to the light. And then God punished me. My head slammed into the bottom of the pool. A spark of pain struck me from pate to jaw to neck to spine, zinging through my body. My inner ears vibrated, and my neck stiffened. I emerged for air, one hand holding my head, and stared at William.

"I just hit my head on the bottom," I said.

"Are you okay?" He winced.

I couldn't break down in front of all of these people. I had to be a tough girl, pretend it never happened, pretend I didn't need anything from anyone.

"I almost got paralyzed," I said. "It's too shallow here." William put his hand on my arm, but I recoiled. "I wanna get out," I said. "I'll see you later."

"But when am I going to see you again?" His eyes said he was drowning in this place, but I could focus only on my injury and had nothing left to give.

"I don't know—Sorry—I have to go."

I wanted to tell him I needed a doctor, that my head felt wet and warm inside as if my brains were bleeding through my skull. But what good would that do? I float-jogged past him to the edge of the pool and lifted myself out. I cried in spurts as I dried off. I told the lifeguard chaperone I didn't feel well. Relieved she didn't demand an explanation, I continued past her and out of the pool area. My face felt full enough to split open.

In my sour-smelling room, I peeled off my tight, dripping swimsuit and slipped into my scratchy community pajama pants and T-shirt. Dizzy, I lay my throbbing head on my pillow. I had to throw up, but I tried to calm my guts. I wanted to be strong, but I was nothing more than an injured baby mouse. And this is what baby animals did. They lay around, squeaking and dying unless somebody happened to notice them, scoop them up, and take them home.

The next morning, I woke up alive, and my brains hadn't seeped onto my pillow.

In the cafeteria, Lupe ran to me, but I barely said hello. I didn't want her to think she could touch me.

We sat together and ate our oatmeal. "Look," Lupe bent her arm and pointed at the crease between her forearm and bicep. She licked her fingers and rubbed her spit vigorously into the crease, creating a matted nest of dark arm hair. "What is it?" she asked.

I shook my head. "I don't know. What?"

"A pussy." She laughed. "See it?" The word embarrassed me, but I laughed. Instead of telling her I thought she was embarrassing and childish for saying sex words and poking and pinching me in my private parts, I busied my mouth with chewing. When she laughed, her boobs bounced. But her eyes were blank, and they made sense to me. She reminded me of the messy shame that swirled in my gut whenever I saw or thought about sex things. She reminded me of Mitch's greasy mouth, the naked man at the community pool, the murdering werewolf, and the shameful secrets I kept about my body's wishes to be loved.

I quietly performed chores and stayed out of trouble, which earned me points to spend at the store. On my way to becoming a top kid, I was benefiting from rewards.

At the video game party, "No Parking (On the Dance Floor)" boomed from the speakers in the ceiling corners.

"Get the scorpion," a voice said from behind me. As the green arachnid raced across the screen, I rolled the ball furiously to catch the pixelated creature with my fire. "1500" popped up in its place, and the voice behind me said, "You got it!" When the spider crashed into me, the voice said, "Oh, you died."

I entered my initials on the high scores list and turned to see the boy who belonged to the voice narrating my arcade journey. We introduced ourselves, and I grew hot under his gaze. Michael had a tiny dip in the tip of his nose, which twitched as he spoke. His black hair almost touched his shoulders, and his onyx eyes sparkled.

"Wanna sit together at dinner tomorrow?"

"Sure," I said. My heart beat faster.

We competed to beat each other's Centipede scores, and when the music stopped and it was time to go to our rooms, Michael leaned in and kissed my cheek. I fell asleep with dreams of love behind my eyes.

At dinner the next day, Michael said, "I get to have a movie night." Movie night, like the video game party, was a big deal, and only the kids with the most points got to attend and bring a friend. "And I choose you," he said as if he'd known all his life that we were meant to be. "Will you be my date?" I hugged him, almost knocking him backward off the bench. He laughed. An awkward silence followed, and we ate our tater tots. My heart seemed to grow inside my chest, and it throbbed with new excitement. I'd have taken it out and placed it in his hand if it meant I'd never be lonely or down ever again.

In class one day, the teacher showed a video about animals mating in the wild. Michael and I sat next to each other and held hands between the desks in the darkened room. When the narrator mentioned polar bear mating patterns, Michael put his velvet lips on mine. Warmth spread throughout my body like a flame. I smiled at Michael and scanned the room to see who had noticed.

"Polar bears," said the video voice, "seek their mates in late spring and early summer."

It was June. Michael and I were polar bears. Even if nobody saw what our lips did, the kiss made me think maybe I was worth something.

The day of movie night, I learned that my social worker had found a foster home for me. Why did I have to leave right when everything was about to happen the way I wanted? I didn't have the courage to question my social worker, didn't have the strength to contest my placement. It might have made a difference, but I was too shy, too quiet, too agreeable, so I said, "Okay," even though nothing about it felt okay.

On movie night, Michael and I sat with a boy named Gio and his girlfriend, Sabrina, on the couch in the cafeteria lobby for our private VHS viewing of *Grease*. As John Travolta and Olivia Newton-John sang "Summer Nights," I told Michael with tears in my eyes that I would be leaving MacLaren Hall the next weekend.

Our thighs touched.

"You got placed fast." He squeezed my hand, and my knuckles throbbed on the release.

It was true that I was leaving right as I was getting used to the place and its people.

"That's too bad," he said, lowering his eyes. A spray of freckles danced across the bridge of his nose. "There was so much I wanted to teach you."

Wasn't there another girl who could take my place so I could stay? It seemed getting what I wanted took some kind of special magic I didn't know how to access. Adults had been deciding who I was and where I went my whole life. Too new, too uncertain to ask questions or make demands of strangers, I had no power to change my situation.

Michael and I didn't talk to each other for the duration of the movie. Lost in a daze of daydreams and *what-ifs*, I spent each song practicing how to hold back tears. When the movie ended, we hugged goodbye, and the death of possibility swelled in my throat.

"Maybe we'll meet again someday." Michael shrugged, and his hesitant smile said he knew loss well.

"Maybe," but I knew the truth—we would never see each other again. We both lived and breathed on the surface of things, never expecting more than we could hold in one hand, always preparing for the moment we'd be letting go again.

chapter 21

1984

AGE 10

I SPENT MY HONOR POINTS ON TWO-INCH-LONG V-shaped earrings with pink and blue chevron stripes across them and the blue and white tie-dyed hoodie I'd set as a goal the night I arrived at MacLaren.

I'd slipped into the oversized sweatshirt and headed toward my dorm when I ran into William.

"I was looking for you," he said.

"Oh, hey. I'm leaving and going to a foster home."

"I know. I wanted to say goodbye."

"Oh." I felt so far away from him, as if I had never known him at all.

"How will I talk to you or see you?" he said. I'd been trying my best to move on, but his eyes told me he was clinging to me, to us, to the only concept of family he'd known.

I'd been focused on myself and on enjoying freedom from Mom. But I wanted to reassure William, so I said, "Gramma and Grampa will know where I am." The truth was I didn't even know where I was going. None of it mattered because I would be leaving the best place I'd ever been. I had gotten a taste of what life could be like without constant fear and frustration, without Mom's stories and violence. Now, I was leaving another place and having to start over yet again when all I wanted was to stay put, reap the rewards of my good behavior, and fall in love with hope and possibility.

"Well, I have to get processed out, so I'll see you later." I hugged William, who was limp and small in my arms. Had we *ever* been brother and sister living the same nightmare? Or were we two people experiencing two different worlds, pulling further away from each other with each passing day?

"Okay, bye. I love you," he said, and I said it back. But like the words had been when I'd said them to Mom, they seemed empty. I knew I loved William, but I'd gotten so used to life without him, I no longer needed him. To need him was to suffer, and I wanted to survive.

The staff girl in charge instructed me to put everything I had earned, bought from the store, or acquired during my stay into a large plastic bag. "For processing," she said. "You have to leave the same as you came in. As long as your clothes still fit." She gave me the bag filled with my belongings and stepped out of my room while I changed. Into the new bag, I stuffed my hoodie and chevron earrings. I picked up the potpourri sachet from my desk. I detested that bag of smelly twigs and had no use for it. I decided I could let it go—I sniffed it quickly and wrinkled my nose before dropping it into the metal trash can like the garbage it was.

When I came out of the room, the MacLaren staff member escorted me to the windowed office at the end of the hall in the girls' dorm where I'd lived for the past month. She took the plastic bag and recorded its contents in a ledger before giving it back to me.

A man I'd never seen before approached. "Hi, Leslie. I'm Mr. Daniels, your new social worker." His hair was a big fluff of white cotton candy. "I'm going to take you to your new home." He pushed his glasses toward his eyes. There was nothing in his voice but sound. I couldn't tell if he was excited for me or merely doing his job.

I looked around for Michael, hoping he had asked for a pass so he could say goodbye. Sharp pain nagged me under one of my shoulder blades.

Once we got into the car, Mr. Daniels became talkative. "How's your day going? This is an exciting day, isn't it?" His hair bounced. I agreed. Could he tell I was lying? "So, this home is great. It's in Pico Rivera." He faced the road. "Do you know where that is? Have you been there before?" Mr. Daniels seemed kind and caring now, unlike in the hallway at MacLaren when I thought he might not even know how to smile. I shook my head. He looked at me. He seemed to be wearing a white rabbit for a hat. "Your new foster mother's name is Mrs. Perez. There's no foster father. Do you have any questions?" Mr. Daniels tapped the steering wheel.

Why would I have questions? Should I have questions? Maybe if someone had prepared me, provided a list . . . "I'm used to not having a father." I grasped the armrest and stroked the rough plastic with my thumb. *Is my brother coming?* I wanted to ask, but I already knew the answer. *Can I see my mom? My grandparents? Auntie Philys?* I exhaled onto the window to leave proof of my existence, but I failed in the warm air. The tuft of white fur on Mr. Daniels's head kept bobbing, the car kept eating the road, and my silence told more lies.

My new home was a corner house with black iron bars separating the yard from the sidewalk. Mr. Daniels walked me to the front door through a jungle of bushes, small trees, and potted plants that grew like a curtain between my past and my future. Mr. Daniels knocked on the door. If I had spoken, my words might have sounded something like, I *don't want to stay here. I don't like it.* My stomach rolled and jumped and burned, turning over on itself.

"Hello, come in," said a large woman in a colorful paisley muumuu. "I'm Mrs. Perez, and you must be Leslie." She spoke with a hint of an accent. After wiping her fingers on a towel draped over her shoulder, she shook my hand limply. Her hand was still damp. Mr. Daniels and I sat on bar stools at a white, tiled counter. Mrs. Perez moved her hands over pans on the stove.

"Rice and tortillas with chorizo—it's Mexican sausage," she said. "I hope you like it."

Mr. Daniels leaned against the island counter. "Do you have any questions, Leslie?"

Maybe *When will William arrive?* Or *When can I see my mom and is she okay because the last time I saw her she was standing in a pile of glass, screaming.* These thoughts made me hot, or maybe it was the chorizo sizzling in the pan, shooting revolting sausage smells into the air. "No." I shook my head. "No questions."

Mr. Daniels patted my forearm and stood up. "I'll let myself out, Mrs. Perez." His rabbit hair shook. "You have my phone number."

Mrs. Perez kept her back to me as she finished cooking. She broke two eggs and scrambled them with the chorizo. "I hope you have a good appetite," she said. "I'm known for my cooking."

"I'm hungry," I said, but chorizo smelled like sausage because it *was* sausage, which meant it consisted of ground-up pig and rat parts and cockroaches. I slipped outside of myself as I chewed, disconnecting my taste buds from reality. She asked if I wanted more. I politely declined. Exhaustion ached in my jaw, throat, and stomach. "Can I go to my—" Was it *my* room? No. Nothing in her house belonged to me. "The bedroom?"

Mrs. Perez said yes and that we'd go over the house rules the next day. "For now, all you need to know is that the cooking and dishes are my job, so don't you worry about that. Let's get you settled into your room." If she referred to it as my room, I supposed I could, too. I put my box of belongings away in drawers. I would get my little silver radio from Gramma and Grampa when I visited. Fortunately, after Mom trashed the Norwalk apartment, Gramma and Grampa had collected and safely stored my things. Mrs. Perez gave me a toothbrush and a towel and left me alone, so I could get ready for bed. I hummed the tune and sang the lyrics to one of my favorite songs, "Do You Really Wanna Hurt Me?" I missed my music and longed to drown in the melody of someone else's pain.

On day two at Mrs. Perez's, I ate Cheerios for breakfast. The kitchen still reeked of sausage. "When you're finished," Mrs. Perez said, "I'll show you how to clean the patio." I followed her to the sliding glass door where she led me onto a cement courtyard surrounded by a low, tiled wall and a landscaped hill ascending to a fence. Potted plants and large planters lined the wall of the house and the parapet. In the center of the courtyard, a large, square planter housed a tree that had shed its leaves everywhere. "This," she put a broom handle in front of me, "is a push broom. You use it like this." Her housecoat danced, and her boobs swayed as she aggressively pushed the broom in several short, forceful jerks. "This is for the dirt. It works better than that one." She nodded at an angled broom. "Which is good for getting the leaves in one place. You gotta get all the dirt, too."

"I like sweeping," I said, and it was true. It was rewarding to make messy, dirty things clear and clean. I swept and swept, jerking the push broom around. The dirt piled nicely, and scooping it with the dustpan made me feel accomplished. Dirt clouds drifted from the bristles like baby powder. If I didn't do a good job, would Mrs. Perez send me away? I jabbed the broom into the cement. A gritty layer remained. Maybe dirt was like a memory. Maybe some things couldn't be cleaned.

The sun bled through the leaves of the courtyard tree as I worked. I couldn't contain all the dirt. It was in my eyes, nose, and mouth, and when I wiped my brow with my forearm, I smeared sweat around like mud. But the sweeping kept me busy, worked my muscles, and took my mind off of the nowhere feeling that stirred in my gut and off of the idea that this stranger was supposed to be my new mom. How would I replace Mom so easily? It was her fault I was here, but Mom was more than just a word. It was blood, connection, a link to myself that grew weaker each day.

Thirsty, panting, and my shirt clinging to my back like a sticker, I stood the brooms and dustpan against the house. All the dirt I'd collected, the layers of filth mixed with sadness, gave me a sense of satisfaction, like I'd done something right.

Mrs. Perez beamed as she pushed her glasses up on her nose. "Next Saturday, same thing."

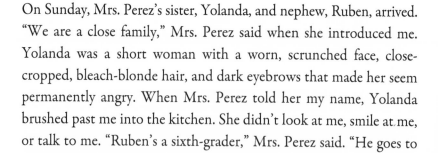

On Sunday, Mrs. Perez's sister, Yolanda, and nephew, Ruben, arrived. "We are a close family," Mrs. Perez said when she introduced me. Yolanda was a short woman with a worn, scrunched face, close-cropped, bleach-blonde hair, and dark eyebrows that made her seem permanently angry. When Mrs. Perez told her my name, Yolanda brushed past me into the kitchen. She didn't look at me, smile at me, or talk to me. "Ruben's a sixth-grader," Mrs. Perez said. "He goes to the school you'll be going to tomorrow."

Tall and tanned, Ruben stood almost as tall as me. His black hair shone like oil. Even though Ruben was my foster-cousin, I secretly hoped he found me pretty. Did he look at me? Would he and I develop crushes on each other, and would my heart flap like it had wings every time he entered the room? I stared at my hands, lines of dirt still under my nails. I stared at the brown stain on the linoleum, the rebel piece of scrambled egg on the counter, the shadowed wall that wouldn't judge me. When Ruben turned away from me, and his slender arm pulled the refrigerator door handle, I imagined touching his elbow.

"So, you're in the fifth grade?" He didn't look at me when he said it. "It's almost summer. That means school's almost out. Everybody already knows everybody."

"Ruben, be nice," Mrs. Perez said. "Leslie will make friends just fine. Can you introduce her to some of yours?"

The next day, Mrs. Perez enrolled me at Rio Vista Elementary School, my ninth elementary school, not counting the classroom at MacLaren. I never saw Ruben at school, but I did make a new friend. Cena Cortes had shoulder-length hair the color of wheat. She said she was Spanish on her father's side, which explained her last name and her fair skin and eyes that shone gray-green with flecks of brown in the light. When she wrote, she held her pencil between her thumb and index finger daintily as if she worried the pencil would break under the slightest pressure. I admired how the lead glided out and made words. She had tight control, even though the side of her hand never touched the page.

"You have pretty handwriting," I said. It was slow, curly, and feminine. She ended her words with upward swirls and dotted her *i*'s with bubbles.

"You're crazy," Cena said. *Don't say that,* I wanted to say. She didn't know the meaning of the word like I did. Maybe nobody liked their own writing. I practiced writing like her, but I couldn't make my curls smooth, and my bubbled *i* was a haphazard halo over a stick-body without arms or legs.

On the blacktop at recess, I followed Cena to the foursquare lines where cliques gathered to sit on the ground instead of playing games. I sat with her as she wrote letters to her other friends, letters she folded in creative ways. The rest of the activity on the playground passed like a silent movie.

I noticed a group of four girls staring at me. They wore black jackets and bright lipstick. I took them for sixth-graders. They stared so long I believed they looked *past* or maybe even *through* me. I turned around to see if there might be something behind me that caught their attention, but Cena and I sat in the last square on this side of the fence. There was nothing behind me but chain link, grass, and the empty street. The group of girls laughed. As they talked to one another and stared, I burned with embarrassment. I couldn't hear their words. They shifted from one foot to the other and threw their heads back in laughter.

Then, all at once, each girl took her hand and swept her long, black hair away from the side of her face. That was my signature move, only I didn't realize it until that moment, as this group of girls repeatedly flipped their hair as they stared at me and then turned to each other, laughing hysterically.

"Look at her," one of them yelled. "She's so full of herself." I turned to the blank paper section in my notebook, and at the top, wrote, *Dear Cena.* My mind fell blank after that, so I folded the page into a rectangle and slid it into my binder's back sleeve.

One day, after the school bus dropped me off, I followed Ruben into the house. We sat next to each other at the kitchen table.

"School was good?" Mrs. Perez flipped a tortilla on the burner. "Leslie, you tell me if Ruben ever does anything to you." Her ashen face caught the dim afternoon light.

"Aunt Maria," Ruben said, shaking his head. She ignored him.

"Okay," I said, and all those guilty feelings came back to me. I thought of how Lupe touched me and then acted like I'd made up the whole thing. I shuddered. Did Mrs. Perez think Ruben would touch me? He was cute, and I did have a crush on him, but we'd barely spent any time together. When would he have put his hands on me?

"Good, because it's inappropriate for him to ever do anything that makes you uncomfortable." I shook my head and stared at her for a moment. The light in her eyes flickered like brown flames. I slowed my chewing, uncertain whose turn it was to speak next. "You tell me if he ever does anything, okay?" She held up her spatula.

"Okay," I looked at the refrigerator to avoid her gaze. "I will." Satisfied, she patted the counter. Maybe Mrs. Perez cared about me.

Ruben sighed, rolling his eyes. "I'll wait for Mom in the living room then." He left the kitchen. Did Ruben have a past record of touching the foster kids? What, exactly, did she think he might do to me? Mrs. Perez had managed to turn a cute boy into a dirty thought.

After a few weeks, Ana came to live with us. She was a small, brown girl with black chin-length hair and a ready smile. But she spoke only Spanish. At night, we lay in our beds in the dark. She taught me how to count to one hundred in her language, and I taught her in mine. She was a patient teacher, and I was a fast learner. In two weeks, we each had a new vocabulary of a hundred words. Other nights, we kept the radio on super low so Mrs. Perez wouldn't hear it. Ana sang along with my music but struggled with the words. She made sounds and noises that weren't the actual lyrics, so I repeated the words, and she repeated them, too, improving every time.

Lionel Richie sang, "Stuck on You." We sang along. Ana picked up the chorus pretty fast even though her accent clung to her words. I pronounced all the words slowly and clearly. She repeated them, and we giggled into the night like long-lost sisters.

When Ana went away for the weekend to visit her family, my stomach ached as if full of poison. Loneliness forced me to feel Mom and William's absence from my life. When Ana returned, we sang songs and counted with each other until my eyelids shut and my ears went deaf with sleep. Every night, we carried on like this, and soon, I realized I was singing Lionel Richie's song *to* Ana. I wasn't a man singing to a woman, but I, too, "needed a friend." We sang along with Cyndi Lauper and Madonna, and during the day, we danced in our room, holding hairbrushes to our lips like microphones. It didn't matter that Ana didn't know the meanings of the words she sang. All that mattered was that she was there with me.

———————

Returning to Mrs. Perez's after visiting my grandparents for the weekend, the faint sound of music streamed from somewhere as I walked to my room. The closer I got, the clearer the music became— "Girls Just Wanna Have Fun," by Cyndi Lauper. I stopped. There was *no way* Ana would be using my radio without my permission. I thought maybe she'd received a radio of her own while I was away. I entered the room.

Ana sat on her bunk, reading. *My* radio was on.

"Why are you listening to my radio?" I shouted. "Did you have my permission to listen to it while I was gone? I can't believe you would just take something that's not yours and use it without even asking. It's *my* radio." I shut the radio off, unplugged it, and hugged it to my chest. Ana looked at me, seemingly stunned, blinking her eyes. She didn't know the words I spoke, but I could tell by her wide eyes and frowning mouth she knew I was angry. Foreign words rolled from her lips.

"What's going on in here?" Mrs. Perez stood in the doorway of our room.

"She used my radio without asking," I said. Tears streamed from my eyes. "Tell her, Mrs. Perez. Tell her it's not okay."

Mrs. Perez said, "It's important to share, Leslie. She wasn't hurting anything by listening to it."

"But it's *my* radio, and she should have asked me if she could listen to it when I'm gone instead of acting like it's hers."

Mrs. Perez snatched the radio from me and wound the cord around its scratched body, and it was like she stole the heart from my chest. She left and slammed the door shut behind her. Ana said more Spanish words. "I hate you," I screamed at her, threw myself onto my bed, and set my lungs on fire with crying into my pillow.

Ana cried, too, like a small, wounded animal. And she counted. "Uno, Dos, Tres..." But there was nothing she could do to bring me back to her. Ana and I continued as roommates, barely talking to or looking at each other. We didn't count or sing or laugh. The music between us was gone.

chapter 22

1984
AGE 10

ON SATURDAYS, I MOVED DIRT AROUND THE BACK patio, becoming filthier with every push of the broom as clouds of dust mottled my skin and drifted into my mouth.

On Sundays, Ruben and Yolanda came over to eat dinner. As Yolanda and Mrs. Perez communicated in Spanish, Ruben and Ana listened, occasionally chiming in, and I pushed food around on my plate.

I didn't belong here with these people who spoke Spanish around me like I was an outsider who deserved no language and no love. Yolanda, who had taken an interest in Ana, continued to ignore me, and I continued to ignore them all. On some weekends, I visited my grandparents, and I always returned with nausea swelling in my stomach. My insides wrestled with reality. Why did I have to be in a foster home? Didn't my grandparents love me? At school, I walked around like an empty stalk of human tissue and bones, hollow of purpose, devoid of meaning. And after my radio was confiscated, and I no longer had music, loneliness swallowed me up.

After sweeping the patio, I showered and dressed, and Mrs. Perez, Yolanda, Ruben, Ana, and I drove to an indoor swap meet in Slauson. "Stay close," Mrs. Perez said. "Don't run off." Ana and I cruised the aisles without speaking. I had never seen so many aisles, so many toys, clothes, and *thises* and *thats* hanging in one place. The glass cases of merchandise reminded me of the glass case in the Golf 'n' Stuff arcade where Auntie Philys took William and me to play video games. She'd save a twenty-dollar bill to feed to the machine in exchange for a pocketful of tokens to keep the three of us busy for a couple of hours.

At the swap meet, though, row after row of cases filled with things I wanted stretched out before me like the future I would never have. There were hair barrettes and pencil erasers and key chains and small stuffed bears and fake flowers and dolls. I pointed to a small baby doll wearing a pink dress. The woman behind the counter lifted her from the shelf and set her on the glass. She reminded me of the sand-bodied baby doll Mom bought me at Stater Bros. the night she kidnapped William and me. I carried the pink doll to the end of the counter.

"You stay here," the lady behind the counter said. "You pay for doll." She smiled at me.

"I have to ask my—" I hesitated because I didn't want to say *foster mother* out loud. Did saying the phrase mean I accepted my role, that I'd given up hope of being reunited with my real family? And I refused to refer to Mrs. Perez as my mother even though the lady behind the counter meant nothing to me and I knew I would never see her again. Setting the doll down, I said, "I'll be right back."

"You buy?" The woman behind the counter wore the same smile she'd put on earlier. My tears didn't faze her.

"I might—maybe," I stuttered. "I'm waiting for my—family." Where did Mrs. Perez go? And Yolanda and Ruben? I'd even lost sight of Ana. I hurried, peeking around the end caps in search of my pretend family, scanning aisle after aisle. Workers stood behind counters, and an occasional *real* family lurked, searching for price tags and turning over shoes or shirts to inspect them. Fearful Mrs. Perez would think I'd intentionally wandered off despite her commanding me not to, I ran. Where were they? I had tried to keep them in sight. I'd only looked away for a moment. Soon, the gleaming floors and fluorescent lights blurred together through my tears. Why did Mrs. Perez let me out of *her* sight? "Mrs. Perez?" I called out. "Ana?" I repeated myself until I choked on my crying and returned to the baby doll waiting for me on the counter.

I was a liar, pretending I had a family. Those people weren't my family any more than this baby doll was an actual baby. But I didn't know what else to call them. The smiling woman placed her hands on the glass counter as if waiting for my money—money I didn't have. And just when I thought I'd been abandoned for good, I saw the back of Ana's head, her shoulder-length straight black hair, as it disappeared behind an end cap. "Ana," I called, shuffling after her. "Where did you go? I was looking everywhere for you."

"¿*Tú?*" she said, pointing at me.

"No, you," I pointed at her. "Where's Mrs. Perez?" She pointed, and I saw her. I wiped my eyes and snorted back snot. "Mrs. Perez," I said, acting as if I hadn't freaked out, as if I'd been in perfect control and had my eye on her the whole time. "Can I buy a baby doll?"

"No," she said, hands on her hips, eyes focused on something behind me.

"We're leaving now." Yolanda's angry eyebrows seemed to say I deserved nothing.

Mrs. Perez and Yolanda walked away from me. Ana and I

followed. Ruben held a pair of black and red sneakers when we found him at a kiosk near the exit. I couldn't shake the thought that I should return to the smiling lady to tell her I wasn't going to buy the doll after all, but I was not in charge of my time, nor did I feel free to ask for anything else. I had already been turned down once, and Mrs. Perez was not my mom. And she and Yolanda walked so fast, the only thing I had permission to do was run after them like a lost puppy.

Ana left Mrs. Perez's for good soon after I'd abandoned the doll at the swap meet. She was there one night, asleep in the bunk above me, and gone the next. I had convinced myself I hated her and didn't need her. But with her gone, I was lonelier and sicker than ever. Nobody else in my world was a foster child, except for William, whom I rarely saw and who grew thinner and thinner in my mind, less like my brother and more like a figment of my imagination. Siblings once, we now inhabited separate worlds that lay many moons and much silence apart. I didn't know his experience, and he didn't know mine. At least when we lived with Mom, William and I had each other. Now, what did we have?

The next time I visited Gramma and Grampa, I begged them to let me live with them again, and Gramma said, "We just can't do it anymore, Leslie." When she put my name in it for emphasis, I knew she meant what she said. Nobody adds your name to the end of a sentence unless they're trying to prove something. I cried into my tissue and forced myself silent so hard I thought the pressure would cause my face to burst. "We can't take the harassment from your mother."

"Please." I begged longer to show her my desperation because it was my last option. I knew what almost dying felt like—I'd been there before, in the grip of Mom's hands and threats—and though nothing pressed on my throat but my grief and loneliness, death would strangle me if I stayed with Mrs. Perez. Gramma heard me, and she reflected myself back to me in her mirror-eyes. But it didn't matter.

"It's going to be all right." She hugged me.

Grampa said, "We can't handle your mother." He looked so tired, like he needed to give up. "You're safer somewhere else. And it's just too hard on Gramma." Sickness sloshed inside of me, and back to Mrs. Perez's I went.

I walked into the house to Madonna's "Lucky Star" booming from her music video. Ruben was sitting on the couch. As Madonna danced and sang, I swallowed my nausea with the joke of lucky stars. Apparently, they existed, and Madonna had one, but where was mine? It wasn't Mrs. Perez's fault, but I still blamed her for being a stranger and not my mother. A gnawing certainty told me I had to leave. There had to be a way to banish this helplessness inside of me, this raw feeling that ran through me like hunger but could not be satisfied no matter how many buttered tortillas I ate. I was sick, growing spiteful, mean, and bitter.

When the music video ended, I walked into the kitchen, where Mrs. Perez was watching a black-and-white TV program. "I want to talk to my social worker."

"Why?" She lowered the volume on the TV. "Did Ruben do something to you?" she said, her gray-brown eyes large and focused behind her metal-rimmed glasses. "Ruben, get in here." Her tight, gray curls shook.

"It's not that. I want to talk to my social worker."

"What did Ruben do to you, because I will kill him if he touched you." Mrs. Perez said the whole thing like a statement instead of a question, so I wasn't sure if I was supposed to answer. She moved her eyebrows up, and she seemed concerned. "It's okay. You can tell me. And then you can talk to Mr. Daniels." I promised her Ruben hadn't done anything to me. She stood in front of me, blinking her eyes a million times, waiting for a reason. I didn't want to tell Mrs. Perez the truth, didn't want to disappoint or anger her. I knew it would be rude to say I hated living in her house.

Finally, I blurted out, "I want to find another foster home." She continued to stare at me and then turned off her show. I knew she cared, and I knew she was a good woman. I shrugged my shoulders. I wanted to give her a reason. How could I explain to her something she could never understand—that there was no *reason* other than I needed to be somewhere I was loved, somewhere I could understand the language, somewhere I didn't feel like I wanted to bury myself in the tree planter in the courtyard and die?

"I don't know what you think you're gonna find, Leslie." There it was again, my name at the end of a sentence. Mrs. Perez walked to the stove and turned to me again. "I've done nothing but provide you with a good home and food and everything you need."

I grasped for a lie, but nothing came to me. "Just somewhere else. I don't know. Anywhere. I just don't feel . . . right. I just want to go home," I said, though I knew I didn't have a home. She and I both knew there was nowhere else for me to go. But if I could hold on to the thought that there was a light out there to guide me, like the light Madonna sang about in her song—a light shining so bright— then maybe my darkness was temporary, and happiness might take its place. I didn't know how to find happiness, but if so many songs had been written about it, it had to exist. It wasn't here in Pico

Rivera. It wasn't in Mrs. Perez's chorizo scramble, nor was it in a Spanish conversation I'd been excluded from. And it most certainly wasn't in a patio of dirt.

Every place was haunted with a coldness that swept through me in layers as if somebody had died and that *somebody* was me. And there was nothing anybody could do about it. How could I tell Mrs. Perez it probably wasn't her fault I was about to vomit every time I walked into her house? That my brain threatened to burst every night? That I detested her for existing because I was there, in her house, and not with my family? Maybe I should have been able to find happiness with Mrs. Perez—and in the fact that she had taken me in. Maybe I should have felt grateful, but I only felt empty.

"I don't understand you," Mrs. Perez said, shaking her head. "You gotta have a reason. He's gonna think you a silly little girl." Maybe Mr. Daniels *would* think that. Usually, I did care what others thought of me, but not this time.

Mr. Daniels found a home for me to visit. I buckled my seat belt.

"Why are you so unhappy?" he said.

I kept my eyes on the road and watched it disappear under the front of the car. "I . . . feel . . . bad . . . all the time."

"Well, I'm not sure we're going to find you a place you like better, and homes are pretty full. There aren't a lot of openings. Let's see what we can do. You can't be too picky." The lump in my throat seemed to increase in size. I was always on the verge of tears, of choking. "Mrs. Perez isn't going to stop you from leaving. She doesn't want anyone who doesn't want to be there. She says she did her best and in her twenty years of being a foster parent, she's never seen such a discontented little girl."

He took me to a small, clean house. The man and woman had a

five-year-old son named Jacob. Mr. Daniels presented a folder. The woman opened it to read some papers, and when she lowered her head, her straight, shoulder-length hair fell forward like a veil against the sides of her face. She said, "Okay," several times in response to what Mr. Daniels said. I waited for instructions.

The table was set for four. I sat in the chair closest to the refrigerator, with my back to it. The nice woman half-smiled, which gave me the impression she didn't like me or trust me. I didn't know what damage I could do in two hours, but letting a strange child sit at her table must have been scary, especially if that strange child had been in and out of homes because her mentally ill mom couldn't handle things anymore. She asked if I wanted milk. I said yes, and when she poured my glass half-full, I asked if she would fill it all the way. I even said please. I knew I'd want more, and I thought I'd save her a trip to the fridge. This way, she could sit and enjoy her meal, and I wouldn't have to ask for more at the worst possible time. She filled my glass to a satisfying level.

When Mr. Daniels returned, I was outside playing on the swing set with Jacob. I thought maybe this could be the place for me. I could swing away and send my worries into the clouds.

I told Jacob not to swing too high, worried he would flip over the swing set and get hurt on my watch. Jacob pumped higher. Swinging with him reminded me of swinging with William. I didn't need a brother replacement, but I knew how to be a sister, so I thought Jacob and I would get along perfectly. I pumped my legs, shaking the swing set on the upswing and on the downswing. I wondered if the whole structure would lift out of the ground. I wondered if I would break it. I wondered if I would get my fingers caught in the chain or if I would swing all the way over the top or fall to the ground and die.

"I'm swinging higher than you," I yelled to the boy. He slowed enough to jump out of his swing. Then he played with a patch of weeds.

The woman appeared at the back door. She still had her apron on. "Your social worker's here," she said.

"I'll race you," I said. The boy ignored me and whacked at the weeds one last time on his way to the house.

We said our goodbyes and it's-nice-to-meet-yous. In the car, Mr. Daniels said, "So, I'll let you know what they thought."

What *they* thought? They were checking *me* out? I prepared myself for compliments and praise. Mr. Daniels said he didn't think it was going to work out. My heartbeat sped up. Tears burned my esophagus. I turned to the window. "Why? What did they say?" I had told Mr. Daniels I wanted to find another home because I questioned my ability to survive. I never thought for a moment that someone might reject *me*, especially not after spending less than a couple of hours with me. What had I done—or not done? Heat pulsed in my cheeks and forehead.

Mr. Daniels's fluffy white hair jiggled. "They thought you were kind of bossy."

Me? Bossy? And how could they even know that? What did we do besides chew food? I didn't know what to say. My mouth quivered. I wanted my Mom—the version of her that would let me lean into her while she stroked my hair and sang me a song—but she was further from me now than ever before. Mr. Daniels, with his rabbit hair, hurtful words, and stuffy car, drove us on the road that led nowhere except back to the place I hated.

"And demanding. They didn't like how you asked for more milk before you drank what they gave you."

I would have told her my reasoning if she had asked. She didn't know anything about me or what I'd given up, and yet she'd already labeled me, pretending she knew me so she could justify rejecting me. How was it that you could be doing the wrong thing even when you thought it was the right thing?

"But I drank it all," I said. "Did they tell you I drank it all?" My eyes blurred, and tears ran out of my eyes like people out of a burning house.

"No," he said. "She didn't tell me that." He patted my knee in a grandfatherly way. "We'll keep searching. We'll find you a home. I promise."

By the middle of summer, Mr. Daniels hadn't yet followed through with his promise. I'd been with Mrs. Perez for two months, twice as long as I'd been in MacLaren Hall. Still, I never fully adjusted to her home, always waiting and hoping to leave.

It was the summer of 1984, the summer Los Angeles hosted the Olympic Games. Mrs. Perez drove Yolanda, Ruben, and me to L.A. to watch the torch relay. Thousands of people crowded the streets. I didn't even know what the Olympics were, and here were all these people excited about seeing runners pass by. Everyone pinned Sam the Eagle to their jackets, hats, and tote bags. To me, Sam symbolized nothing—he smiled with his orange beak, pretending to be a person when he was only a dumb drawing. Mrs. Perez gave me a pin. I held it in my hand like a silver dollar and rubbed its surface, tracing the metal etchings of its design with my thumb. I shoved it in my pocket.

I couldn't see past the back of the person in front of me. People all around me, only sky above me, I wished I could fly, rise among the clouds and float where everything seemed simple, where there was no sound, no heartache, no fear. In the streets on that day in July, a wall of bodies surrounded me. How could I care about athletes winning medals when I'd lost the most important thing of all—my family?

"It's the chance of a lifetime," Mrs. Perez said, resting her hand on my shoulder. Her eyes lit up. My vision dulled as my world closed in. I could have taken a step back, blended in with the crowd, shrunk myself, and throngs of people wouldn't have had any idea they were clapping and cheering as I vanished.

chapter 23

1984
AGE 10

ONE SEPTEMBER AFTERNOON, MR. DANIELS PICKED me up. "I think this is going to be a good one," he said as he buckled his seatbelt. "The Poplawskis live in La Puente. They are excited to meet you." I wondered what they knew about me, especially since the previous family I visited hated my guts. I wiped my clammy hands on my pants. As we drove along the highway, the world passed by in blurs of color. A flash of light danced in my heart. Was this hope? Happiness?

We arrived at a small house set back from the street by a patch of lawn. An awning made it dark and ominous-looking, even in the bright sun. Mr. Daniels stood behind me, radiating heat against my back as he leaned over me to knock on the door.

A short, blonde-haired girl stuck her upturned nose into the narrow gap. I guessed her to be about eight or nine—at most, a couple years younger than I was.

Mr. Daniels said, "And who might you be?"

"I'm Katy." She didn't smile.

We entered to find a large woman reclining on a brown couch. Next to her, another girl, about my age, sat forward with a white poufy dog on her knees. The dog reminded me of Mr. Daniels's hair.

"You can call me Iga," the woman said. She wore jeans, a button-down blouse with the sleeves rolled to the elbows, and light blue Dearfoam slippers. The dog ran at me and yipped. I jumped back. It panted and let its pink tongue dangle from its smiling mouth.

"And I'm Andrea," said the girl with the dog. She wore a red ribbon as a headband around her shoulder-length bob of dark brown hair. "I'm not a foster kid. I'm their *real* daughter. And this," she said, petting and shaking the fluffy pooch, "is Tippy. I named him that because he has a lazy eye and tips his head to the side." Tippy licked Andrea's chin and mouth. "He's a Pomeranian. Pure breed. He's mine. My little bay-bay."

"So," Iga said. "What do you want to know about us and our home? Please, sit." She gestured to the rocking chair opposite the couch. "Katy, get Mr. Daniels a chair from the dining room."

"I—don't know," I said. My cheeks grew hot, and my hands became aimless. I wiped them on my pants, which were cool to the touch. Slightly sweaty but cold, I tensed my torso. I made eye contact with each of them. They stared at me. I looked at Mr. Daniels.

"What she's hoping to find," he said, "is a place that feels safe, that feels right. We spoke about this on the phone. The home she's in now isn't a good fit." I interlocked my fingers in my lap. "Leslie is very pleasant."

"We are like one big, happy family," Iga said. "You'll have chores. It's part of learning responsibility. And we go to church on Sundays. And we go out to eat afterward. I'm sure you'll like that." I did, in fact, like the idea of that. With Mom, we rarely ate out except for McDonald's on occasion and a pizza or a bucket of fried chicken here and there. And I could go to church. As long as I didn't have to wait in line to eat a plastic wafer and grape juice like the time Mom took us to the most boring Catholic Mass ever, with a priest in a white robe and velvety blue floor-to-ceiling curtains against the walls.

"My mom taught me how to say the Lord's Prayer," I said, hoping to impress them, especially now that I knew they could turn me away.

"Come on," Andrea said, "I'll show you my room." I followed her past the dining room and down the hallway to her bedroom, the first one on the right. "This is mine and Katy's room," Andrea said. "And this is my TV. We play video games here. And this," she patted the top of a large, black stereo system "is my stereo. Nobody touches it but me." Next to it, my little silver radio would look like nothing more than a cheap, plastic toy. But my heart leaped. We both gravitated toward music. She snapped a cassette tape into the deck. "Do you like Prince?" she said. "He's my favorite. I'm going to marry him."

"Andrea," Katy said, standing in the doorway. "Your mom says to show her the other room—her room." "Let's Go Crazy," a song I'd heard on the radio, boomed from the speakers. Andrea sang the words and cut the air with her hands.

"Just a minute." Andrea sang, pointing at me and swaying her head back and forth with the words. Why would anyone *want* to go crazy? Did anybody choose crazy? I didn't think so. Prince must have meant something else. I thought about Mom and her fear of trucks, but we weren't going to be thrown into them like in the Prince song. Mom had said we were going to be rammed by them. The more Andrea sang, the more I missed Mom. I thought it was possible I had an actual hole in my heart. Andrea spun around and stopped singing. Tippy waddled in, and Andrea scooped him up. He looked like one of those muffs you can put your hands in when it's freezing out. In a gross display of affection, Tippy licked Andrea's mouth. "Come on. Let's see *your* room," Andrea said.

We left Prince going crazy by himself. I followed Andrea into a room on the left at the end of the short hallway. It had bunk beds like the room I'd shared with Ana, who used to be my friend but now existed somewhere else in the world. And like some of the rooms I'd slept in with William, who used to be my brother before he became a memory.

Andrea said I could choose the bed I wanted. "Always turn off the lights, Okay?"

Straightforward and reasonable. Rules didn't scare me. Every place had rules. Even my grandparents had rules, such as no sugar cereals, no crayons or markers in the living room, no talking about Mom, and no nail polish remover in the house because if the remover spilled, it would drain the color out of everything it touched.

"And that," she pointed to the room opposite the one I'd be sleeping in, "is my parents' bedroom. Don't ever go in there unless you have permission. It's off limits." *Understandable.* The grown-ups needed their own space. The ajar door invited me into the darkness, but I followed rules well, especially rules others imposed on me. I hated to disappoint.

In the kitchen, a door led to the garage, and in the garage, a door led to the backyard. Andrea still held Tippy, who licked Andrea's mouth like an ice cream cone. Outside, crabgrass and dirt led to a rusted swing set. Andrea sat in one swing with her dog in her lap. I took the other swing. "So, what do you think?" Andrea asked, licking her lips. She pulled Chapstick from her pocket and vigorously applied it to her mouth. Katy stood next to the swing set, folding her arms across her chest.

I said, "It feels like the right place." The sun sank behind us, its light making the kitchen window sparkle like jewelry. The lingering heat of the summer sun warmed my skin, but something else happened, too. Andrea made me feel welcomed and safe and hopeful that we would have fun together and that she wouldn't touch my radio without permission because she had a stereo of her own.

"I think it's a perfect fit," Andrea said, scratching Tippy behind his pointy ears. Katy dragged a stick across the dirt close to the house. She followed Andrea around like Tippy did. *I could fit in here. I could be like a puppy, too.* People adored puppies. We could be puppies together. As long as I didn't have to lick Andrea on the mouth. Maybe if I lived here instead of with Mrs. Perez, the sickness in my stomach would dissolve and happiness and safety would bloom there instead.

We reentered the house and stood together in the living room where Iga and Mr. Daniels sat. "How soon can she move?" Iga asked. Too white, too wide, and every one identical, her teeth were too big for her face, and they clicked when she talked. But I didn't care. I was getting a new home.

"I love it there," I said as soon as we got into the car.

"Are you sure?" Mr. Daniels asked. His expression said he doubted I knew what I loved. He rubbed his stubbly white chin. "I will talk to them later and see how it went on their end, to make sure they didn't feel, you know, pressured, with us standing there. And if they have no complaints, we'll get you moved." I didn't want him to talk to them later. That would give them a chance to think things over and change their minds. I wanted Iga's word to be as good as gold, written in stone, stamped and sealed with an unbreakable promise.

"When? How soon will you know?"

"Calm down," he said. "Everything's going to be okay." How could he be so sure? What did he know about feeling stuck and unanchored at the same time? If I could move in with the Poplawskis, they might cure my aching existence. If I couldn't... I was terrified of what might happen next.

Summer was over when I moved in with the Poplawskis. I only had a few things, including my little silver radio, which Mrs. Perez returned to me now that I was leaving her home. It *did* look like a cheap toy compared to Andrea's beast of a stereo system with detachable speakers. I learned all the words to her Prince album while taking turns on Atari, playing Crystal Castles and Pac-man and while combing the hair on all her My Little Pony ponies. Andrea controlled what we did, when, and for how long. She determined whether I brushed the bubblegum pink hair of Pinkie Pie or the rainbow hair of Rainbow Dash. I didn't mind. Not having to be the one in charge of all the decisions relieved me. I could be a ten-year-old instead of a grown-up. I could play instead of worrying about William and Mom and all the ways we might die.

It didn't seem to matter anymore that I had to leave Jellybean in a shopping cart by the freeway. Having fewer toys meant I wouldn't have to search for them. They wouldn't go missing. I left that fear behind. It lay in my past like clothes that no longer fit.

Katy butted in, and Andrea put her in her place. "It's Leslie's turn," Andrea shouted, stealing the plastic pony brush from Katy. "You've had your turn. Give her a chance." Her protectiveness gave me confidence. She chose me first, and like when Mom scolded William, I reveled in my place as the favorite. Katy sulked and dragged herself from the room. I didn't care where she went, didn't care if she bawled her eyes out.

"Let's play Pac-Man," Andrea said. She got thirty restarts to every one life I got because the game belonged to her and not me. Andrea regularly reminded us we were foster kids, and she was the *real* daughter. At first, all of this almost went unnoticed. But soon, I learned how insignificant we foster kids were.

Katy and I cleaned the house every weekend. This included removing every trinket from the particle board curio cabinet and dusting every nook, cranny, shelf, and surface. A pair of bronzed baby shoes sat in the cabinet. Were they Andrea's real baby shoes? I had known of babies' feet or hands being cast in clay and the age of the baby carved with a toothpick before the clay had dried. The round clay slab hung on a wall as proof of life.

Going through some of my mom's papers once, I came across a lock of hair in a slim envelope with light blue writing on it that said, "Baby's First Haircut." "That's your hair," Mom said.

"Why do you have it?" I placed my hand on my head.

"To mark the milestone of your first cut. I hated to do it. Your hair was so beautiful." On the lines below, Mom had written my name and the date of the trimming.

"But why did you keep it?"

"To remind me of you as a baby, so I could keep a piece of you from the time before you grew up." A pink ribbon tied the silky strands together. I petted the hair like a soft animal, and my joy blossomed in the comfort of Mom's admiration.

Weekends provided plenty of time to learn how to properly do our chores—the way Iga liked them done. Since Andrea suffered from allergies and asthma, Katy and I cleaned the house, cooked the meals, and washed and dried the dishes. Katy showed no excitement or relief about teaching me how to do everything, which surprised me because I cut her work in half.

Katy, an emotionless, shy girl, kept mostly to herself. We never dove into deep conversations about how we ended up parentless, but I believed, somewhere along the line, she must have learned to handle unpleasant situations with silence. We worked side by side, cleaning wordlessly except to give instructions. "Put things back exactly where they go," Katy said, adjusting a picture in a blue frame that showed a younger version of Andrea smiling at something above the camera. I registered each item's position and placement before I lifted it and turned it ever-so-slightly to the right or left to match its previous orientation exactly. Katy supervised, making sure I learned.

Excited about using a vacuum, I sucked crumbs from the poo-colored carpet with pleasure—it beat sweeping Mrs. Perez's endlessly dirty patio or scooping dirt and hair with my hands like I'd done while living with Mom. When I'd finished, Katy came in from the kitchen with widening eyes and a frown. "Oh, no," she said, evaluating my progress. "Line up the vacuum lines perfectly with the sliding door, like this," Katy said, showing me. "No crazy lines and patterns, okay?" I re-vacuumed the entire living room and dining room. I had to agree that straight, perfect carpet lines were better than the chaos I'd created with my first, uncontrolled pass.

The days ran together. Each morning, I followed the same routine. I made my bed, allowing enough bedspread to be tucked under the pillow and the rest over the pillow entirely. With my palms, I smoothed out the scratchy blue polyester bed cover, eliminating lumps and wrinkles. I went to the bathroom and back to my room to dress before heading to the kitchen for breakfast.

Katy and Andrea had explained the rules. "Fill the cereal to this line here." Katy pointed to a notch that lined the inside of the bowl about halfway up. "And then when you pour the milk," she looked at me, "the milk can only go to that line and *no* higher."

"What if I want more?" I asked.

"That's it." Andrea laughed. "There are no seconds, and if you want an Eggo . . ." She dropped two frozen waffles in the toaster. "You get *one* and butter *or* syrup. Not both. It's wasteful." I poured myself some Lucky Charms, careful not to fill the bowl above the line, and I ate slower, hoping it would make me feel fuller. Katy sat opposite me at the small Formica table against one wall in the kitchen.

When Andrea's waffles popped up, she pulled them from the toaster and squeezed fake liquid butter onto them. "You can fill each hole in the waffle grid," she said. "That way, you don't waste it. I like my waffles with just butter and no syrup. Oh," she said, as an afterthought, "remember, you only get one waffle."

"Why do you get to have two?" I asked. Andrea, smaller and shorter than I was, couldn't need more food than I did. My Lucky Charms crackled in their milk.

"She has different rules," Katy said.

"I'm not a foster kid," Andrea said and walked her plate of waffles to her bedroom.

I picked up my bowl, but as I headed for the hallway, Katy stopped me. "We have to eat in here. No food in the rooms." When Katy finished eating, she took her bowl to the sink and left the kitchen. The quiet made the muscles in my face throb to the beat of my heart. After eating my cereal, I debated pouring another. Who would know? I would. Besides, if Mr. and Mrs. Poplawksi perceived me as difficult, or if Andrea disliked me, they might send me away. The only thing worse than living with the Poplawskis was the fear that they might reject me. Then where would I end up?

My real family, more distant from me than ever, became a knot in my belly. The courts had rescinded visitation rights. Would I ever see Mom again? I coped by never asking about her out loud. Emptiness replaced her in my heart. Holding a bowl of stars, hearts, and four-leaf clovers didn't increase my luck.

chapter 24

1984
AGE 10

SINCE I WAS THE NEW GIRL, IT WAS MY DUTY TO clean the toilet. The stench of urine stung my nose, and Mr. Poplawski's pubic hairs kept sticking to my fingers. Even though he and Iga had their own bathroom, he used the hall bathroom for convenience. I dumped Comet in the sink and toilet, and a green cloud exploded in my face.

"This is for the toilet." Katy handed me a sponge. "Never use the same sponge for the sink and the toilet because that's gross." This all seemed simple enough, but I worried I might forget. They wouldn't know if I used the wrong sponges. But *I* would know. What if I used the toilet sponge to wipe up Mr. Poplawski's pubic hairs, then used it to clean the sink, and then dropped my toothbrush in the sink? Gross. My attention to detail made me an overachiever, even if I worked slowly. More Comet. More scrubbing. More rinsing. Did I get all the Comet lines? Did random hairs cling to anything? Had I polished the faucet to a shine, rubbing away every water spot?

Nobody would have noticed if I'd strayed from the rules here and there. But this home belonged to someone else, and I longed for praise and favorable impressions. I meant nothing to them, but somehow, their opinions meant everything to me. I did my chores without complaint. The thought that the Poplawskis might become unhappy with me encouraged me to slump into my quiet, insecure, rule-following self.

A little housework never hurt anyone. Unless you were Andrea.

"Don't vacuum when Andrea is in the room," Iga shouted. "I can see all the dust floating up, and you know she has asthma. Do you want her to end up in the hospital? Do you want her to die?" Andrea sucked on her inhaler once more to prove she did, in fact, have asthma.

Certain that vacuuming or dusting or scrubbing a toilet would not kill Andrea, I rolled my eyes, but I had no intention of speaking up. I wanted to ask for some medical proof, a doctor's note, that specifically outlined the dangers of doing chores. Andrea seemed conveniently allergic to the things she wished to avoid. While Katy and I sweated our weekends away, Andrea sat with Tippy in her lap, and the two of them kissed each other's faces off. Katy and I swept and mopped the bathroom and kitchen floors. And after every meal, which we prepared, we washed and dried the dishes. Our duties rotated for many of the chores like dusting and vacuuming and bathroom duty, but since the Poplawskis signed on to have Katy "long-term," they treated Katy like a second-rate daughter.

My rank lay a step below that. The new girl, I made no decisions. Katy chose dishwashing, which, though I preferred washing, meant I did double duty as dryer and put-away-er. I had arrived almost a year after Katy, so I fell in line and did my part. But resentments stacked inside me like cement blocks, building a wall so thick and high, nobody could break through.

One morning, I failed to make my bed properly.

"Do it again," Iga said as she passed from her room to the kitchen. "Do it right." I tugged on the thin cover to smooth it out, and I pulled the top high enough to tuck under the pillow, in a fold, and over it like I had watched Gramma do. "Did you do hospital corners?" Iga shouted. "I will check, so you better do it right." I did it right, but my tears left dark wet spots in the royal blue cover. "And don't forget the lights," she said, returning to check my bed-making skills. "Remember, it's five-hundred sentences as punishment. You must learn not to be wasteful. And is it you who left the toilet seat up?" Her teeth clicked. I told her I didn't think so.

"Good, because you know what that means. You're still new, but soon, I won't be reminding you of these things. You're old enough to know better." Iga waddled like Tweedle Dee, huge and round in her baby blue housecoat with white snaps down the front. She never took her false teeth out in front of me, and I never saw her without them. Even so, she was like a ventriloquist's dummy. *Click. Click. Click.*

Mr. Poplawski stood about six foot four, broad-shouldered, and big-boned. With his underbite and slow, lumbering movements, he reminded me of Herman Munster.

They intimidated me. The Poplawskis' rules were opposite those of my upbringing. Never in my life had anyone told me I had to close the toilet lid when I was finished going to the bathroom, not even after we ran from the living room to the toilet, carrying fleas on our legs and brushing them into the water for a mass flea-icide flush. Never had anyone made me feel like a servant, like my only purpose was to meet expectations or suffer consequences for not living up to them.

I'd begun silently crying every night and kept my wet tissues wadded under my pillow. How many tissues could I take at once without being wasteful? Was crying even allowed? Or was I going to have to write a million sentences promising, "I will never cry"?

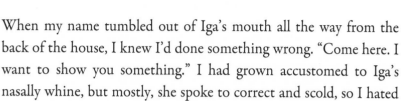

When my name tumbled out of Iga's mouth all the way from the back of the house, I knew I'd done something wrong. "Come here. I want to show you something." I had grown accustomed to Iga's nasally whine, but mostly, she spoke to correct and scold, so I hated her voice. I left the kitchen to find her. "I'm waiting." She stood outside my bedroom door. I tried to swallow, but cotton stuck in my throat. "What is the consequence for wasting electricity?" she asked, arms folded.

"Sorry." My voice trailed out of my mouth in a whisper, and I flipped the wall switch. How could I have been so stupid? I turned to go back to the kitchen.

"Excuse me." Iga's teeth clicked.

"But I only *just* left the room. The lights were on for not even a minute. I'll remember next time. I promise. Please?" The punishment itself paled in comparison to the shame of it. I lowered my head.

Iga did not let me win. "If you keep arguing, it'll be a thousand."

"A thousand sentences?" I deflated. Daylight waned. I turned the light back on and sat cross-legged on the floor to serve my sentence of sentences. The sentences had to be numbered, neat, and perfect, no spelling errors or scribbles allowed. I thought about all the electricity I was wasting sitting in my room for hours writing five-hundred perfect sentences.

Tippy stood in the doorway, his tongue gently bobbing in his mouth like a pink feather. I shut the door in his face.

And I wrote. I enjoyed writing, so the punishment did not affect me as Iga had intended. *I will remember to turn off the lights when I leave a room.* I spelled "remember" wrong a few times and had to start over. I crumpled page after page until my writing pleased me. Soon, I found my groove. I took care in forming my letters, changing my penmanship from cursive to printing, and dotting my i's with hearts. I wrote like my friend Cena from Rio Vista Elementary with the elegant and delicate hand. I wrote and wrote and wrote, denying thoughts of hatred and loneliness as ink and paper took me away from myself. Beautiful sentences leaked out, uniform on each page, each word aligned with its matching word above. I alternated between writing whole sentences at a time and writing columns of words.

"Here." I handed Iga my pages. "I'm done." My hand throbbed.

"Good," she said. "I hope you've learned your lesson. Now throw it away."

I was *not* confident I had learned anything. However, I *was* sure I hated Iga and her tent of a housecoat, blue slippers, fat face, and false teeth. Still, I wanted to explain myself to her so she would know I wasn't a bad girl. I wanted to tell her that no matter how many sentences she assigned, I might still forget to turn off the lights, and it didn't mean I needed to be punished into remembering. Sometimes, I wanted to say, *you just forget, and it's not that you're stupid or selfish or purposely trying to run up the electric bill. It just means that maybe your head holds too many questions like where is my brother and is he okay? What if my mom tries to kill him or herself again? Will I survive here? Or will I die without understanding how or why?*

Iga thought Andrea pooped hearts and could do no wrong. "Remember her asthma," she said to Katy and me. "You know she can't be around dust. Clean the bathrooms first. Wait until Andrea leaves the living room before you dust and vacuum in here. God, you guys." She shook her big moon face, and her frown deepened the creases at the sides of her mouth.

"Yeah, you guys," Andrea said, swatting the air and running to her room. "The dust." If a wayward particle rose up, she coughed and carried on like she was dying. We foster kids obeyed. Did Katy see me roll my eyes? Did hers roll, too? Were we going to have a secret eye-rolling club and bond over our mutual disgust? Why didn't all the French-kissing with Tippy make Andrea's allergies act up? I'd heard that dog mouths are cleaner than human mouths. Maybe it was true. I didn't know how it could be possible since dogs lick their buttholes and eat poop.

I scrubbed the toilet more vigorously, shoved the vacuum around faster. Under my breath, I cussed Iga and her daughter out all the way to hell and back, and each night, tears drenched my pillow, snot stuffed my nose, and pressure filled my head and lungs. When I made my bed in the morning, I crammed my snotty, crusty tissues under my pillow and pulled the thin blue blanket perfectly over it. If there was no visible evidence, and if nobody knew I had cried, had I cried? Only I knew the truth. Until Katy ripped my bed apart on laundry day. I was stupid to think I could have secrets.

"Ooh, I'm telling!" she said. "That's so wasteful!"

"They're there so I can reuse them," I said. "See?" I pulled at the tissues, one at a time, tugging at their edges and flattening them between my hands. "It's not wasteful at all." Terrified for Iga to know the truth, I begged Katy to keep my secret safe. But she didn't.

"That's disgusting," Iga said. "Five-hundred sentences. 'I will not be wasteful, and I will throw away my trash.'"

"But they're not trash yet," I said. "There's still room on them. I'm keeping them to use at night in case I need them." I searched for soft, unused sections as proof, but she scowled and swatted at my germy hands. Trying to defend myself was a useless pursuit.

She told me to stay in my room until I was finished writing. "And don't forget to number them."

One Friday while wrapping leftover liver and onions, Katy cut her thumb on the serrated edge of the plastic wrap box and couldn't peel potatoes the next day. She couldn't do dishes either because she was *wounded*. I thought maybe she'd injured herself on purpose so she could take a break from all the servitude.

After gorging on kielbasa and buttery mashed potatoes, I stood at the kitchen sink by myself and washed and dried the evening's mess. Facing the darkness in the backyard, I searched for my eyes in the kitchen, and my reflection came into view like a holograph, like a ghost in the carriage at the end of the Haunted Mansion ride at Disneyland. I dried a knife. I hated knives. I feared I might stab myself or drop one on my foot or bleed to death.

Like those hidden pictures in repeating designs of optical illusion posters filled with the colors of the rainbow, my eyes came into view for a moment. Afraid I might lose them again, I tried not to blink. In the window, my irises were black, but they pleased me more than they did in a real mirror because my blue eyes looked like zombie eyes, blind, dead, and hopeless. Dark eyes made me look like somebody else, somebody exotic, tough, and unfazed, who might fight back and *win*.

My entire existence was a question mark. Who was I, *really?* Would my grandparents ever save me? Would Mom ever get well? And what about William? Where was he now—had he moved into another home, a place taking advantage of him instead of appreciating him for who he was? And who *was* he? Staring at the fake me, I turned pots and pans over, transferring water to the towel as I dried them. Then I lost my eyes again and faded away in an instant. After stacking the last plate in the cupboard, I hung the soaked dish towel on the oven door handle and turned off the lights as I exited the kitchen.

chapter 25

1984
AGE 10-11

THE SCHOOL YEAR HAD ALREADY BEGUN WHEN I moved in with the Poplawskis. I enrolled in the sixth grade at my eleventh school, Yorbita Elementary, in La Puente. My teacher was a woman with blonde, shoulder-length hair and sparkly gray-blue eyes. She wrote her name on the board in pink chalk and welcomed me, her *new student*. "The rules are to be kind and to do your best," she said. "Ask permission before leaving the classroom. And no eating in class."

My classmates, a bit fidgety but quiet, respected Mrs. Ferguson and her classroom. I tried to memorize them, wondering if I'd have a chance to make friends. I'd moved around so much over the years; the idea of leaving didn't disturb me like it used to. I expected to leave. I'd never *stayed* anywhere.

I wanted friends but knew getting attached made leaving difficult. If I hovered on the surface and kept to myself, maybe I could avoid sorrow altogether. When grief layered itself in me like bricks, I broke through the wall of loss by focusing on my schoolwork.

"When you get an A on a test or finish your work first," Mrs. Ferguson said, "you get a prize." She was speaking my language. I had always earned good grades, and I read above-grade-level and finished math worksheets faster than my peers. Mrs. Ferguson held a small, cardboard box with a flap lid. She flashed us its contents. *Stickers.* Teddy-bear stickers and sparkly heart stickers, flower stickers and balloon stickers. "Or you can choose pencils or other school supplies." Mrs. Ferguson pointed to a clear plastic bin on her desk. "Or you can choose things like extra-credit or free-time. It's just an incentive to reward you for working hard and doing a good job. It's more like the real world."

I was in love with this school and this classroom, this woman and this day. This was going to be a great year. I hoped I would make it to the end.

Katy stuck the knife in the mayonnaise jar and scraped a dime of mayo onto a slice of bread in a thin layer. "You can have one piece of bologna, remember," she said. "Or a piece of cheese. And mayonnaise *or* mustard. And you have to put it on like this." I pictured those commercials where the mom makes a sandwich and layers the mayo in a thick, delicious swirl. But we were *not* in a commercial.

I told her I knew the rules. I should have been used to them, but I missed Gramma's pickle and cheese sandwiches and her grilled cheese with dollops of mayonnaise and mustard together to create salty-sour heaven on my tongue. Gramma laid the mayo on thick and delicious, the way I liked it, just how they did in the commercial. This was nothing like being at Gramma's.

I had never eaten bologna. Meat made me gag in general.

Katy put the knife back in the jar. It still had some mayonnaise on it. She ran the blade against the lip of the jar to put the unused mayonnaise back. I wanted to throw the jar of mayonnaise across the kitchen. I wanted to smash her sandwich into her face. I knew Katy wasn't the one who made the rules, but she followed them and was now enforcing them like someone had made her my boss. Katy and I were allowed the same amounts of food despite her being several inches shorter and tens of pounds lighter than me.

I chewed my dry Wonder Bread and bologna sandwich. I swallowed without breathing through my nose so I could avoid smelling or tasting the foul slab of congealed rat parts becoming mush in my mouth. I wanted Home Pride or Roman Meal. That's what Gramma always served. Or sliced French bread like Auntie Philys ate. The cold, wet bologna was meat-flavored pudding crust—like when the pudding is old and gets all peely along the inside of the plastic container.

Iga bought frozen bean and cheese burritos by the box and kept them in the freezer in the garage. Katy and I served Andrea and her parents steak and potatoes. Then we microwaved our burritos. We blew on them to cool them before each bite. The beans tasted chalky, but the cheese was good, so gooey I had to cut it with my finger to keep it from falling against my chin.

One afternoon, Iga said to Katy and me, "Hotdogs are in the fridge for you two. I've got a migraine, so I'm laying down. Don't disturb me for anything. But Katy, when you're done cleaning up, come and scratch my back, okay?" Her slippers snapped against her feet as she faded into her room.

"Gross." I meant the back scratching *and* the hotdog situation. Katy smiled at me nervously and dumped two hot dogs in the pot of water on the stove. After the water boiled, I checked the dogs. "Do they look green to you? They look green."

"They're not green," Katy stabbed one with a fork. "They're fine. They look how they're supposed to." She stuck each wiener in a bun.

I believed her when she said they were fine, but I also believed my eyes when they told me the hotdogs were green. My wiener tasted metallic, somewhat off. I'd never cooked a hotdog before, so I thought maybe that's what pan-boiled hotdogs tasted like. Pup 'n' Taco served my favorite hotdog ever. Mom drove us through, and we ate in the car in a parking lot, washing down lunch with cold, crushed-ice Cokes. This hotdog tasted like garbage, literal garbage.

I said, "It's rotten, I think." After a few bites, the thought of green meat sticking to my insides intensified the rancid stench and taste. I gagged and spit the half-chewed bite-in-progress into the sink. I rinsed my mouth out with water from the tap. "I can't eat it. I'm asking Iga for something else."

"She's napping," Katy said. "She has a migraine, and we aren't allowed to bother her, *remember?*" So, I went hungry. I knew Katy would tell on me if I ate something else, so my increasing hatred of her burned in me, and I kept my mouth shut—no food in, no words out. Insecure and afraid, I belonged to others and their judgments. This wasn't like fighting with Mom. With strangers, I belonged to rules more than ever.

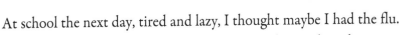

At school the next day, tired and lazy, I thought maybe I had the flu. When I slid out of my seat, I almost fell over. Christopher, the cutest boy in class, caught me.

"Leslie," Mrs. Ferguson said from across the room, where she was helping somebody read. She rushed down an aisle of desks. Her hands on my shoulders, she led me to the door.

"I'm sick," I said. "I feel like I'm going to throw up."

"You look pale, too. You'll be okay going by yourself?" Her kindness was soft like a blanket, and I wanted to lean into her.

In the bathroom, I hung my face over the toilet bowl. It smelled like Pine-Sol and pee. I gagged. Then, everything in my stomach came bursting forth like lava. And there they were—my Lucky Charms—bobbing in the peachy water like tiny life preservers, fully formed, as if I had swallowed them whole without chewing at all.

I rinsed my mouth at the sink and coughed up bits of phlegm and food. I heaved. My glassy, dead eyes in the dimly lit bathroom creeped me out. Who was I? My face gray, thin, and long, I thought maybe I would collapse right there onto the sink, hit my head, and die. They'd find me eventually and carry my body out on a stretcher. I'd be covered up, so everyone would whisper, gossiping and asking questions about who had died. My arm would drop off the stretcher, causing my classmates to gasp. And then I'd be gone, and everybody would go back to doing what they did before I existed. But I didn't collapse. I was too strong for that, too good at pretending nothing was wrong. I wiped my mouth and chin with the scratchy paper towel and went back to class.

Sundays were the one day of the week the foster kids ate what the Poplawskis ate. If we went out after church, Iga selected our meals and portions for us. If we stayed in, since Mr. Poplawski and Iga had Polish roots, they often had Katy and me prepare boiled Polish *kielbasa*, canned green beans, and mashed potatoes. My right hand grew into a claw from peeling a dozen potatoes like a world champion. I had to be the faster peeler. Katy probably never realized I counted my potatoes, and I smiled at the fact that I beat her every time, peeling two or three for every one she peeled. We cut the potatoes before boiling, and I mashed them and salted and buttered them. I took lots of tastes to make sure they were perfect.

Mr. Poplawski forked his *kielbasa* and dipped it in ketchup. I copied him. *Kielbasa* surprised me by being delicious, especially when smothered in ketchup. Sausage links made me throw up in my mouth. But Polish sausage was different. When I bit into the link, it snapped, and juicy meat burst out. After eating, I felt sick to my stomach, like I could vomit up all of my insides. But then I'd be hungry again. And who knew how big or small the next meal would be? I had to stock up, fill my *hollow leg*, as Grampa called it. I had to eat until stuffed, which bloated my gut and made me regret eating at all.

I never appreciated rules about food, not when Mom refused to cash her checks or spend money that symbolized my death, and not now. I doubted Iga would let me starve to death, but I also doubted she cared, so my loneliness and sadness created a void—a hunger more figurative than literal. When food presented itself, I devoured it, gorging myself to the edge, so stuffed sometimes I thought my stomach would rupture right there at the kitchen table. Still, I could never get enough.

chapter 26

Winter 1985
AGE 11

ON A SATURDAY IN FEBRUARY, I WAITED ON THE curb for Auntie Philys, but her white Mustang stopped at the end of the street instead of in front of the Poplawskis'. She stuck her arm out the window, motioning for me to come. As I approached, I saw another person in the car, a blurry, fuzzy-headed someone, in the middle of the back seat. My stomach lurched when I understood who it was.

I hadn't seen Mom since Christmas. She was only allowed to see William or me while my grandparents supervised. How could my aunt bring her without telling me? I didn't want to spend the weekend shielding myself from her verbal attacks and defending my every word and action. I didn't want her to beg me to run away with her or guilt me into acting more loving and caring than I felt. When I sat in the passenger's seat, Mom and Auntie spoke simultaneously.

"Oh, my baby," Mom said.

"She made me bring her," Auntie said. The car stank like ash and smoke. I sank into the vinyl seat and rolled the window down.

WHEN I WAS HER DAUGHTER

"Aren't you happy to see me?" Mom asked. I said I was. "How have you been?" It was the first time anyone had asked me that in a long time, and a lie rolled out from the surprise of it. I said I was fine, though I felt far from it. Mom acted so normal, I wanted to soften and tell her everything. But I knew how distant we were, how different and separate we'd become over the past year. "Give me a kiss." Mom leaned between the seats. I kissed her.

We drove to Thrifty's.

"Your mother used to work at Thrifty's, scooping ice cream," Auntie Philys said. "Everything was fine, but she quit because she didn't want to get fired. That's your mother—makes no sense." Mom told her to quit talking about her and defended herself by saying she knew she was going to get fired, so she wanted to beat 'em to the punch.

Auntie Philys never acknowledged Mom's illness for what it was. Her comments and frustration came across like those of an annoyed younger sister. "Your mother's just stubborn and selfish, and she doesn't think. Once, I asked her the time, and she turned her wrist over to look at her watch, but she had a can of Pepsi in her hand, so it dumped out all over the ground."

In the drugstore, Auntie and I considered all the Revlon lipstick colors and tried on our favorite earrings. Mom perused the refrigerated sodas.

"What about these?" Auntie Philys shook her head to make a pair of shiny, dangly earrings jiggle. I liked hoops and long ones that didn't dangle much. "Look to see if anyone's looking," Auntie Philys said. "And drop what you want in your purse. Easy. Just like that."

Auntie didn't know William and I tried to steal food from Lucky's. She let a pair of silver earrings that sparkled like fish scales fall from her hand into her pleather handbag. I scanned the store as I put my hand on a lipstick. I made sure Mom didn't notice. She would surely lecture me about the immorality of theft. We bought some cashews and Pepsi, but that was mostly a cover so we could steal makeup and jewelry.

When we got to my aunt's, we dumped all of our loot out on her bed to show each other what we got. Earrings, pens, lipsticks, and keychains. I ran my hand over the floral bedspread. My lipstick was missing. All I'd had to do was choose one and drop it into my purse—nothing could have been easier—but I'd failed.

My aunt heaved her emphysemic laugh into her hand and coughed. "At least you didn't pay for it."

"I can't believe you stole, Leslie." Mom stood in the doorway, with her arms folded under her boobs. "Philys, stealing is wrong. I'd appreciate it if you wouldn't teach my daughter to be a criminal."

My aunt told her to stop being such a fuddy-duddy. "They'll never miss these things."

Mom and I colored in my Sanrio coloring book. My picture was of a bunny holding a lollipop in the shape of a star, and her picture was of a boy and girl sitting in a crescent moon bathtub in the sky. "I've missed you so much. Soon, we'll be a family again—you, me, and William." She pressed salmon pink into the page, shading the bathtub moon, with her nail-bitten fingers, her hands covered in constellations of freckles.

"I miss you, too," I said. I thought it would make me cry to look in her eyes, so I concentrated on coloring, on making my flat, fake lollipop red-orange.

"It's just a matter of time," she said, "before the judge is going to let me have custody of you and William again. Wouldn't that be nice?"

"Do you like my picture? I messed up the bunny's ears. I tried to stay inside the lines, but I couldn't." I didn't want to tell her I didn't think I should live with her.

"Leslie, it's beautiful," she said. Mom was the only person in the world who would think my sloppy outside-the-lines work was perfect. Her devotion magnified my betrayal and my emotional withdrawal from her. At the same time, I knew she had betrayed me again and again. Would I forever be stuck in an endless loop—loving her only to hate her, hating her only to love her?

When it was time for Auntie to drive me back to the Poplawskis' Sunday night, I blubbered and begged. But like always, I had to go back to my foster home. Mom hugged me longer than I wanted. I softened in a gesture of pulling away, but she hung on.

"I love you," I said to her. And I meant it. Mom held my hand until I slipped away from her to step off the stoop in front of my aunt's apartment. The crisp wintery air sent a chill through me, and I looked back at Mom, her figure silhouetted by the light emanating from the living room lamp behind her.

In the car, I tensed with mixed emotions deep in me like an iceberg. When we arrived at the spot around the corner from the Poplawskis', I leaned over the console to hug my aunt goodbye, inhaling the fragrance of her frizzy hair. If only I were small enough to crawl into it, build a nest, and stay cozy forever.

As I walked into the house, I shook off tears, but they found me again when I slid under the covers in my dim, cold room.

My school desk had a metal cubby for books, papers, and pencils. One day, I thought I'd sat in the wrong desk because there were items in my desk that I hadn't left there—a shiny red apple, some tiny twist pretzels in a baggie with a twist-tie, and a lump of something wrapped in tinfoil. But I was in the right seat. Somebody's *food* was in *my* cubby. What if someone thought I had stolen *their* food. I looked around the room. Or maybe it was a trick, and they were watching to see how I'd react. I tried not to look at the food. I wanted to unwrap the foil lump to see what it was. I pressed it with my finger, and it gave slightly. *A sandwich?*

Mrs. Ferguson had started class. She was talking to all of us, but I could only focus on my cubby food. I tuned in when Mrs. Ferguson said something about class rules. You couldn't be the best and favorite student if you weren't a good rule follower. "I've just been thinking," she said. "This 'no eating in class' rule seems a bit unreasonable." Was she talking about the food in my desk? She continued, "because you might be hungry, and if you're hungry, you should be able to eat." She looked at me. Now I knew *Mrs. Ferguson* had put the apple, pretzels, and tinfoil lump in my desk. "So, if you have a little bag of something, like grapes, or whatever, you can eat them. As long as you're careful not to make a mess."

I smiled and then hid it. I didn't want anyone to see me—to see that Mrs. Ferguson had done this especially for me. The smile crept back onto my lips. Nothing funny had happened, yet I couldn't erase the smile. The food was for *me*. *My teacher* brought me *food*. I gazed down. I didn't want Mrs. Ferguson to call on me and say something about the food in my desk or why she put it there. I leaned my arms on my desk and scooted in close, to hide my cubby. I didn't want anyone to see the food in there because they might know I was hungry and receiving special treatment.

The classroom went about its business, and when Mrs. Ferguson assigned reading and questions to answer about Egypt for our social studies lesson, I took out my tinfoil lump. I unwrapped it inside the cubby, careful not to make any crinkle noises, and discovered it was a peanut butter and jelly sandwich. The jelly was strawberry, the peanut butter was crunchy—my favorite—and the bread had pieces of seeds in it, which I thought was strange. I'd never eaten that kind of bread before. I couldn't concentrate on Egypt; I was still focused on the fact that there was food in my desk, food that was all mine, and it made me feel like a person.

After my classmates left the room at lunchtime, I said to Mrs. Ferguson, "Thank you, for the sandwich and stuff."

"You're so welcome," she said, eating a sandwich that resembled the one she gave me.

"Why did you bring it for me?"

"I just thought you might want a snack."

When I brought home all A's on my report card, Iga offered me a reward. I had the choice of a Take Five bar she'd had in her purse for over a week, a five-dollar bill, or a hot fudge cake at Bob's Big Boy. The candy bar was a joke. I wanted to choose it so I could throw it at her. And five dollars? What the heck was I going to do with five dollars? True, that could buy me a lot of pencils and erasers and notepaper at the discount store, but I already had plenty of office supplies, most of which I had acquired for free at school or as gifts from Auntie Philys. I chose the hot fudge cake.

All day, I dreamed about eating that square piece of moist, warm chocolate cake, with vanilla ice cream in the middle, drenched in hot fudge. I would scoop some of the whipped cream onto every bite and save the maraschino cherry for somewhere toward the end, before the last mouthful. I pictured myself scraping the hot fudge off the plate with the side of my fork, barely leaving a trace, and licking the left-over bits from the corners of my mouth. Man, was I going to *eat* that thing.

When the waitress approached our table, I was ready to order the Big Boy combo. "Can I get—"

But Iga interrupted and ordered for me as usual, a junior hamburger with fries. "Two please," Iga said and nodded at Katy.

I raged inside.

Iga ordered herself the combo. Mr. Poplawski ordered the double-deck hamburger and a salad.

By the time Andrea ordered, I had spiraled so far into my anger that I failed to hear her words. I ate my limp burger and tiny fry pile. I obsessed about the dessert I knew was coming, my reward for a perfect report card. I could practically smell its chocolaty deliciousness from across the restaurant. I searched for our waitress, and my eyes caught her pale pink uniform and white waist apron.

"We'd like to order a hot fudge cake," Iga said to the waitress.

"Just one?" The waitress tapped her pen on her pad. Did she know the cake was mine and she might need to call an ambulance because I was going to inhale it and choke to death?

When the waitress emerged from the kitchen, I locked eyes with her. She floated like an angel to our table and placed the piece of perfection in front of me. The chocolate sauce glimmered under the restaurant lights. Putting my arms around the plate, I brought it close to my chest—as close as I could without dumping it in my lap. I gripped my fork—and that's when Katy asked me for a bite.

"It's *my* reward," I said.

"Don't be so greedy, Leslie," Iga said. "All children must learn to share and be polite to others. Let her have a bite. It won't kill you."

Katy stuck her dumb spoon into my hot fudge cake, and I imagined stabbing her pale, freckled hand with my fork. I could barely swallow because my frustration fought the cake for space in my throat. *Maybe this is how craziness begins.* Maybe someone asks for a bite of your cake, and you just lose it. I took bigger and bigger bites to ensure I'd get more than she did.

"Slow down, Leslie," Iga said. "Don't choke." By that time, I was already scraping the chocolate off the plate with my fork.

chapter 27

1985

AGE 11

A HOLE OPENED IN THE TOE OF MY DINGY WHITE tennis shoes, so Iga went to the discount store, Pic 'N' Save, to buy me a new pair. "New shoes," she said when she returned, holding a pair of lightweight, felt tennis shoes with a thin rubber sole. Baby pink and attached to each other with a plastic ring through the laces, they had a white stripe on the side and a Velcro strap across the foot. "Aren't they great?" Iga asked. "And they're pink. Do you like them?"

I did until I showed them off to my teacher the next day. I modeled them for her, pointing my toe to the ground and back again so she could see all sides. Mrs. Ferguson's forced smile told me I should be embarrassed by my cheap shoes. Their newness wore off as the day passed. And I was stuck with stupid pig-pink shoes. After that, how could I ever trust my own instincts? *Of course* the shoes were embarrassing. I should have realized that from the start. Maybe I was trying to make the best out of things—when someone buys you shoes and you don't get to choose them, you have to convince yourself you like them because they're the only ones you have.

It was Wednesday, which meant my greasy hair stunk and scalp itched. Iga allowed the foster kids to wash their hair once a week, and my day was Friday. "We have to learn to conserve water," Iga had said. "And you can't be running up the water bill."

I smelled like bacon and milk.

That night, after the water rose to the limit—a smooth, rounded ridge along the inside of the tub that was maybe a foot from the bottom—I got in and slunk way down, as low as I could, to wet the underside of my hair. Iga made sure I didn't turn the water back on—made sure I wasn't rinsing my hair. Katy listened like a guard outside the bathroom door. At least I had some privacy. I was surprised Iga didn't make Katy sit on the toilet and watch me. I tried to make my body flatter so the water would cover my stomach and private parts. My knees hit the spigot. I was sliding around like a snake. The water cooled fast, and before long, I shivered, so I sank to rinse my shoulders. I dunked my washcloth in my dirty water and squeezed it out onto my chest, stomach, and knees. There was a gurgling at the drain, and the water level lowered. I pressed the stopper with my toe, but it was as low as it could go. It was *my* water, and it was leaving me.

I wrung my washcloth out and threw it over the shower rod. Katy, sounding like Darth Vader with her mouth right against the door jamb, said, "It's my turn."

"I'm drying off," I said.

"Time's up. I'm telling." I dried off and slid my blue nylon night-gown over my head. When I exited the bathroom, Katy bumped me on her way in. I was so much bigger than she was. I should have shoved her, pushed her face against the wall, punched her in the gut. Something to let her know not to mess with me.

Minutes later, from my room, I heard Iga say, "That's just disgusting."

"Katy, that's so gross," Andrea said.

Then, Iga called out to me. What had I done this time? I stepped into the hall, where Andrea and Katy stood. Iga approached from her room and stood before us, arms folded across her ginormous chest. "You rinse your washrag out after using it, don't you?" Iga said. Her brown eyes drilled me.

Not sure of the right answer, I made a quick assumption. "Yeah. Why?" I lied. I pitied my unrinsed washrag, which hung over the shower rod. Did it appear unrinsed?

"Katy, here, doesn't rinse hers." Iga gave an up-nod to indicate Katy.

"Everyone knows you're supposed to rinse the dirty bathwater out of it," Andrea said.

"That *is* pretty gross," I said. "I always rinse mine under the faucet afterwards. *Everybody* knows to." Katy's eyes pleaded with me to back her up. Did she know I most definitely had not turned the water on after my bath—that, even if I did know I was supposed to rinse my rag, I had been prescribed an exact amount of water and wouldn't have dared defy the rule? Katy retreated to her room, and I rested comfortably in my lie because it took the negative attention away from me and placed it on Katy.

In bed, my ears pulsed in what would soon become a headache. I lifted my hair over my pillow to avoid sleeping on it and to avoid getting my dirty hair on my clean neck, back, and shoulders. Hair-wash Friday was still two whole days away.

On my next visit to Gramma and Grampa's, to celebrate William's tenth birthday, I wore my best outfit—a thin yellow cotton dress with two layers of ruffle in the skirt and a thick sash tied in a bow at my waist. I put a neon pink lace bow in my hair because I wanted to be cool and pretty like Madonna, and I wore tan flats on my feet because my only other option was the pig-pink felt shoes Iga had bought for me. I pinned a tiny fuzzy bear to the spot above my flat chest. He was cute and naked, wearing only a red bowtie.

"Your bra is showing through your dress." Grampa lowered his eyes to my boobs as if I didn't know where my bra was. I hung my head and folded my arms across my chest. In the bathroom mirror, I noticed my white underwear with pink and yellow flowers were also visible if I pulled my dress tight against my body. Frustrated by my failure to look good, I remained quiet the rest of the day.

William blew out ten candles on a homemade chocolate cake, and Grampa took a picture of William seated, a bunch of balloons tied to the chair, and Gramma, Auntie Philys, and me standing around him.

William and I both seemed like fake versions of our real selves. William forced smiles and lowered his voice. We didn't talk about Mom, our foster homes, or our emotions. I had come, hoping to win my grandparents over, hoping to impress them by dressing as stylishly as I could because if they saw how pretty I was, they might want me to stay. Maybe they'd think, *Isn't she the cutest? We have to keep her.* I was going through the motions, detached from my body and heart, light and heavy at once. Why were they making me stay with strangers? Didn't they love me enough to let me live with them?

"Why do I have to leave?" I asked.

Gramma said, "You know why. It's best this way." I thought I saw tears in William's eyes.

Grampa said, "It's because of your mother. Your grandma is getting too old for this. We just can't do it anymore." He scooped his keys off the desk in the kitchen nook.

I threw my arms around Gramma. "Please don't make me go back," I said. "I'll die."

She pried my hands off the back of her neck, set me up straight, and told me I would be okay. "You're embarrassing yourself."

Wiping my tears, I tried to convince myself I *was* okay. The Poplawskis didn't beat me or give me black eyes or broken arms. What could I tell my grandparents was wrong, exactly?

Auntie Philys drove William to his foster home, and Grampa drove me to mine. My grandparents' house was the closest thing to "home" I'd ever known. It was the only stable place I'd ever slept, the place I'd lived for the longest amount of time. I said nothing during the drive, convinced Grampa hated my guts. Saying anything more would only send me further down the hole of rejection.

We pulled up to the house, and Grampa must have sensed that my anger and desolation were about to erupt because he said, "Keep it together, now." I slunk away from him and into the Poplawskis' house, feeling exposed and raw, and I skulked straight to my room to take off my stupid, yellow see-through dress.

Outside, the whole sky was an even blue, and the sun lit the back-yard. Andrea, Katy, and I took turns teetering on the lop-sided seesaw and swinging on the rusted swing set. "Maybe you could be long-term, like Katy," Andrea said.

"Maybe," I said. The entire swing structure vibrated wildly every time I pumped to fly up, and it jerked with every descent.

"It would be cool if my mom and dad promised to keep you as their foster kid until you turn eighteen."

Katy closed her smile. I scanned the space above the telephone wires, past where trees poked the sky. Swinging made me breathe better, made me feel like I was flying away.

"Want me to ask?" Andrea stopped pumping her legs and stared at me.

Guilt stirred in my mind about the secret I'd been keeping from the Poplawskis about how much I despised them. Katy subtly kicked at the dirt.

Months earlier, I might have squealed with excitement at the thought of a promotion like that. But now I knew the truth about all of them. No respect for foster kids entered their home, and no genuine concern or interest for my well-being accompanied their intentions.

"I don't know, maybe. I think I'm going to live with my Mom when she gets better." I hoped I wouldn't be with the Poplawskis for six and a half more years. But I also had a sinking feeling Mom's condition would not improve. So, where else would I go? It was best for me to keep pretending and to keep following their rules.

Soaring in the swing, there was so much air—so freeing. The swing lifted me higher and higher, and it seemed that if I focused on the clouds, the ground wouldn't matter so much anymore.

Andrea said, "I'm sure my parents will let you. You've been here a long time. They trust you. We all do." I had been with them for about eight months. "And you could be my roommate," Andrea said, slowing her swing.

"But what about Katy?" I said. Andrea shrugged, and Katy avoided making eye contact with either of us.

Often, nights went like this: Iga said, "I have a migraine, Katy." Katy disappeared into Iga's room. At first, I was jealous, curious about their connection and longing for one of my own. But when Katy forgot to close the door once, I caught a glimpse of Iga and Katy lying on the bed in the dark, watching TV. Iga was stretched out on her side like a beached whale, plastic curlers in her short, brown hair. Propped on one elbow to see the TV over Iga, Katy ran her fingernails over Iga's back. For hours.

I snuck away, into my room, and closed the door. Grateful I wasn't the favored one, I sympathized with Katy and decided I didn't want to trade places with her for anything. I had always wanted long fingernails, but at times like these, I was glad I'd started biting my nails again. Katy didn't seem to mind her task. She was a good servant to Iga and did what she was told. After all, she couldn't risk losing her "long-term" status. If Katy was demoted, she might be on her way out of the Poplawskis' and into the world of nothing and nowhere else to go.

The next morning, in my half-sleep, I shifted and dreamed that my body would explode if I ignored the fire burning in me. I awoke to reality—my bladder was screaming that I needed to pee. I rubbed my eyes free of the dark morning-blur and rushed down the hall. The bathroom was a few steps from my room, so I knew I could make it in time. But the door was locked. I knocked. "Please hurry," I said. I tried to be polite. I didn't know who was in there, but surely it couldn't take long. We bathed in the evening. No one took morning baths, not even Andrea. I wished I could run into Iga's room and use her bathroom, but I wasn't allowed in there.

"Be out in a minute." It was Katy's man-child voice. "I'm in here."

I put my ear to the door. I couldn't hear anything. "Just let me in. I really gotta go bad."

She shouted in the whisper of a demon girl. "I'm going to the bathroom." Was she mad at me? I begged and begged. I should have said I was going to come for her in her sleep and cut her long blonde hair off with a paring knife if she didn't let me in. I should have said her real mom was in the living room waiting to see her and take her home. I should have kicked the door down.

I pounded. It didn't matter anymore that Iga was sleeping. My brain grew dizzy. No longer was anything in my control, so pee rushed out of me, sending a hot stream of liquid down my legs and onto the hall carpet.

It felt so good. And so bad. Then, Katy opened the door. Her eyes widened, and her jaw dropped as she witnessed my urine splashing at my feet. "I told you I really had to go," I said. I peed and cried at the same time. There I was, standing barefoot in a marsh of hot urine, the front of my blue nightgown soaked. It didn't matter that it had a delicate white ruffling of lace along the edges of the sleeves. It didn't matter that it was the only nightgown I owned. My bladder had a rude mind, a determination to ruin clean, girly things.

Iga burst out of her bedroom, wearing her floral muumuu and Dearfoam slippers. She rushed at me and yelled, "What have you done? Did you piss yourself? You're too old to piss yourself!"

I apologized and promised it was an accident. I doubled over in shame.

Iga lurched into the kitchen, a few feet farther down the hall. Cupboards creaked and slammed—*whap whap whap.* She returned with a bucket, a sponge, and a bottle of Pine-Sol. "Clean it," she said and shoved the supplies at me.

"I have to get ready for school," I said.

"You're not going to school today. You created a mess. I don't suppose you think I should clean it?" I did suppose she should clean it, but I didn't have the courage to tell her so. "And you better stop crying," Iga said. Andrea was awake now, and she and Katy stood over me. I was Cinderella, performing chores as the evil step-sisters watched, victory tickling their greedy hearts. I filled the bucket with warm water from the bath faucet and added Pine-Sol. On all fours, scrubbing the dark-green shag carpet, I grew chilly in my nightgown, which stuck to my thighs in a cold, wet sheet of polyester. I could handle the cold pee on my body. I could handle the sharp scent of ammonia and the shrinking and shriveling of the skin on my hands as cleaning chemicals sucked out their moisture. I could even handle the embarrassment.

What I couldn't get over was the idea of missing a day of school.

"Stop your blubbering," Iga repeated. But my tears fell onto my nightgown, onto my hands, onto the floor, and so I absorbed them with my urine into the mildewed yellow sponge and squeezed them into the bucket. And I scrubbed and squeezed until Iga said that would probably be enough but she still couldn't believe I would do such a stupid thing.

Every day, I anticipated finding another lunch in my desk, and every day, another foil-wrapped sandwich and baggie of pretzels from Mrs. Ferguson greeted me. In April, for Dress-up Day, Mrs. Ferguson helped me braid my hair before school, and she handed me a paper grocery bag with a costume in it, which included a button-down shirt with felt letters and numbers glued onto it.

That day, Mrs. Ferguson's husband visited our classroom. In the Reading Center, which included a couple of bookshelves in a corner at the back of the room, Mrs. Ferguson had arranged five chairs in a small circle. Baggie of pretzel twists in hand, I rushed to the circle and sat in a chair opposite Mr. Ferguson.

He asked who I was supposed to be in my shirt and tie.

"Boy George. From Culture Club." Did he know Mrs. Ferguson had made me a costume from his clothes? Was I also wearing *his* wide-brimmed hat? I munched a pretzel and brushed crumbs off my (his!) shirt.

"I know who that is," he said. "Some of my favorites are the Rolling Stones and the Beatles." He adjusted his glasses. "Ever heard of them?"

"I think so," I said. I tucked my pink shoes under my chair, hoping Mr. Ferguson wasn't judging me for them. Mr. Ferguson made simple conversation with some of my classmates, and then it was time for him to leave. The class waved goodbye, and Mr. Ferguson smiled one last time before he left.

"Your husband is so nice," my friend Gracie said.

"I like him," Mrs. Ferguson said. We all laughed. After school, Mrs. Ferguson told me her husband had come only to meet *me*. It had been a long time since I'd felt like anyone's reason for anything good.

One day, Katy lost her status as the favored foster kid.

"What happened?" I asked Andrea, who ignored the question.

Katy shook her head. "Not supposed to talk about it." I stared at her little piggy nose and downturned eyes.

"You and Andrea are like sisters, anyway," Iga said to me. "Andrea wants to room with you now."

Katy moved her things into the bunk bedroom, sniffling and wiping tears from her cheeks. The only other time I'd seen Katy cry was during onion chopping. She released sobs and chokes, shaking and gasping. Redness made her blue eyes brighter and her blonde lashes less visible, and she looked like an albino rat. I had some compassion for her, but mostly, I hoped to God I wouldn't become Iga's new back scratcher. My promotion to favorite foster-child was a triumph, but I was now a big, fat fake and a liar. I had said I wanted it, but I didn't—I didn't care anymore because moving up in the ranks meant I had to act excited to be there and grateful for every bean burrito and rotten hot dog I got to eat.

I was numb to the Poplawskis' false shows of interest in me. Mrs. Poplawski and Andrea felt proud of themselves for offering me garbage that I should have accepted with utter pleasure. They didn't care about me. They only cared about themselves.

I placed my clothing in a drawer and my small silver radio on the floor by my bed. No more bunk beds. I hated bunk beds ever since that day William kicked my bed out of the frame, making me fall and making Mom come in and beat me senseless. Memories like those don't fade.

The comforter was soft. The bed was so high I had to jump to sit on it even though I was tall. Andrea and I played video games until our hands hurt from holding the controller in one hand and working the joystick with the other. I thought I might finally have a chance to eliminate the Crystal Castles witch. We laughed. We talked about our disdain for Katy. We exiled her from our club. We listened to Prince every night before falling asleep, singing the lyrics as if we were him, or the Revolution at least. We laughed some more. I wore my fake happy face and made Andrea think we were best friends.

It felt good to be "in," liked, popular, *chosen*, as if I'd won something even if it meant Katy lost. It was the same as when Mom used to get mad at William and favor me, which didn't happen often, but when it did, I became queen and relished my position where life temporarily held promise and hope.

After lights out my first night in Andrea's room, I noticed the glow-in-the-dark stars and planets on the ceiling. I imagined a hidden universe among them, one I'd always dreamed existed beyond the clouds. Maybe things weren't so bad after all. I matched my breathing with Tippy's so I could sleep. His white fur glowed like the greenish-yellow solar system above. I wished Tippy were *my* dog. I wished this room were my room and this bed, my bed. But for now, it was enough to borrow these things. It was enough to pretend.

chapter 28

1985

AGE 11

I MET MRS. CUNNINGHAM ONE MORNING WHEN I was called to the office.

"I'm your social worker, here to check on you and to make sure you're doing okay with the Poplawskis." She clicked her retractable pen. You may not know this, but your teacher, Mrs. Ferguson, and I have been talking . . . about your situation. She has reason to believe you aren't getting enough food. Are they mistreating you?"

"Well, we can't eat very much. But Mrs. Ferguson brings me food, so it's okay."

Mrs. Cunningham slid her hands over the table toward me. For a second, I thought she wanted me to hold her hands, but thankfully, I figured out the truth before lifting my hands from my lap.

"Are they hurting you?" she said.

I froze. Abuse, to me, meant a physical, maniacal beating, like the time Mom hit me so viciously my nose bled for an hour. The Poplawskis had never laid a hand on me.

Mrs. Cunningham's question made me wonder whether my

loneliness and emptiness had anything to do with the Poplawskis. Was I a miserable child who would never find happiness anywhere? Was I a "silly little girl" like Mrs. Perez thought? It was impossible to know how foster homes were supposed to be and how I was supposed to feel. Everything had been so messed up for so long. Maybe *every* place other than with real family would cause my spirit to cave in. Maybe I couldn't reasonably expect anything better.

I studied the poster on the wall behind Mrs. Cunningham. A kitten hung from a tree branch, and the caption read, "Hang in there."

"Your teacher cares about you. You're a lucky girl." Mrs. Cunningham stood, so I did too. She hugged me. "It's going to be okay, Leslie. Just hang tight."

"Like the kitten," I said. I pointed to the poster.

She turned, and when she saw the poster, she gave a short laugh. "Yeah. Like the kitten."

I walked back to class with a sour bubble in my gut. My lie about being fine was also the truth. Nothing had a simple answer. I wished I'd been more prepared to talk about my feelings and desires. If I'd had time to practice answering questions—if I knew Mrs. Cunningham were coming to talk to me—I could've rehearsed and painted a clearer picture.

It didn't matter that I'd failed to rant about the details of my misery, did it? Articulating my unhappiness seemed impossible. I'd told my grandparents I wanted to live with them, and they ignored me. Couldn't they see in my eyes how incomplete I was, how dejected? Maybe Mrs. Ferguson could see it because I sat in her class every day. Maybe she was better at seeing the real me than my grandparents or aunt ever were.

At lunchtime, Mrs. Ferguson let me alphabetize papers, organize books, and place math worksheets on the desks. I was useful and helpful, and being around Mrs. Ferguson made me feel calm. One day, we walked side by side to the copy room to get the next day's handouts ready. On the way back to the classroom, we walked for a while without talking. When we were under the big tree and almost to the classroom, Mrs. Ferguson said, "I'd like to ask you an important question." We walked over a raised, cracked patch of asphalt. "I was wondering... if you would like to come and live with me. And my husband."

What? Maybe I hadn't heard her correctly. "Really?" I said. The thought had never occurred to me. Did teachers do this—give sad, unlucky students a place to live? The ground smoothed out.

"You don't have to answer now. But think about it. I just wanted to see if that would be something you'd want."

"So, you'd be my—*mom?*"

"Well, we'd be your foster parents. The important thing is we want to get you out of the home you're in now."

I didn't need time to think. Mrs. Ferguson was the best teacher I'd ever had. And she was telling me she wanted me as her foster daughter. *To come and live with her.* "School's almost out," she said, "so it'll just be for a short while that we have to hide it from your classmates and from the Poplawskis. No use mentioning it because it might cause confusion and questions. And I don't want to create any more problems for you."

I understood everything she said. More importantly, I understood this to be the happiest question anyone had ever asked me. I wanted everyone to understand *Mrs. Ferguson was going to be my mom.* But this wasn't like when I told the whole neighborhood which house was giving out money on Halloween. This was an important secret, so I had to keep it. It was better to stay quiet, too, because I'd been let down enough times to know a good thing could be ripped away in an instant.

Mrs. Ferguson's class piled into the bus for the tide pools field trip. Christopher took me by the hand and pulled me after him into a seat at the back of the bus. Mrs. Ferguson saw us, so I leaned my upper body away from Christopher. Our thighs touched, which sent a shiver through my thighs and crotch. "Have you been to the tide pools before?" I asked him.

"No. This is so cool." Christopher smiled, revealing a chipped front tooth, which only made him cuter. His brown eyes deepened, and I looked away, down, and then at his neck, where a freckle sat below his ear.

"Yeah, I'm glad we're going together," I said. His sweaty hand in my sweaty hand made me fluttery on the inside and safe on the outside. He ran his other hand through his blond hair.

The bus jerked into motion. "I'm glad, too." He shifted his torso toward me and turned his face to mine. For a moment, I forgot Mrs. Ferguson was going to be my new mom, so I let Christopher kiss me on the mouth. My breath stopped, collected in my head, and then pulsed and spun me. When I exhaled, floating on the idea of being loved, I raised my eyes. Mrs. Ferguson was staring at me. She shook her head in a way that let me know she didn't approve. Shame tugged at my happiness, and I yanked my hand from Christopher's. He didn't seem to care.

Mrs. Ferguson's disappointment colored the bus ride gray for me. Christopher put his head to the window, and the breeze lifted his hair like a flap. Would Mrs. Ferguson still want to be my mom now that she saw me kiss Christopher?

I followed Christopher to the tide pools under the gloomy sky and back onto the beach, where someone brought out a football. The gritty sand scratched the spaces between my toes. I hadn't been to the beach since I was six—the time Mom, Auntie, William, and I were saved by the man who looked like Jesus.

"Go long," someone yelled.

Christopher ran from me and caught the football. "Touchdown!"

I lowered my butt in the sand and wrapped my arms around my knees. My classmates and Mrs. Ferguson moved in slow motion on the beach, at the shore, and in the rocky pools, bending over to poke anemones and gawk at crabs. My whole life was about to change. Could I be good enough? *Would* I be good enough? Faint hot dog smells lingered in the air. And coconut suntan oil. Seagulls squawked.

The bus ride back to school took a bazillion years. I sat alone in the front, hoping to show Mrs. Ferguson I was a good girl.

She sat across the aisle from me. "Did you have fun?"

"Yeah," I said. "It was awesome."

"What was your favorite part?"

Kissing Christopher. "Poking the anemones."

"I'm glad you had fun. You should be careful with boys. I didn't say anything earlier because I didn't want to embarrass you. But that was inappropriate."

I said I was sorry. It was only partly true. The kiss made me feel like I had worth, so I basked in it. But Mrs. Ferguson made me feel like I had hope, and I needed that most of all. I couldn't risk Mrs. Ferguson thinking I was a slut. Then she'd change her mind, and I'd have to stay with the Poplawskis forever.

The night was like any other. Mr. Poplawski lay asleep on the couch, stretched out with one foot on the floor. Katy had been summoned for the nightly back-scratching session, and she and Iga lay alone in the dark bedroom as the television glowed and flashed. I watched Andrea escape the moving trees in Crystal Castles, anxiously awaiting my turn. How would I improve if she barely let me play?

Then Iga yelled my name. "Telephone. Your social worker." I picked up the handset from the base on the dining room wall. I usually didn't get calls, especially not on weeknights.

"Hello?" A creepy, crawly feeling circled the inside of my stomach. It was my new social worker, Mrs. Cunningham.

"Everything's all set. We're gonna come and get you tonight, so get your stuff ready and we'll be there soon." She breathed heavily as if she'd been running from something.

I waited. "Okay," I said softly, worried that Mr. Poplawski had heard me. His eyes were shut, and he remained still. My heart pounded against my ribcage. Weren't my bones supposed to protect me? Why did it feel like I could explode, crumble, vanish? My ears were hot. I hung up the phone. My hand shook, and a flutter beat my stomach. Things were happening so fast.

Iga rushed into the dining room. "Why, you deceitful, lying, sneaky little bitch." She bent toward me and pointed in my face. "I heard everything. What did you tell them about us?"

Shocked to learn she'd listened in on my private call, I grew hot as if my body would burn, one part at a time—first my hair, then my face, my heart, my knees—until I were nothing more than a pile of ash. Iga's liver-and-onion breath burned my eyes; her dentures clicked in their gums. Too scared to wipe her spit from my lips, I pressed my hands onto the dining table to balance myself. I couldn't speak. I knew the truth—I hated the Poplawskis even though they thought I should worship them. My teacher had asked if I wanted to live with her and her husband, and tonight, I was getting moved. I had done such a great job of keeping the secret, it seemed more like a faded dream I'd once had and less like a new reality. Where else were my secrets supposed to go if not absorbed by my wishful thinking, swallowed by my fear, and dissolved by my knowledge that past experiences often indicate future performance—failure or success?

"What's going on?" Mr. Poplawski boomed into the dining room and stood behind me.

"She's been telling her social worker lies about us," Iga said.

"I didn't—She came to the school and asked me questions. I told her the truth." I took a step back so I could see both of them. *In fact, I should have said, I actually lied and said I was fine.* Mr. Poplawski towered over me like a tree. The hanging light swayed above the polished wooden table.

"Well, for how long, you little sneak?" Iga said. "How long have you been spreading filth about us? This whole time, she's been playing the *angel* while she's been telling stories behind our backs. Stuff that's bad enough to get them to call out of nowhere and come and get her in the dark." Iga's eyes were black. And huge and round. They seemed to spin in their sockets as if they might fly out of her face any minute.

I had nothing to say. *Just hang tight,* Mrs. Cunningham had said. Why did it feel like it was taking forever for her to arrive and save me from the wolf pack? I kept my eyes down. I tried not to make noise, but emotion surged so fast in my throat I thought I might never be able to stop it.

"They're coming tonight to get her?" Mr. Poplawski asked. By now, Andrea and Katy had emerged from their rooms to join the ambush. All four of them against me, arms folded across their chests, scowling at me as if I'd killed Tippy.

"What did you tell them?" Mr. Poplawski shouted.

"Nothing. I just—"

"You just what?" Iga's eyes were beetles about to fly out of their holes and bore into my skull. Her lips shook. Her dentures clicked.

Her jowls jiggled. "All we've done is be good to you," she said. "Treat you like our own. We bought you stuff at Christmas. We brought you into our home, and this is how you repay us? With secrets? Lies? Talking about us behind our backs?"

I twisted the bottom of my T-shirt with my fingers.

"You ungrateful shit," Mr. Poplawski said, all the fire gone, nothing but disgust left in his voice. "Good. Let her go then. We don't want her here if that's what she's about. Social worker can have her. One thing's for sure, social worker can't get here soon enough." He shooed me like an insect, like he couldn't be bothered with my existence. "Sneaky bitch."

"And I let you move into my room," Andrea shouted, before stomping down the dark hallway. A door slammed.

Mr. Poplawski sauntered back to the couch, put his shoes on, and tucked his shirt into his pants. "I'm going to work, and I'll be glad as hell to know you'll be gone when I get home." Iga shook her head, turned, and walked away, her slippers snapping against her heels.

Katy stood for a moment, staring at me. She shook her head and huffed. "How *could* you?"

I leaned against the table. There was nothing to say.

I knocked on Andrea's door.

"Go away," she yelled. I could tell she was crying.

"I have to get my stuff." Iga dropped a cardboard box at my feet as Andrea, sniffling, opened the door and pushed past me. I licked my tears as they fell onto my upper lip. I put my things in the box—some clothes, some cassette tapes, and my little silver radio. I left the few Pic 'N' Save trinkets the Poplawskis had given me for Christmas. I left the yellow see-through dress that let everybody see my underwear. I thought twice about a green roller skate sweatshirt with shiny arms Iga had given me for Christmas. I wadded it up and closed it in the dresser drawer.

Katy slammed the door behind me. I didn't have a free hand to wipe my tears. Snot trickled into my mouth. Nobody said goodbye. They wouldn't miss me, and I wouldn't miss them. *Then why did this feel so horrifically awful?*

The scent of jasmine punched me in the nose. It was the scent of roaming the city at night with Mom and William, the scent of hunger, fear, cold. I was older now, and the streets were in my past, but I'd learned scent memories are the strongest memories of all. My cardboard box of belongings was lighter than I expected. Maybe it meant I'd left all the heaviness behind.

The yellow light gave my arms and the dried grass beneath me a sickly hue. A brown sedan pulled up to the curb. Mrs. Cunningham exited the driver's side. "They made you wait out here in the cold? Are you crying?"

"Mrs. Poplawski stayed on the phone and heard our conversation. I'm okay."

Mrs. Cunningham pulled my box from my hands and placed it in the trunk of her car. I sighed. She asked if I had a jacket. I told her I only had the vest I was wearing, the ivory one my gramma had crocheted for me. I tugged on it. A layer of defeat lifted from my shoulders, and I straightened a bit, stood taller. It didn't pull the tightness out of my back, but I blamed the chilly May air for the sharp needle stabbing me under my shoulder blade. Not even an hour ago, it was any other day—a homesick day, purposeless, dead-ended. And now, I was in my social worker's car, driving away in the dark but toward some kind of new light. I could feel it.

chapter 29

1985
AGE 11

MRS. CUNNINGHAM WAS SILENT DURING THE DRIVE. My brain knocked around all the things I should've done at the Poplawskis'. If I'd had more time, advance notice, and if I hadn't been caught off guard by all the angry words and pointing fingers, I might have run through the house, turning on every single light and flipping up the toilet lid. I might have turned on the bath water, let the tub overflow into the hallway, into the yard, into the street. I might have set fire to the perfectly vacuumed carpet. I might have torn my bed apart, shredded the thin, pilled cover into bits. I might have tossed the plates from their cupboards or flung them like Frisbees at Iga's head.

Streetlights lit dark roads. The car smelled like wet paper, hairspray, and pine air freshener, reminding me of the dumpster smell at Corn Nuts when Mom made us stay outside and awake all night. Maybe I'd smell memories my whole life.

I was cold but almost didn't care because I felt as if I'd broken out of jail. I didn't know where we were going on the map, only that

Mrs. Cunningham, whom I trusted, was taking me to my teacher. I focused on the streets and the stubborn pit in my stomach.

After turning off the main road in a city far from the freeway, we drove by a school that had a small playground with a swing set. I thought of Andrea and Katy and how glad I was I'd never swing with them again. And I thought of William, of how our childhood had come to this—separation and fear. When we'd seen each other a couple of months earlier, he wore his fear in his eyes, eyes full of longing and concern. I'd probably never swing with *him* again, either.

Onto the curvy, twisty, unlit streets, we drove up up up and around. Where was Mrs. Cunningham taking me? Were we in the mountains? I let out all the air in my chest and head and sucked in the damp car smells. For a moment, I thought maybe it had all been a trick. Maybe Mom's stories of torture and rape would come true. I squeezed my eyes shut, and my eyeballs pressed into the jelly of my brain. When I opened them, stars flashed.

It had been over a year since the police took my brother and me away from Mom. If the government had wanted me, they would have captured me a long time ago. *No*, I thought. *Those stories were not real.* Maybe, if I knew *that*, I could start to trust myself.

We pulled into a steep, curved driveway. A dim light illuminated a path from the porch, along the side of the garage, to us.

Mrs. Ferguson greeted us, and when I heard her voice, I sighed, and my shoulders dropped in relief. Her husband walked behind her. Mrs. Cunningham thanked them and said they were doing an amazing thing, as if nobody in their right mind would want to take me on. She said something about this being an emergency. Mrs. Cunningham shook Mr. and Mrs. Ferguson's hands.

Mr. Ferguson stepped toward me. "I remember you." He smiled under his mustache.

"I remember you, too," I said, as Mr. Ferguson took my box of belongings from the trunk. The house was small and dark, with wood paneling on one of the walls, which made things seem even more ominous. But it was nighttime, and that meant reality was skewed. The world was a much different and scarier place at night than during the day.

Mrs. Ferguson said, "Let's take this to your room." *My* room. I would be all alone now, but I'd wanted it, didn't I? When I lived without William at Gramma and Grampa's, everything had been not only lonelier and quieter but also simpler. Maybe I needed some isolation, some freedom from the mess Mom had made of everything. I'd come to prefer loneliness to fear and loss of control.

My teacher thanked my social worker and led me along the carpeted hallway. I heard the front door shut. Mrs. Ferguson stopped at what seemed to be the middle bedroom in their house. But this middle bedroom smelled of wood and not blood. No bad memories seeped from the walls. No eeriness like that of the ghost boat painting and the things that happened below it I wanted so badly to forget.

The bedspread, lacy and girly, was white cotton with eyelets. The daybed's metal frame was painted white. It was so perfect, so *clean*, I didn't want to touch it. Was I clean enough for this place?

Mrs. Ferguson pointed to the bed and to the built-in dresser with a hutch and mirror. "These drawers are for your things," she said. The wood floor creaked a bit, like an old haunted house, but this house held hope. Maybe the missing person from the ghost boat didn't drown at all. Maybe she was a princess who found safety on dry land before the boat drifted among the loose pink flowers.

Night air had chilled the room. Blinds were drawn over two large windows, and a dim overhead light emanated from four chandelier bulbs in the ceiling fan. It was all the light I needed.

The top drawer of the built-in already held six folded shirts. I pulled one out: a pink polo shirt. The remaining three drawers were empty. I wiped tears away and placed my old clothes in the second drawer. I set my little silver radio on the dresser, and the cord dangled to the floor. I caught myself in the hutch mirror. Redness ringed my eyes and blotched my pale skin. I smoothed my hair with shaky hands, my breathing shallow. When was the last time I'd taken a deep breath? Had I ever known how to breathe correctly?

A cork board hung on the wall to the left of the door. Extending from a baby blue ribbon on a clear plastic push pin was a carved wooden heart, painted with a teddy bear and the words, "You're Beary Special." Mrs. Ferguson had put it there to tell me something about myself the same way she'd put food in my cubby. Mrs. Ferguson was the nicest person I'd ever met, and if *she* thought I was special and deserving of her time and effort, then maybe I *did* deserve these things. Maybe I wouldn't have to drown anymore—maybe I had a chance to swim, and if I sank, Mrs. Ferguson would be right there to pull me up. I smiled, touched the heart, and flipped off the light switch as I followed my teacher out of the room.

Mr. and Mrs. Ferguson didn't want Mom to have my new address—their address—so all correspondence went through my grandparents.

"We don't know what she's capable of," Mrs. Ferguson said. "It's best this way. Do you understand why?"

I nodded. I imagined that Mr. and Mrs. Ferguson had talked beforehand about how my living with them would change their lives and introduce new fears. Would Mom arrive on their doorstep, waving a knife or holding a lit match to a line of gasoline, and demand I leave with her? Would she kidnap me in a stolen car, drive me to the desert again, and maybe drug me, strangle me, shoot me, drive over my head?

The next time I visited my grandparents, Gramma handed William and me letters from Mom. I sat with William in our old room, and we read our letters silently. In my letter, Mom wrote that she was living in Bell Gardens Manor, an assisted living facility for poor and disabled people. She talked about how much worse she was doing since she couldn't see William and me all the time.

"I will get a car and an apartment," she wrote. "And then the three of us can be a family again, just like we used to be. Mommy misses you so much."

The next line proved how sick she still was: "I'm so sorry they took your brothers and sisters away when they were born. I would have stopped them if I could." She listed the names of my fake brothers and sisters with the real William and me: "Twins: Louis and William and Triplets: Leslie, Elizabeth, and Julie." I remembered the poster Mom drew that I found under the bed the night we left the Corn Nuts apartment. And I thought about the story Emily and Sarah told us in Bell Gardens about the twins drowned by their mother in the lake.

If William and I had survived Mom, maybe those boys never drowned at all. Maybe they were a creation—a *story*—like the twins on Mom's poster.

The rest of Mom's letter cheered me up at first, but then it left a lingering sorrow in my chest: "I know you can't get me cigarettes," she'd written. "Ha Ha. Wouldn't that be nice. Send money. Cigarettes are expensive. And I'd like to buy some Pepsis from the machine here."

She signed the letter, "XOXOXOXO, Mommy."

Written along the side of the page was a request: "If you see your brother, tell him I love him, too. All of this is for William, too. Mommy loves you. You are my sunshine, my only sunshine. Remember when I used to sing that to you?"

I supposed I was her sunshine and she did love me, but too much distance had separated us. I was still huge in her world, but like each person is miniscule compared to the sun, she seemed so small to me now.

Mom's letter and my memories hurt my heart, but I didn't have time to break, so I focused on more recent memories—of my teacher bringing me home and of becoming someone else's daughter.

In the living room at my new home, I often lay on the couch, thinking about my past and fearing my future. Would the Fergusons like me enough to keep me? Or would I be rejected and forced to search for yet another home, another place that felt right and good? My teacher sat with me, caressing my back, sincere concern in her big blue eyes. "Are you all right?" Her voice was soft, wading between voice and whisper, sincere unlike any voice I'd ever known.

I shook my head. "I was wondering if I should call you *Mom*."

"I guess that would be okay," she said. "But at school, you should still call me Mrs. Ferguson." A sense of order and calm spread through me, and I hugged her, appreciative of her willingness to let me in, to lead me to safety when I was certain I would never be safe again.

Despite hopeful moments, grief overwhelmed me.

We started seeing a family therapist (my first) who said instant, unplanned parenthood was about one of the most challenging things a person could face.

"And you, Leslie," the therapist said, "have some adjusting to do as well. Your new foster mom tells me you're sad quite often. Can you tell me about it?" I stared out the window, arms and legs crossed, guarding my heart, keeping everyone out.

"I just don't know how to help you," Mrs. Ferguson said. "I'm so sorry you're sad. I'm here for you." That soothed me because I knew she was trying. It also terrified me because if *she* was trying, it meant there was pressure to appreciate her efforts and to be the version of myself she expected. Mrs. Ferguson pulled a Kleenex from the box on the coffee table and pressed it to her eyes. My head throbbed.

"It's normal," the therapist said, "for pre-teens to carry angst. I think the important thing to remember is that you're here and trying to help each other. That's what families do. Can you see there's hope in that, Leslie?"

I shrugged. If I admitted I could see hope, would I no longer be protected by the tough armor I'd spent so much time building?

"I try so hard," Mrs. Ferguson said.

The therapist said, "It will take time, but I believe you will work it out. I can see it in your eyes. You care for Leslie very much."

"I do," Mrs. Ferguson said.

I sighed, and my shoulders relaxed. Through the window, leaves flickered in a tree. The colorless sky peeked through the branches. Parked cars in the lot sparkled from the sun blasting their windshields. I reached for a Kleenex, and Mrs. Ferguson held the box out to me.

I was in junior high now. I immediately began using *Ferguson* as my last name, but I often forgot to write it on my homework. My real name kept showing up first, and sometimes, when the eraser didn't remove it enough to satisfy me, I crumpled the paper and started over. Soon, it seemed I'd always been a Ferguson, and the word flowed straight from my dreams onto the page.

My volleyball coach, a small, weathered Japanese woman with a reputation for being strict and mean, stood on a chair and hit balls over the net for each player to practice blocking. When it was my turn, she hit the ball at me and repeatedly yelled how useless and ugly I was. "You can't block. You're so ugly. You're so stupid." And it rang like a mantra in my head, like a song about my true identity.

I didn't ask why I was the only one she said those things to. Her brutal training style drove anger, frustration, and determination into me. I'd been through worse. She couldn't hurt me. I'd joined the volleyball team because I wanted to hit something—or maybe I wanted to be hit and to recover as a sign of my unrelenting toughness. Physical exertion and the repetition of practice forced my melancholy mind to toughen up, so I could stop thinking about Mom and William and how broken we'd become. When the ball smacked my forearms, inner pain dissipated. When I spiked the ball, my anger subsided. It was exhilarating to pound. I made it my mission to prove my coach wrong, even if it meant looking uglier and stupider as I practiced, with tears streaming from my eyes, until I got the drills right.

At home, my armor fell away, and pain replaced it. Dejected and hollow from defending myself from Mom's madness over the years and now from my coach's cruel tactics, I became both numb and pathetic.

When I threw myself onto my bed after storming straight to my room, Mrs. Ferguson followed. She reached out tentatively as if to touch my arm. I flinched. She pulled her hand away and brought it toward me again, letting it rest on my back. My face hot and wet from my tears, hair clinging to my forehead and temples, I sobbed. I didn't know why, if I finally had a safe place to land, I felt so small, so angry, and further from peace than ever.

chapter 30

1985–1986
AGE 12–13

AFTER SCHOOL, I SAT IN THE LIVING ROOM CHAIR, inhaling Chips Ahoy! cookies one by one, sucking on buttery, sugary crumbs and chocolate, letting that feeling of goodness replace my emptiness. Still hungry, I gorged myself at dinnertime, filling myself so full I could have thrown up, but I wouldn't be caught dead doing something so clearly wrong. Wedged between that desire and the knowledge that vomiting after eating meant I would be ill, flawed, less than perfect, I kept the bloat and sickness in my body, allowing myself only enough strength to commit to the easy half of bulimia.

"Don't you think you've had enough to eat?" Mrs. Ferguson would ask, worry in her eyes. I also saw disappointment settling in them, under her furrowed brow, an indication that I should be ashamed. And so, I was ashamed. "You're eating way more than you should." She tried to tell me gently that I was a pig, and it only made me want to eat more.

Sometime after that, my frustration and embarrassment confirmed what I needed to do. I needed to leave before I was rejected and sent away. It was only a matter of time before the Fergusons would realize they'd taken on more than they'd bargained for. I told them I wanted to live with my grandparents.

Mr. Ferguson said, "Why do you think you aren't already with them?"

Maybe I *was* the problem. I was unwanted everywhere and unsatisfied no matter where I lived.

"Call them right now," Mrs. Ferguson said. "If that's what you want." I called, and nobody answered. I called Auntie Philys. She apologized and said she couldn't take me. She reminded me that we'd been through this before, and nothing had changed. As if I'd forgotten one of the worst days of my life, as if I'd forgotten she didn't want me.

Mrs. Ferguson had tears in her eyes. I enjoyed hurting her and didn't realize she might be crying because she knew how much I was hurting. My aunt told me to write a phone number down. Then she said it was an abuse hotline, which made me know my aunt didn't understand one bit what I needed or what I was going through. I folded the paper and held it in my grip.

When I was off the phone, Mrs. Ferguson pulled at my hand to make me show her the number. "Why does she think you need that?" At that moment, I knew my situation was hopeless. Nobody understood me. And worse, I had no idea how to make them understand. I shut myself in my room. Facedown on my dumb lace bedcover, I let everything out, soaked my pillow with tears, and screamed into the cotton.

Mrs. Ferguson let herself in. She placed her hand on my back. "Can we talk about this? I know what you're going through is hard." She drew away and sat on the wooden floor by the window. The last bit of daylight streamed in from behind the blinds. "We're trying to be a family. The way you're acting is not normal."

I glared at her. Maybe nobody had invented a way to speak aloud the fear, anger, ugliness, and frustration that could haunt a person on the inside. I didn't have the right words, so instead, I yelled, "I hate you." The power of my growl startled me. Now I sounded as ugly as I felt. The words were out of me, I couldn't take them back, and I'd done my best, which was also my worst. Somehow, I had to let Mrs. Ferguson know I hated her because, that way, if it turned out she did, in fact, hate *me*, we would be on even playing ground. The sting wouldn't hurt as much when it came time for her and her husband to reject me. "Send me back if you want to," I said. "If that's what you're going to do, do it now and get it over with." I turned my face to the cool wall, and it eased the heat of my suffering.

"We're the ones who took you in, not your grandparents. And you're angry at us?"

This is it. She is going to send me away. I was impossible and cruel and sad and stupid, and I loathed myself for ruining everything, but I could do nothing more in that moment than stare at the wall.

After several minutes, Mrs. Ferguson sighed, wiped her tears, and rolled me toward her by gently pulling my shoulder. She said my name, said it like it was the most important word she'd ever uttered in her life. Another wave of crying rose in me in anticipation of the truth I knew was coming next. But her words didn't match my prediction. With slow deliberation, as if to make certain I would grasp the meaning of her words, she said, "There is nothing you could ever say or do to make us send you back. This is it. And you can hate us all you want, but we are not giving up. You are *our* kid."

I didn't know how to respond. I had been so bitter and scared, and Mrs. Ferguson, instead of showing me my own ugliness in return, gave me the most unexpected thing—a thing I didn't understand or have a name for—a nothing that became the greatest something of all—a *lovething*.

Maybe I did belong somewhere, and maybe that somewhere was with Mr. and Mrs. Ferguson. If they didn't give up after all that, maybe I *could* trust them. In Mrs. Ferguson's clear gray-blue eyes, I saw commitment and honesty, though I barely knew how to identify those qualities. Her dedication despite my belligerence knocked the fear and howl right out of me.

On Christmas Eve that year, I visited my grandparents. Mom, William, and Auntie Philys came, too, and it was our first time together since March. I wore black jersey pants with pockets and a white sweatshirt with lacy arms. I'd recently gotten my hair cut short for the first time. It was a mistake because the hairdresser either misinterpreted my instructions or chose to ignore them altogether. The result: I looked like a boy. Even our school counselor thought so. While sitting in the car, waiting for Mrs. Ferguson to return from the front office one day, I overheard the counselor ask, "Oh, is that your son?"

Now, reaching to touch my head, Mom said, "Oh, Leslie. Why did you cut your hair? You had such beautiful hair."

I pulled away. "Well, it's short now, and there's nothing I can do about it, so there." She didn't know I made a nightly ritual of tugging on it forcefully, in an attempt to make it grow. She didn't know I berated myself every time I looked in a mirror.

Mom wore a powder-blue chiffon wrap-front dress. When she was well, she'd always prided herself on being presentable, but this time, the dress was wrinkled beyond all hope, and what appeared to be burn lines, perhaps from an iron, marred its pale color. Even though she was my mom, and she was there with us, I had never felt so lost to her as I did in that moment.

"My eyesight is so bad," she said, clutching her can of Pepsi in a tremulous hand. "I can barely see to write." No wonder her skin was so bad. No wonder her eyeliner was crooked and lipstick bleeding out from the corners. I thought she looked like a wreck because she was crazy and that's what crazy became, but she was going blind. "And this medicine they have me on gives me the shakes so bad, I can't do my makeup like I used to. I probably look so bad to you, huh?"

Mom had always been alluring. In my favorite photograph of my mom, she's in her early twenties, standing on a towel at the beach. She's wearing a dark one-piece bathing suit with pointy breast cups, and she holds a floppy-brimmed hat in one hand at her hip. Her eyes hide behind a pair of oversized sunglasses. She's looking straight at the camera.

When she looked at you—when she smiled—the whole world stopped spinning for a second.

But now, her aging skin, pimples, and clown makeup embarrassed me for her. Mom used to smell like Ivory soap and pancake makeup. Now she smelled dirty, stale, and rancid. Her face had changed in the past six months since I'd last seen her—or maybe it had changed incrementally over many years, too slowly to discern. Almost distorted—her features were those of a stranger and also those of someone I used to know.

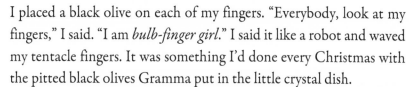

I placed a black olive on each of my fingers. "Everybody, look at my fingers," I said. "I am *bulb-finger girl*." I said it like a robot and waved my tentacle fingers. It was something I'd done every Christmas with the pitted black olives Gramma put in the little crystal dish.

Mom crossed her arms and legs and scowled at me before avoiding my gaze. "Don't do that. That's bad; very, very bad." My face flushed with heat at the humiliation and at the slow knowing that crept into my brain. Mom was not well at all. She sat before us, able to talk, eat, and breathe, and she looked like any other disheveled person might, but she was indeed very sick. I sucked the olives off my fingers. Mom threw me a scowl as if to say I'd purposefully injured her and I would have to pay for it.

"Roberta," Gramma said, coming in from the kitchen. "Knock it off. She's not hurting anybody." The kitchen timer dinged, and Gramma went to pull the enchiladas from the oven. Grampa was in the kitchen, too, helping with the final preparation of the meal.

Mom glared at me and said, "And why would you wear black? Don't ever wear it. The color of death, funerals, torture. All things evil."

"They're just pants." I tugged at the thin jersey material to show her, wanting desperately to undo her years of paranoid thinking and bring her to my rational side of the world.

Mom furrowed her brow, mumbled something imperceptible, and studied a corner of the ceiling. "Cross your legs. Ladies do not sit with their legs open like that and private parts accessible for everybody to see." I crossed my legs, knowing my crotch was not showing, given I was wearing pants. I glanced at my crotch anyway.

"Stop saying that," I said. Instead of showing compassion, instead of being satisfied to be wrong, I broke. "Nothing is bad. Olives aren't bad. The color black is not bad. I can sit any way I want. You don't know anything. You don't even know me anymore. Why can't you leave me alone? Why am I the one who's always doing something wrong?" William leaned into Mom on the couch, and Mom hugged him with one arm as if she wished to protect him from my jealousy.

We ate in silence and exchanged gifts afterward. Mom handed me a gift, wrapped in green paper with Santa Clauses on it. When I unwrapped it, Mom said, "I painted it myself. Do you like it?"

On a white mug, she'd painted a deformed Santa head with wonky, black, dead eyes. I caressed the bad Santa and wrapped him in the crinkled tissue paper.

I set the mug on the couch and left the room for Grampa's bathroom. I locked the door behind me and dry-heaved over the sink as acid threatened to come up. Then, as if things weren't bad enough, I saw Mom's face in the mirror—but it was *my* face. I was already starting to look like her—and not the beach bombshell version. I was the miserable version, a girl with too many freckles and moles from the sun and a downturned mouth sucking in the truth about her life and family. I calmed myself, patted my skin with water, and slowed my breathing.

The rest of the night, I suffered from guilt because I was relieved and happy my teacher was now my new mom.

"Do you like the mug?" Mom asked again, seemingly desperate for my approval. I couldn't look at her. I'd always wondered if she were going to leave *me*, but now, I had left her in a more real way than ever before. I sat quietly on the couch, arms folded across my chest, legs crossed to protect myself, staring into the colored Christmas tree lights. They blurred before me like the clouded definition between my old life and the new, showing me my necessary detachment from my old mom and sorrow over having to choose one or the other.

Less than a month after Christmas, I received an envelope in the mail from Gramma. Inside there was another envelope, addressed to me from Mom, containing a letter. I shut myself in my bedroom, sat on the edge of my bed, on my white eyelet bedcover, and read.

January 18, 1986

Dear Leslie and William,

Your Dad wanted to name you Michelle don't use it. These are possible names I almost named you, too. Julie, Linda, Elizabeth, Anne, Susan, Cheryl, Ann.

Leslie, (don't use the other Karen name).

I'm unhappy that I had to be away from you. I'm better now. I'm so unhappy you and Julie, i.e., Leslie, Louis, and William had to be away from me. (I was unconscious when the Dr. brought you & my second and another child into the world. I also was unconscious when the second pregnancy child) (Johnny I named him Johnny William Newson) (He Johnny was brought into the world). (He may have a turn. I doubt it). You can tell if it's me if I have funny shaped small ears; it's me. Johnny doesn't have funny shaped ears. At least I didn't notice if he does.

I hope you will get married and stay married and not have any children and stay away from people that have a family (You don't want to be responsible for other people's children). Having pets is enough. Pets are fun.

Avoid black in everything. Black represents death or a person you don't know exists in the family could be a cat. Don't wear black. Wearing black represents death. Black is to wear to funerals and not after. I had a black cat when I was in grammar school living in Norwalk. I used to get its fleas off with tweezers. I really don't know what happened to the cat. It was terrible to be without you, Leslie, and Linda and Johnny that should be Louis.

P.S. Please don't use rubber bands and keep the speed limit pay any tickets immediately in cash or they'll put a person in jail if you don't pay your ticket. Stay out of the ocean it's dangerous. Don't be with anyone you don't want to be with. It's better if you don't marry. Don't wait on anyone. Just think of yourself. Keep away from men. Please. If they want to, get married. Don't just accept an engagement ring and think you are married—

wait until you get married, don't lay down with men at all. Make him pay his way in marriage or forget it. Give yourself all the confidence. Don't feel sorry for people. They really act up here (they do) It's an education. I'll be on my way from here. Don't ever be in here if you can help it—Go somewhere else if you ever get here right away. Don't stay here at all. If you keep a job and keep an active life you shouldn't have to have Social Security Income like I have. Religion is good to have. Reading the bible is educational.

I hope you haven't been too unhappy away from me. I have a birthday on April 15. I'll be 45 years. I've tried to have a normal managed life. Maybe I'll be seeing you soon at Mom & Dad's.

Love, Mom

The letter showed me that Mom was still suffering—and unable to separate truth from fiction—and still attempting to mother me by sharing *her* reality, her guiding truths, which she must have viewed as crucial to my well-being. Her nonsensical advice didn't instill values or ideas about how I would live my life. It increased my sorrow, and it convinced me further that I needed to move on without her. There was no hope of ever going back, of ever being her daughter again.

I didn't respond. What was there to say? *I've chosen to abandon you? I'm trying to forget you, so please leave me alone?* Instead, I continued living as a Ferguson as if I'd only ever had one family, as if I'd never had a mentally ill mother who threatened my existence.

I carried on with life as "normal," doing my best to be a regular *tweenager*. At the mall, Heidi, Kassandra, and I ordered pepperoni pizza by the slice and large Cokes from Antonio's, and we scoped out the scene, hoping to scam on cute guys.

Mrs. Ferguson, whom I now easily called "Mom," picked us up, and after dropping Heidi and Kassandra home, she asked what I'd been doing at the mall, sounding more accusatory than curious. "I smell smoke." She leaned toward me, both hands on the wheel, and sniffed. "Were you smoking?"

"What? No. Why?" I pulled at my T-shirt, brought it to my nose, and sniffed it. "I don't smell smoke." I held my thin cross-body purse closer to my stomach, thinking about the black kohl eyeliner pencil I'd been hiding in the front zip pocket. I felt terrible for sneaking around but entitled to wear makeup. My eyes, my decision.

"I got a call from someone today about you." She looked at the road.

"From who?" I stared ahead.

"They wouldn't say. Do you promise you weren't smoking or doing anything wrong at the mall with your friends?"

"I promise. Swear. Cross my heart and hope to die." I rubbed my eyes with my fingers and discreetly checked for lingering black. It seemed I'd wiped it all away. "Why? What did they say?" I knew I'd been sneaking around, knew it might make Mrs. Ferguson send me away.

"They said, 'You'd be *very disappointed* to know what your little *angel* is doing at the mall.'"

"What? I swear I have no idea what they're talking about." The lies turned sick on my tongue. "We walked around, got pizza." I put my hands on my bloated stomach, aching from the pressure of my buttoned jeans. "That's it."

Would someone really call about eyeliner? That didn't seem like something worthy of a phone call claiming I was less than angelic. Neither did sitting around, hoping to meet cute guys to make out with.

"Why would someone call to tell me that unless it was true?"

"If I knew who it was, I might have a clue. You believe me, don't you?" I stared at her profile, at her mouth turned down in disappointment.

"What choice do I have? All I know is you better not be smoking, or you're grounded for life."

I rolled my eyes. But secretly, I worried someone was out to get me.

My friends wore makeup, but when I asked if I could, Mom said I was too young, so the answer was, "No, but you can ask your father and see what he says."

"It'll make you look older than you are." He emptied his pockets and placed his wallet and keys on the island separating the kitchen and the dining room. "You don't want people to think you're hot to trot—do you?"

I scrunched my nose, confused.

"Looking for sex," he said.

How embarrassing. But was I . . . hot to trot? I thought about how my friends and I searched for guys, hoping we were pretty enough to attract them. "Everybody's wearing makeup. I'm in the eighth grade now, and only some of the seventh graders don't wear it. I want to do what my friends are doing."

"If your friends jumped off a bridge, would you jump, too?"

"Yeah, probably." I laughed.

"Leslie, come on," Dad said. "Really? I'd like to think you have at least half a brain and would make a better decision than that."

"It's only makeup. It's not hurting anybody. It's not like I'm asking to smoke or drink or do drugs. I'm not asking to stay out all night." Believing I'd made excellent points, I folded my arms across my chest. He'd have to give in. "Please?"

He said to ask my mom, and with that, I knew this was a battle I would not win.

"Ugh! *So* lame." I stormed off and slammed my bedroom door. Dad unlatched it, and I closed it again, and we went back and forth like this five or six times. Finally, I opted to solve the problem another way. I slid my toddler-height wicker clothes hamper into the doorway and on top of it, I stacked textbooks, clothes, shoes, and anything else I could find, to make my fake compromise door as tall as possible.

Dad walked by and laughed. "I can still see you," he joked. I huffed, but the fire in me died, and I conceded. Lying on my bed, staring at the ceiling, and listening to Wham!'s *Make It Big* album on my little silver radio, I pretended I was all grown up and things were exactly as I'd intended them to be.

At dinner, Dad said, "Glad you decided to join us. I was wondering if there might be a hunger strike." He laughed, and I rolled my eyes.

In the locker room mirror, Kassandra, Heidi, and I stood side by side, sharing eyeliner, applying it to the inner rims of our eyes before school.

At the end of the day, after volleyball practice, I used a Kleenex to wipe my eyes clean. Then, Heidi announced she had pinkeye so we couldn't use her eyeliner anymore. I purchased a Wet N Wild black kohl eyeliner, and I kept it in my crossbody purse. How would my parents ever know?

But I was a terrible secret-keeper. While I sat at the dining table, finishing my homework, Mom asked, "Do you have any gum?" I told her to check my purse. She walked toward me, holding my secret eyeliner pencil. My stomach turned. I'd been caught and hadn't thought at all about how I would cover it up. So, the truth came out with my tears, and Mom cried, too, the corners of her mouth crinkling, her hope and trust seeming to crumble at once.

"I can't believe you lied and have been sneaking around." Her voice shook and cut out. "For how long? When did it start?"

"Just this school year—for a couple of months—I promise. After you guys said no, I realized it wouldn't hurt to wear it only at school. Nobody else cared but you, so if I kept it from you, you got what you wanted, and so did I."

"That's funny logic. You should be a lawyer since you're so good at manipulation."

"Mom. I'm sorry. I really am. Don't be mad. Please."

"I'm not mad," she said. "I'm just so disappointed. It makes me wonder what else you're lying about." Silence followed. Knowing I'd disappointed her shot me in the gut. How could I have lied to this woman, the only one who ever cared enough about me to save me? Mom confiscated my eyeliner, and I stopped wearing it. Now that I knew how dreadful it felt to lose her trust, I needed it more than ever.

For eighth-grade graduation, Mom took me shopping for a dress at Broadway. I settled on a floor-length baby-pink strapless Jessica McClintock gown with a damask print. It made me feel so grown-up, I barely cared that my braces made my smile gray.

"And your father and I," she said, "have decided you can wear makeup to graduation."

I threw my arms around her. "Thank you!"

My whole family, except for my biological mom, came to the ceremony. I sat next to my friend Kassandra, who wore a light blue strapless dress and white elbow-length gloves. The sun beat down on us, but we didn't care because we were about to be high schoolers.

The principal gave a speech about moving on, toward success. Kassandra and I whispered about how we'd be friends forever, hang out all summer, and start high school together.

The principal said something about an award—Girl and Boy of the Year. These awards were voted on by the entire staff, taking into account grades, attendance, attitude, and school involvement.

"The boy of the year is . . ." Everyone clapped, and some hooted and hollered as the recipient accepted his trophy.

"Girl of the year is . . ."

Kassandra jabbed me with her elbow. "It's you," she said. "He just said your name. Go!" I raised my head to see my classmates looking at me.

"Go, Leslie!" someone shouted. The audience hooted and clapped as I stood. Shaking, I slid from my row and walked to the podium. The size of a small child, my trophy almost slipped from my sweaty grasp. I gazed out over the audience, hundreds of people watching me accept an award I hadn't even tried to win.

After the ceremony, I joined my family. They hugged me and congratulated me, loading me up with cards, balloons, and flowers.

"You won," William said. "That's so cool." William now lived with Gramma and Grampa, so, it seemed, neither of us would be shuffled around anymore. He stood away from me a bit but offered a small smile. I smiled at him, but I avoided his eyes, terrified I might not find him there. He was my brother, but we now belonged to different families, different lives, and my guilt over having been chosen and brought into favor and fortune prevented me from connecting with him.

Mom asked if I had known I was getting the award. I said I was shocked, and Dad said he wasn't. "I think you're better than you think." His words took hold of me. I couldn't stop shaking, couldn't stop the chill of nervous excitement running through me.

Gramma and Grampa praised me. Auntie Philys told me not to ruin my makeup by crying. Mom and I locked eyes for a moment, and I looked away, still embarrassed and ashamed about having worn eyeliner behind her back. We all laughed and went to Lascari's for pizza and tiramisu. I was on top of the world—or at least—on top of *my* world.

chapter 31

1987
AGE 13–14

TOWARD THE END OF THE SUMMER, MOM AND DAD sat me at the dining room table. Through the sliding glass door, the foliage shimmered in the sunlight. The clear sky shone blue for miles in the distance. The view from our house stretched out over the valley and to Catalina Island, a faint outline at the farthest point to the west.

"We always wanted kids," Mrs. Ferguson said. "But I had a miscarriage. We finally decided if it was meant to be, it would happen. And then you came along." Her eyes turned glossy. She sniffled, and I stood to hug her.

I said, "I'm really glad you're my mom now."

"You should thank *him*," she said, pointing to Mr. Ferguson.

"She came home from work every day," he said, "and all she'd do was talk about you and how worried she was for you." He leaned back in his chair and crossed his arms. "Finally, I said, she'd better shut up about you or bring you home."

"Thanks ... Dad." I hugged him. I'd never had a dad before, but when I called Mr. Ferguson *Dad,* I meant it in my heart like an honor. He hugged me back and patted my shoulder.

"Only time will tell if we made the right decision," he said with a laugh.

I thought about how Katy got demoted from "long-term" to a regular foster kid. I wondered if my place here could be ripped away in a moment. But somehow, I knew Mr. Ferguson's joke meant we were on our way to becoming a real family.

"We've been talking," Mom said. "And we've decided we would like to adopt you . . . you know . . . if you want us to."

I beamed and then reined in my excitement. We'd been living like a true, *normal* family for two years. Still, I worried adoption *would* change things, maybe everything. I had finally become settled and calm, and I wanted to continue without upset. I didn't want to anger or sadden my biological mom any more than necessary.

My new mom said, "The counselor thinks it's important for you—to help you feel safe and secure. We want to do everything we can to let you know you are our kid."

"Ah, Mom. I know that. You keep telling me."

"But we want you to know we love you and want to be a family in the eyes of the law."

"Will my real mom know?" There was that guilt again. Would it ever let me go? Was I about to abandon my other mom permanently as if she never existed?

"I'd appreciate it," Mom said, "if you wouldn't call her that— *Real mom.*" She looked down as if she understood the gravity of what she was asking.

Confused and stunned, I said, "What should I call her? She is my mom, you know." Now, I worried she'd be upset not only if I got adopted but also if I no longer referred to her as my mom. Hadn't she been through enough heartache? At the same time, Mrs. Ferguson had done so much for me, couldn't I easily comply with this small request?

"What about if you refer to her as *Roberta*. Just around us—because we are trying to be a family, and it's hurtful to have you think I'm not your *real* mom. Blood isn't the only thing that makes families." I didn't want my new mom to be hurt, so I agreed. She explained how the adoption proceedings would happen. If Roberta failed to show in court the day of the hearing, I would be free to be adopted. But if she came, she would have to sign me over, granting the Fergusons permission to be my permanent parents in the eyes of the law.

"She'll never sign me away," I said, depressed about the idea of Mom no longer referring to me as her daughter. I didn't want her to be my mom, but I also didn't want her to willingly give me up. I couldn't give voice to my thoughts because they revealed how selfish I was. "What about William? Will he still be my brother if I'm adopted?"

"Of course, he'll always be your brother. This would make you our kid by law—you're already our kid in our hearts. If adopted, you will be entitled to inheritance without question. It solidifies what we already know to be true for us. Want some time to think about it?"

I didn't need any more time. I was as eager to be a part of a real family as they were to let go of the fear that someday, Roberta might knock on their door, demanding I leave with her. Mom furrowed her brows, but light flickered in her eyes. And I understood that, perhaps for the first time, the Fergusons needed me as much as I needed them.

To celebrate our adoption decision, Mom, Dad, my best friend Kassandra, and I went to Rudy's, our favorite hole-in-the-wall Mexican restaurant. After I'd stuffed myself beyond capacity with chips, salsa, and a chimichanga slathered in sour cream sauce, Kassandra and I walked across the street to the cemetery. We hoped to meet cute boys who might be slightly morbid like we were, stalking around tombstones at dusk.

"It's cool you're getting adopted. I can't believe you never even told me about your situation." Kassandra fiddled with the collar on her pink polo shirt. She wore two pairs of socks, one pink, the tops sticking out from the second pair, white.

"Nobody ever asked, and I just didn't want to talk about it. It seemed like they were my real parents, so I pretended they were."

"Well, I'm happy for you guys," she said. As we entered the iron gates of the cemetery, grass and dirt scents surrounded us, and full trees swayed in the cool breeze. The sun was setting behind houses at the far end of the property, and the color faded out of the green, turning the world gray. We didn't see any boys, but we read tombstones.

"Think about all these people who died..." Kassandra turned her attention from the gravestones to the full, green trees.

I thought about Mom and William and how, even though they still lived, being apart from them sometimes made it seem like they had died. "What do you think happens when we die?"

"We go to Heaven," she said. "But only the good people." Then I asked if she believed in ghosts. She said, "I believe in ghosts and angels. One time, my aunt's car died in the desert, and she prayed, asking God to send angels to help her, and she said her car started rolling as if angels were pushing it."

I widened my eyes. I thought about some of the things I'd seen and heard, and about the ghost boat painting above Roberta's bed at Gramma's house. The idea of ghosts and haunting, unexplainable events made me feel like almost anything was possible, like even if I died, it would still matter that I'd lived. Somber and slow, we walked a line as if paying respects to the decomposing bodies beneath us, bodies we'd never known.

A loud sound started up, a whisk and spurt, sputtering fast and seemingly out of nowhere. Screaming, we ran to the entrance as the sprinklers shot on and sprayed us, soaking our hair and clothes.

"Oh my god," I said. "That scared the shit out of me."

"Me, too," she said. "I can't believe you said 'shit'!" She laughed. And we heaved and giggled, hands on our knees at the front gate, before calming ourselves enough to walk back to the restaurant in the thickening twilight. "That was fun," Kassandra said, adjusting her white headband.

"The best." I pulled the cuffs of my green Generra sweatshirt over my hands. My jaw ached, and my stomach tensed from cracking up. The safety of friendship and a sense of belonging flooded me as if I'd finally left my old life behind, buried it in the graveyard beneath the setting sun, so I could start over on a better path, one where fear was nothing more than a moment.

The day of the adoption hearing, Dad drove us to the courthouse in downtown Los Angeles.

"And you're still okay with what we talked about?" Mom asked, filing her fingernails with a metal file, something she often did in the car. I gave a closed-mouthed smile, and Mom reached back to hold my hand. I held on, but she slipped from me to resume her manicure.

In the courtroom, my social worker, Mrs. Cunningham, whispered "Good morning" as if she were afraid to wake the dead. Mom, Dad, and I sat in wooden chairs alongside her at a table in front of the judge, who seemed eight feet tall at his bench.

"I'm so nervous." Mom crossed her arms and held her elbows as if she were more cold than nervous. But I knew how easily emotions could freeze or starve a person. I looked at her, concerned. She smiled.

Dad said, "There's no use worrying. When have things not worked out?"

"I know, I know. But still." She whispered now, leaning into my dad as if to keep me safe from her words, from her anxiety. I knew this was a big day for us all, and only one thing—one person—could stand in our way. But she wasn't here. I hadn't seen or spoken to her in months, and part of me wanted to keep it that way, let her slide away from me more and more so I could forget the past and focus on my future.

"Susan." Dad shook his head, ready to lecture her with logic.

"Shh," Mom snapped. "I don't want to scare Leslie." Did she think I couldn't hear her? Her hand covered her mouth as she spoke, but she failed to shield me from her voice.

Still as stone in his khaki-colored uniform, the bailiff clasped his hands in front of him, shiny handcuffs and a holstered gun hanging from his belt. I was safe. We all were.

Security would come from finalizing an adoption, but at what risk? I imagined someday telling Roberta I'd been adopted. Her face—her trembling lips and beckoning eyes—would draw down in recognition of the ultimate betrayal. What she wanted most was to reunite our family, but there was no chance of that now. I held my clammy hands in my lap. My stomach keeled on the sea of my nerves. Mom placed one hand on a manila folder that included paperwork for my adoption. I'd signed my consent; Mom and Dad had signed theirs. Now, I needed my biological mom to stay put, wherever she was, and to ignore the court's request for her appearance, so I could move forward. I watched the clock.

I leaned my arms on the table. *Please don't come, please don't come.*

Mom and Dad looked ahead. The judge, glasses toward the tip of his nose, scanned documents before him. Rushed feet and muffled voices raced about in the halls on the other side of the closed double doors. I shook my knees, couldn't calm them. I tucked my hair behind my ears. Annoying and out of place, the hair itched me, so I untucked it; it flounced, so I held it back with my hands, which made my arms tired. I held my breath, counting how long I could go before dying, and then let it go.

"Well," the judge said, "it's time to proceed. Are all parties present?"

Mrs. Cunningham said yes and stood, brushing the wrinkles from the front of her blouse.

I stared at the clock.

"And the biological parents? Should we assume they have decided to terminate parental rights voluntarily?" The judge removed his glasses and held them in one hand.

"Yes, your honor," my social worker said, moving toward the bench, manila folder in hand. The judge held his free hand out to receive the folder. Mrs. Cunningham brought it to him. She wasn't coming. I was about to be free.

But then a thump of wood and creak of hinges sounded behind me. I turned around. The double doors had been thrown open.

"Leslie, Leslie, my baby." It was *her*, in a teal dress, a mess of auburn hair puffy around her face. "Mommy's here." She held her arms out and approached me, zoomed toward me like an arrow to a target. Her voice punctured me. Tears burned my eyes, blurred my vision. I hugged her because she hugged me, because it's what you do in a situation like that.

The bailiff came near, hand on the butt of his gun. Mr. and Mrs. Ferguson turned, waiting for something, maybe for the unexpected embrace to end. She held me tight; she meant to keep me. No money, no car, no job, no custody, and now no surrender, either.

"Mommy loves you, Leslie. I've missed you so much," she cried into my hair. Her hair stuck to my wet face. I held on to her as if letting go meant I would plummet into a bottomless pit. And I let go as if holding on meant I would alienate my new parents, the people responsible for my new life and who hadn't broken a single promise.

She let me go and turned to the Fergusons. "Thank you," she said. "For taking good care of my little girl. I did my best, but I just couldn't. Maybe someday . . ." Her voice turned hollow and soft, and it trailed off.

A squeak came from somewhere inside of me. She *wasn't* a monster. I'd spent so much time making her out to be the villain, I'd forgotten she was in there somewhere, with some sanity left. She loved me first in the world, and she did her best. She'd battled, in her way, to keep us safe, but her mental illness and the sum of her failures had broken her.

Suddenly, the idea of being adopted made *me* feel like a monster. Did people do this—abandon their mothers, ditch them for better parents?

"You're welcome," Mr. Ferguson said. "It's our pleasure."

Mrs. Ferguson and Mrs. Cunningham had approached the judge. I couldn't hear what they said, but I knew they were making new arrangements.

I would not be adopted that day. Relief and loss tightened around me. I thought being adopted would help me discover who I was, but now I would continue to straddle two families, two worlds, and I would remain pulled in opposite directions. I wanted to let go, but the defeat of this day would keep me hanging on.

The judge's loud voice said for everyone to have a seat.

"Mr. and Mrs. Ferguson, Leslie, is this what you want?" said the judge, with compassion in his tone.

Roberta sat at the next table. The room swallowed us with its many rows of bench seating, its beige walls, and old wood. Mrs. Ferguson placed her hand on my arm. Involuntary shakes forced their way into me as if sending me a message—I was chilly, scared, angry, sad, or all of these things at once. I was so hot, my ears burned, and my neck, too, in that smooth place above the collarbone that tenses under pressure.

"She can't be adopted," Roberta blurted out, arms crossed. She didn't know we had already backed down. "I won't let them do it. They don't have my permission. She's *my* daughter."

My nose tingled like it did whenever I tried not to cry, whenever I tried to prevent my face from bursting. Mrs. Cunningham told the judge it was what we wanted. She glanced at Mom and Dad one final time as if to say this was their last chance.

I couldn't speak because how does one say *I don't want you to be my mom. I want new parents and a new life so you can never, ever hurt me again?* I was fourteen, but in her presence, I regressed into a helpless child, the same helpless child who'd had to fight to survive and beg and plead for safety. My throat made a noise. I took in a big, long breath as if I'd just emerged from water.

Mr. Ferguson put his arm around Mrs. Ferguson as she slumped in her chair. He held out his handkerchief. She pulled it from his hand and put it to her wet eyes. Caught between *them* and *her*, I sat in silence, numb. It was as if I'd agreed to stop caring and pretend I wanted nothing from this day.

The judge adjourned the hearing. We all stood, and *she* hooked her arm around mine, linking us together in a symbolic gesture, pulling me toward the doors. Were we making a pact to always be mother and daughter? To be best friends? Or were we saying goodbye? Her body became rigid, determined to keep me as long as possible. I softened and then stiffened and held back, waiting for my new mom and dad, but my old mom gripped my arm, so I went back to her, hoping to appease her demons and walk the path of least resistance to keep everyone happy.

Before we reached the double doors, Mr. Ferguson said my name. I froze as if suspended in time before pulling away from Roberta slightly, then leaning toward her, while she held on. I did and did not want her to let me go.

"I know," I said, though I didn't know what he meant. Maybe it was *don't go too far,* or *it's time to let go.* Maybe my name in his mouth meant for all of us to stop because this was where we went our separate ways—*her* to wherever *she* would go, and us to our home where we would continue being a family.

"Roberta," Dad said, "you take care, now."

She hugged me again. "I love you. Mommy loves you so much. You be a good girl, okay?" She said it as if she had control over my goodness, as if she hadn't stopped being the voice of morality and education in my head long ago. It occurred to me that she missed me more than I missed her, that I remained her whole life while she had been reduced to a nightmare in mine. She embarrassed me, scared me, and saddened me. And I could never let her be my mom again. We were over.

"Okay. I love you, too." The words burst out. As she exited the courtroom, her hands pressed the sides of her head as if putting hair in place after being hit with a gust of wind. The khaki bailiff stood at the door.

In the car, Mrs. Ferguson said, "Leslie, we want you to know this doesn't change *anything.* You understand what happened, don't you?" I knew what happened was that my old mom showed up, and it meant I couldn't be adopted that day. "We didn't want to make things unnecessarily harder for her. *We* know we're family, right?"

I sat in the middle of the backseat, where I always sat so I could see where I was headed. "I understand." I caught my eyes in the rearview mirror. Ringed with red, and swollen, they said I was a coward—a despondent, nervous, ugly coward. Mr. Ferguson's eyes caught mine in the rearview mirror. My body sank into the seat, the heat of emotional exhaustion swirling in my head. I was and was not okay. Bitterness replaced my hope of freedom and sat at the back of my tongue like a rotten meal. We would go on, living as a family like we'd been doing. Nothing had been lost, had it? Then why did I feel so empty?

chapter 32

1987–1996
AGE 14–22

I EXCELLED IN HONORS AND AP CLASSES AND PRAC-
ticed diligently every day during volleyball and basketball seasons. I
had friends, boyfriends, wins, and losses. On my sixteenth birthday,
Mom and Dad bought me a safe, used car. I still gorged when I ate,
stuffing myself so full I dry-heaved over the toilet.

To celebrate birthdays and holidays, my first family and I
gathered at Gramma and Grampa's over feasts cooked in the kitchen
where my first mom almost forced my head into the oven that one
scary night. Even after all the sadness and terror, I still felt guilty, as
if I'd abandoned them to accept a better life without them. Being an
only child without William made me sorry for him most of all
because I got a second chance to have a fresh start with a new family
while he was stuck with the old.

I pressured myself to earn all A's and maintain a perfect record
and do no wrong, continuing to deny where I came from and focus
on who I was meant to be, not that I knew who that was, exactly.

Playing sports brought out my competitive nature and taught

me the importance of hard work and accountability to others. My mom and dad attended all of my volleyball and basketball games, and my dad started keeping stats on scratch paper to help correct any errors in the official record book.

I graduated sixth in my class, a top-ten senior, and an All-CIF dual-sport athlete—a two-time state-championship volleyball winner and one of the ten best female basketball players in Orange County.

I planned to study psychology in college because it might help me understand my biological mom and the harrowing experiences of my childhood. Or maybe I would study education and earn my teaching credential. When I was in the third grade, I thought, if I lived long enough, I would probably want to be a teacher.

My parents said, "We want you to be happy and choose a college without thinking about the money." By the time I applied to colleges, I no longer doubted their love for me, so I believed them, and to their financial dismay in the end, I declined full-ride athletic scholarships from schools across the country. My visit to the University of Redlands, a small liberal arts college, showed me it was where I belonged. My parents funded my tuition, less a small academic scholarship and meager financial government support received over the previous seven years of my life in foster care.

My parents emphasized that my job was to go to school and play basketball. They worried that, since the risk of developing schizophrenia is higher in those with family members who suffer from the disease, the stress of college might trigger its symptoms. However, to fulfill my work-study obligation, and earn a stipend, I secured part-time employment at the writing center, helping others improve their essays.

Nobody knew that, despite my smile and seemingly perfect life, I sometimes sat on the floor of the shower in my dorm, hugging my knees, sobbing. I couldn't have articulated why I felt so unhappy beneath the surface. My life was turning out fine after all, wasn't it?

At mealtime, I filled my tray with heaping salads, convincing myself I wasn't eating too much. I ate without ever feeling connected to my body, without ever registering fullness until I was stuffed enough to pop. The goal was to extinguish all other feelings that might creep in—pressure, responsibility, low self-worth, and guilt about everything I'd ever done that might have led to others' sadness (mostly Roberta's and William's). My freshman year, almost twenty-five pounds crept under my flesh and flooded me with more guilt. Why couldn't I be skinnier? Why did my stomach hurt all the time? I couldn't control my portions. Food was my therapy, my comfort, my surrogate mother who never judged me, never asked anything of me, never returned my gaze with disappointment.

Still, I excelled on the basketball court, practicing, pounding, and playing for hours every day, choosing exhaustion over acknowledgment of the truth of my past. I napped in my room before and after practice, and I dragged my body around even though I felt as if I'd been hit by a truck. I thought often about the irony of that phrase, given my memory of Roberta's certainty that semi-trucks were after us. I was chronically fatigued and unable to recover. But I kept pushing myself.

When I turned eighteen, I was an adult, aging out of the foster care system, and I legally belonged only to myself. The Fergusons wanted me to be their daughter anyway, which proved how much they loved me. They could have released me to the wind and let me fend for myself, but they didn't. They adopted me in a quiet ceremony in the judge's chambers.

"I feel so lucky I found you," I said.

Mom hugged me. "We are lucky we found *you*." She was crying, so I started crying.

And the two of us crying put a tear in Dad's eye. "Who knew you'd turn out to be such a good kid?" His mustache twitched when he smirked. "I guess this means we're stuck with you." He had become an official expert at making dad jokes.

I rolled my eyes and hugged him. "I guess *so!*"

We all felt as if our union had been too lucky of a thing to be a coincidence. We believed we were meant to be a family.

Even though I had a secure place to land, I was nervous and anxious all the time, worried about making mistakes and prompting the disapproval and disappointment of my parents who had made sacrifices to give me a full, stable life. I gorged myself, kept secrets, and played basketball until it tired me out, so I could sleep and not have to think about how fearful I felt. That's the thing about traumatic childhoods—they leave us empty. No matter how hard we try to fill ourselves up, our insecurity is too big to be sated.

While I didn't think my parents would disown me, I thought they might stop loving me, and my newly constructed world would eventually come crashing down.

When I was little, I couldn't make my mom well, and I couldn't quell my fear. Growing up in foster homes and in my new permanent home, I couldn't make my sadness disappear. In school, I focused on academics and athletics, moving forward one step at a time so I would never have to look back, ever again. I couldn't change the past, but I could pretend it never happened by throwing myself into the fantasy of the good. I believed my survival depended on my denial.

As a member of the women's basketball team at the University of Redlands, I became the first player to make the starting lineup all four years and the first to receive Southern California Intercollegiate

Athletic Conference (SCIAC) first-team honors all four years. My senior year, I was chosen as the (SCIAC) MVP and a first-team CoSida Academic All-American. By the end of my senior season, I'd broken nine school records, including most career rebounds, out-rebounding even the top rebounder in the men's all-time record book.

The next fall, I was awarded an NCAA postgraduate scholar-ship. I stayed at the University of Redlands to complete my teaching credential. In the fall of 1996, at twenty-two years old, I secured a teaching position at La Habra High School, my alma mater.

In 2000, I started graduate school at Chapman University, where I later earned an MA in English literature and an MFA in creative writing. In 2001, I was inducted into the University of Redlands Intercollegiate Athletics Hall of Fame.

chapter 33

WHEN MY SIXTH-GRADE TEACHER AND HER HUSBAND
rescued me from drowning in the foster care system, grit, resilience,
and serendipity collided.

After I graduated from college, William and I reconnected. For the
first time since junior high, I was without a boyfriend and didn't
know how to be unattached. I packed an overnight bag and drove to
Occidental College to grieve in the company of my only sibling. My
retreat from William over the years hadn't been conscious or intentional. But he was a collateral piece of the dysfunctional family I'd
needed to shed in order to survive.

William and I didn't talk about the abandonment he felt in
my absence. Or about the otherness I'd achieved by turning my
back on my past and neglecting him in order to fully integrate
myself into a new family. We simply came together as if no
distance or tragedy had ever split us up, and while I knew I'd

forsaken him, he never laid guilt on me for my choices.

Surrounded by him and his friends one morning at Roscoe's Chicken and Waffles, a sense of calm enveloped me. Even after what we'd been through, William and I still belonged to each other. For the first time in my life, I was present with William; he included me in a way that made me feel as if nothing I said or did could alienate me from him ever again—because we were blood. I devoured my plate of food, partly because I was amazed by the surprisingly delicious combination of fried chicken and maple syrup and partly because I'd lived for so long, starving for more than food. I picked at others' discards. I'd eaten enough but could not get full. Eating became a mindless activity and a shallow comfort. I needed more than food if I were ever going to heal.

That day existed for me as if to teach me that everything before it was my childhood and everything after it would be my adulthood. Now, William and I are like best friends brought together by a shared tragedy, confiding in each other and recalling bits and pieces of the past. We console and protect each other, but whereas William doesn't like to talk about the past, I want to dig deep. It is as if our childhood lies buried at the core of a graveyard and each question leads us beyond more bones that reveal yet another missing chunk of my memory. I want to dig deep because if I can make sense of everything, I can heal.

One day, over the phone, I asked William why he had always agreed with Mom and why he'd repeatedly offered himself as the one Mom could kill first.

"I always knew she'd never kill us," he said. "I was just trying to keep her calm."

Then, holding back tears, I asked him why he left me in our Aunt's apartment that day I chose to stay behind.

He said, "I left you alone because I knew you'd survive, but if I would've left Mom, she *would've* killed herself."

Choking on my sorrow for my brother, for all he'd suffered, I said, "I never realized you were so strategic about everything. How were you able to think like that—to know so much—when you were so young?" But I knew the answer to that. William is an old soul, wise beyond his years. He is now, and he was then. All that time, I thought I was protecting William and myself, but *William* was protecting Mom and me.

"Why do you always want to relive the past?" he asked. "Didn't you get enough of the bad stuff the first time around?"

"I want to understand it all," I said. "I need closure. Don't you?"

"I got closure when Mom tried to kill me."

"But you never gave up on her, and you still send her cards and care packages. It will always sadden me to think back to the time you were alone with her on the streets."

"You can't blame yourself," he said. "You were just a kid."

I laughed at his irony. He was just a kid, too. I cried and thanked him, with a laugh tucked into my gratitude, for being such a caring brother. He didn't cry. He hasn't cried since he was eight. He shared with me that in the middle of the night once, when he and Mom were homeless without me, he was shivering, starving, and sad. He composed himself and made a silent promise to never again cry or suffer cold or hunger. William is impeccable with his word—that promise became his armor, his defense mechanism for surviving the past and moving forward into the future. I lean on him, perhaps more than I should, and he allows it, tolerating my neediness. I admire and respect him for his perspective and ability to love without judgment. He represents all that is right in my world.

In my thirties, I lost contact with Roberta. Neither William nor my grandparents knew where she was. Then, William received a call at work from a woman claiming to have found her lying in a gutter. Roberta had suffered a massive stroke that rendered her partially paralyzed and unable to walk or speak.

I drove two hours to visit her. Upon seeing me, her eyes widened, and her jaw shook. It was as if she had seen a ghost. Hadn't she? I'd been absent from her life for more than two decades—I'd replaced her, mind and deeds focused on my future, willing myself not to turn back, as if she were my Medusa and I her weakling mortal.

Unable to feel genuinely happy she was still alive, I was preoccupied by my guilt and shame, a kind of morbid sorrow for what I'd lost over the years. When I left her room, left her sitting in her wheelchair in her tarnished brass earrings and sloppily applied eyeliner, I ran down the stairs and sat in my car. Heat washed over me like a shroud, and I leaned over my steering wheel and sobbed.

My complicated grief knew no logic. But often, I wonder, *Wasn't it always supposed to be like this—wasn't she supposed to be ill—so I could have this beautiful life? Didn't everything lead me here, and didn't I have to be lost so I could find my way home?*

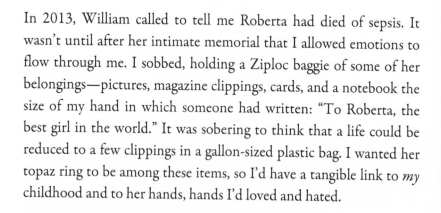

In 2013, William called to tell me Roberta had died of sepsis. It wasn't until after her intimate memorial that I allowed emotions to flow through me. I sobbed, holding a Ziploc baggie of some of her belongings—pictures, magazine clippings, cards, and a notebook the size of my hand in which someone had written: "To Roberta, the best girl in the world." It was sobering to think that a life could be reduced to a few clippings in a gallon-sized plastic bag. I wanted her topaz ring to be among these items, so I'd have a tangible link to *my* childhood and to her hands, hands I'd loved and hated.

I wiped away my tears, but my hands smelled of cigarette ash, and the scent brought everything back—the tender moments and the harsh, under the pressure of her loving yet unpredictable hand, all of the gut pain, sorrow, and striving for approval, all of the hoping and believing life could be better without her. I was no longer her daughter—I hadn't been in her life for over thirty years—but she would always be my mother, continuing to show up in my DNA, my memories, and my trauma.

There are four photographs I turn to when I want to go back to before this all began:

One is that favorite photo of mine—a black-and-white image of Roberta at the beach. From the photo, I understand why women wanted to be her and men wanted to be with her; she was smart, gorgeous, and mysterious. Her behavioral idiosyncrasies began to appear when she was a child, stubborn, discontented, and fast to pull pranks on her siblings and friends. Exactly when she crossed over into paranoia and psychological turmoil, I will never know. I suspect, back when she was coming of age, my grandparents didn't have a word for my mother's affliction, so they assumed she was a contrarian simply because her charm and wit helped her get away with it.

The second is a photo taken during my fifth birthday party in my grandparents' backyard. Fuchsia bougainvillea blossoms cascade over the brick wall that divides the yard from the neighbor's property. A Pin-the-Tail-on-the-Donkey poster has been taped to the mint green stable-style gate. I stand patiently in my navy dress with white polka dots and Peter Pan collar. I'm wearing my red knee-high socks. Mom, in a pale-yellow T-shirt, denim bell-bottoms, and flat leather sandals, ties a blindfold around my head. William, wearing a rainbow-striped party hat, stands to my left, seemingly less patient than I am;

he holds his hand to his mouth, and one foot is lifted off the ground. He is in motion, ready for what comes next. Four other children in pointed party hats wait their turn, watching raptly as I prepare to make my mark.

The October afternoon is sunny, and friends and family have come to celebrate me. Nothing injurious has yet rocked my world. My socks are just socks, and I am just a naïve girl, blind to the turns my life will take once my mother journeys into the dark cave of her illness.

The third photo was taken at Disneyland. I'm five years old, standing at the Carnation Plaza Gardens outdoor café, watching Minnie Mouse and Pluto dance to the music. A vertical beam, painted red and white, obscures the singer on stage, a man wearing baby-blue trousers and a white shirt with a baby-blue bowtie. I've turned to find the camera. Maybe my mom has called my name because she wants to capture my candid smile and because she adores me more than life itself. Or maybe I seek her out and wish to pull her into this experience with my need for her attention. I'm holding a cake cone topped with a scoop of strawberry ice cream, my favorite, which is smeared across my lips, making them appear fuller than they are. Brown bangs hang over bright blue eyes.

The fourth is a faded photograph Auntie Philys took of Roberta, William, and me at Seal Beach the day we almost drowned. The expanse of water sparkles as white foam dances at our ankles. I stand at Mom's left, and William stands to her right. She looks down at him; his head is turned, and he looks toward his hand in hers as if making sure they are secure in each other's grip. I stare straight ahead as if mentally preparing myself to fight the ocean's power.

Life was still a fairytale then, before my mom's illness took over. Whether I remember these times accurately, or whether the photographs inform my memories, does not matter. What matters is that someone who loved me took my picture, hoping to record glimpses of my happiness as part of a larger story, a childhood, a legacy. When I study these photographs, the flood of simpler times rushes in. Still, I know the years have tainted these memories with a strange sense of *saudade*, a feeling of sorrow and nostalgia for what has been lost, for experiences I will never have again. I am grateful those terrifying, harrowing days are gone. I find solace and gratitude in the thought that the grief I experienced as a child opened me up to boundless parameters of joy.

I've come to appreciate the past as not only an unchangeable, unforgiving force but also a source of hope and healing. For these reasons, the past is like the ocean. I used to wish I were a mermaid, graceful and mythical enough to survive any struggle. I accept the trauma that has impacted my life, but I refuse to let that trauma define me. I confront my childhood as it curls in like a wave from a seemingly infinite horizon—to capsize me or to offer me an opportunity to alter my perspective. Testing my lungs and my resilience, I breathe deeply before I go under, and I remember I have *always* been able to find the light. I am not drowning. I am free. I close my eyes, stretch out my limbs, and swim.

epilogue

SOMETIMES WHEN I VISIT MY PARENTS IN ORANGE County, I get the desire to travel to the cities I lived in as a child, before I became someone else's daughter.

This time, I've driven to see my parents because it's been too long since we've talked face to face. I am about to head out on my own, but I reason that it's rude to take off when I am supposed to be spending time with them.

I ask them if they want to join me. My dad doesn't want to. Spending hours in a car with no real destination sounds dreadful, even to me, unless I am the one actively seeking something.

My mom wants to come, and her eager *yes* gives me the validation I always need, the reassurance that I am not alone and I still matter even though I come from my past.

Still, I say what every insecure girl says when she doesn't want to burden someone else. "Are you sure? You don't have to." Why would she *want* to come? She never lived in those places. She didn't even know me when I lived in those places. Why would she want to spend her afternoon driving into oblivion just so I can maybe find a few sad apartments down the winding road of sorrow and nostalgia?

"Yeah," she says. "I'm sure. Let's go."

I feel so loved, seen, understood. And I am reminded that my mom is ultimately the most selfless person I've ever known. I don't know why it surprises me that she volunteers to be my passenger on this day. I suppose she wants to spend time with me; the location doesn't matter.

As we drive, we talk about some of our shared memories and piece broken stories together. Or we don't talk at all, and the warmth mixes with silence in that comforting way that is easy between two people who have known each other for a long time.

We first do what I've never attempted—we roll up and down all the streets of Bell Gardens, searching for the duplex I lived in with Roberta's boyfriend Jerry the summer I learned that friends can guide you to excitement and men can trick you with a lie. The summer I learned that even though Roberta showed improvement, her illness still had the power to destroy me.

An hour passes. We never find the duplex. I'm not surprised. I never learned the name of the street. What use did I have for it when I was eight? I had nobody to tell where I lived or who I was. It was a summer that left almost as quickly as it had arrived. The details of that street itself lifted from me, maybe, so I could make room for the details of what happened on that street. And for everything that came after.

"Sorry," I say. "I know this is boring. Are you regretting coming with me?"

I can't see her eyes behind her sunglasses when I look to her for her answer. "Oh, no. It's a lovely day. A bit warm out, though. And the sun is so hot." She shields her face with her hand. I adjust the AC. "I hope you don't mind if I drift off to sleep. Being in the car just makes me drowsy."

I don't mind. How many times has she accompanied me as I slept? Like the several nights she spent on my bedroom floor so she'd be there when I awoke from a nightmare. Or the times inexplicable despair drained me, and she caressed my head and reassured me everything was going to be okay. Or as I got older and suffered from restless legs and pain so bad I wanted to chop my limbs off at the hips. Or when I was twenty-two and she drove sixty miles every day for a week, after a full day of teaching, to take care of me when I was hospitalized with a blood clot after I broke my foot playing basketball.

Having her next to me is enough.

We drive to Bellflower to see the apartment on Cornuta Avenue. I can't find it, but in the place it's supposed to be, there is a mosque set back from the street several hundred feet beyond a gated parking lot. I get out of the car, take some pictures.

"That's weird," I say to my mom as she bobs in and out of consciousness. "But kind of funny, right? That the building is now a mosque?" Still, I know it can't be true, nor do I want it to be true. I need to see that apartment building again with my own eyes to prove it ever existed at all. I laugh, but on the inside, I'm crying.

As we drive away, toward the main cross street, Alondra, I see 5 Star Liquor on the corner, and I am reminded—my brother and I walked to this liquor store a hundred times to buy candy, Pepsi, and chips on days we were supposed to be in school. Gaining my bearings, I learn I have turned the wrong way onto Cornuta.

"It's this way," I say, feeling stupid for really believing my old apartment building has been razed and replaced by a religious temple. Although, I can't think of a more fitting or ironic end.

As we pull up to the apartment building, relief spreads through me. "Here it is." It's gated. A moment later, the gate opens to let us in. *Why have a gate,* I am about to say, when I glimpse a car in my rearview, waiting behind us, its driver trying to get in, to get home.

I stop inside the gate and let the other car pass to park. I take pictures and walk between the brick wall and the laundry room and pebbled stairs where Roberta kept us awake all night when she was convinced a revving semi-truck was going to crash through our apartment and kill us.

After standing before the stucco apartment where I'd smashed my left fingers in the wooden door, where my mother, brother, and I hid from the outside world, where my mother got better and then a whole lot worse, I snap a few more photos. I'm a damaged tourist carrying around this longing to exist inside my past. I want to get closer, knock on that door, enter the dark cave of a dwelling, and *feel* my childhood, *absorb* it—because writing about childhood is cathartic, and I can feel the details of those days leaving me. I want to hold on to them forever. If I let them go, might I be giving the universe permission to erase who I was and all the things that helped make me who I am?

I rush back to the lot where the man who drove in behind us waits so he can click the gate open and let us leave. Don't those gates always have an automatic sensor that opens by the weight of the approaching car? Isn't it against some code or law to keep a car trapped inside? It's silly how, all these years later, I still think of everything in terms of capture and escape, fight or flight.

Next, we stop at the liquor store, and I take pictures of the sign. I want to go inside, to see if feeling the floor under my feet might teleport me back to the past—to the times my brother and I walked the half a mile or so without our mom's permission, and while she slept, to cross the busy intersection and throw coins onto the counter in exchange for Doritos and Nestlé Drumsticks on a perfectly fine Tuesday. It is a happy memory. We were perpetually hungry and worried about when our mom's mental tide would turn, but we were also having an adventure.

This time, though, I don't go inside. I think I should because maybe I will find something I can write about, some connection to the past that has since evaded me. I am self-conscious and don't want the clerk to look at me, don't want to explain why I'm there, don't want to buy anything. Opening my mouth, my purse, my wallet will only make me vulnerable. If I stay closed up, I won't stretch myself too far on this journey into the past.

Back in the car, my mom navigates to Downey, to my aunt Philys's apartment. To make things more difficult, the name of her street has been changed.

Deleting "Clark Avenue" seems like a denial of my aunt's existence, and an alteration to the course of history and of my time in that tiny apartment that was never truly mine. The building has been painted taupe and named "The Apollo Apts" as if inhabited by the Olympian god of sun and light and healing. The irony makes me sigh a hesitant laugh that sometimes precedes a cry.

Being on that property makes me think about the couch where I was strangled by Roberta, the couch I returned to over the years to sleep on when I visited my aunt, the couch that was loaded into a U-Haul and carted off to Goodwill after my aunt died. Mostly, being there makes me think about my aunt's unapologetic laughter and the carefree disposition she had until she got cancer, until she was laid off from her job, until clinical depression sent her further into the abyss of despair. I think about how, all those years ago, I called to tell her I would visit her soon but then didn't and she died.

Near tears, I slide behind the wheel, and my mom says, "It's only natural for you to be sad."

Her words mean she *understands* me, and I feel close to whole.

I place my hand on her hand and squeeze gently. "Thank you for coming with me today."

She gives me a closed-lipped smile that I've learned is her way of showing appreciation for what I've said.

We proceed to our last stop: my grandparents' house. I exit the car for some quick photos, hoping not to alert the Neighborhood Watch. The birch tree is long gone. The seafoam green has been covered with canary yellow. Being there makes me shaky as if I've had too much coffee. Too many losses to handle in one day. The last thing I want is for the current homeowner to tell me to leave. The house had never been *mine*, but it was mine before it was theirs. I practice what I might say if someone approaches me. "I used to live here." *I almost died here.*

"I think we should head home," my mom says. "We still have to pick up dinner."

It's about 5 p.m., and as committed as I am to the idea of searching for old streets in the dark, I know it's time to leave the skeletons alone. I've taken enough of my mom's day with my agenda to travel back to another life. I am disappointed our journey must end. I am certain, if we had more time, I would find what I am looking for—even though I know what I seek is an intangible sense I can't fully describe or define. Maybe one more turn, one more street, one more glance will fill the grave of loss I carry deep inside. Auntie Philys and Grampa always used to say about Roberta, "Give her an inch, and she'll take a mile." I've spent my entire life trying not to be like her.

On the way home, my mom takes a phone call, so as we pass through Norwalk, instead of asking permission, I turn into the neighborhood where I left Roberta standing among glass shards, crying at the sky. *What's one more quick drive-by?* But as I weave through the streets, I remember the apartment is never where I think it is.

Why do I care so much about seeing these places now? Don't they represent loss and insecurity, neglect and hunger, cold and uncertainty about everything? I have moved on; I've had an entire life away from those places and those feelings. What do I need from them now? What am I hoping to find?

The answers to these questions seem as lost to me as the peace I crave like sustenance. The logical part of my brain knows that when the past is ripped away, even if that past contained horrible events, we don't have a chance to achieve natural closure. As a child who was separated from my first family, I experienced an undefinable, inexplicable grief that became embedded in my DNA. I was lucky to have an opportunity to move on physically to a stable, healthy place, but the pull of the past remains buried in me like a stone. Every once in a while, that stone must be uncovered, and the soil must be brushed away so I can look at the stone and say, *Here, see? It did really happen.* If the stone is forgotten, or if it is cast into eternity, something even more important becomes lost: sense of self.

To ignore or forget everything I experienced when I was young threatens my understanding of truth and self. What happened can never be retold with perfect accuracy, but in experiencing the events, I became a part of them, and they became a part of me—parts of me. To excavate and discard is to cut away the heart and soul of my *becoming,* of my compassion, my sensitivity, my desire in this world.

That my mom has accompanied me on this journey to revisit my past means she accepts my past. Her bearing witness to these streets and to my hunger for revisiting such turbulent times is something I accept as one of her most loving and blatant acknowledgments of who I am, who I was before she entered my life and changed it forever with her compassionate and loyal magic.

The next day, my mom encourages me to go skating. I've recently taken up the sport as a hobby—a fun way to get some exercise while desiring to prove my body isn't nearing fifty (and hopefully without breaking my skull). We think of a place close by that might have a perfect, even slab of cement on which to skate. *And she wants to come with me.*

I skate and laugh, and my mom takes pictures and videos. It occurs to me that, like those childhood places of mine are my past, I am my mom's past. I am the daughter she thought she'd never have.

"Thanks for making me come," I say. "And thanks for coming."

"Oh, it's been fun." She hands me my phone. "It's a beautiful day, and I thought it would be good to get outside and enjoy it."

Then I say, "Me skating and you watching and taking pictures makes me feel like I'm a kid all over again and like we're making up for so many things we missed out on before you became my mom."

I wipe the tears from my eyes.

"Yep," she says. "I'm glad." She might have tears in her eyes, too, because she is sensitive like I am. But I am no longer looking at her. I sit on a metal bench to remove my skates and protective gear. I stand and hug her.

And we go home.

That night, we eat Thai food from a favorite restaurant. I show my mom some pages of this memoir and share a few stories about events from my childhood before I became the Fergusons' daughter.

My dad simply accepts my tragedies without much response. I suppose he considers the past nothing more than dust in the wind. He never dwells too much on errors, miseries, or the what ifs of a life lived. He is good at focusing on the present.

My mom shakes her head and says, "It's a miracle you aren't totally fucked up." We all have a solid laugh about it, and my dad, ever the joker, chimes in with a comment about how the jury is still out on that verdict.

As I slurp the remains of my tom kha and rice, I contemplate how far we've come—how far *I've* come. It strikes me that maybe I don't need to go back to the past anymore. I am who I am despite those distressing days, but also *because* of them. They exist in me. I don't need to search for something undefinable that might still haunt the grounds I once walked. Those places don't hold the key to the meaning of life, they don't reflect gems of wisdom, and they most certainly cannot bring back what I've lost.

Normalizing my experiences has always been integral to my survival and to my ability to keep my head above water while treading furiously to avoid being swallowed by the vortex of trauma. I think the real miracle is a grand stroke of luck—many lucks over time—that I found my mom and dad (and that they would say they found me) and that they have continued holding the light steady at the surface, unconditionally welcoming me home from the deep.

ACKNOWLEDGMENTS

Mom and Dad, thank you for your constant support, guidance, and unconditional love—who knows where I'd be today if you hadn't opened your hearts and your home to me. Thank you for always reminding me I was (and still am) easy to love. I am in awe of your generosity, compassion, and integrity. I sometimes still can't believe you were willing to sacrifice so much for one lost little girl. Mom, thank you for always being willing to read and edit early drafts of anything I write and for offering crucial advice with candor and humor. Dad, thanks for being the backbone of our family and for leading with consistency, loyalty, and commitment. I've learned so much from both of you about hard work and perseverance, and look! After two decades, I finally finished this book!

To my brother—my first best friend—my greatest witness and connection to my past: Thank you for welcoming me back into your life after the years pushed us apart. I appreciate your taking time to read early drafts of this book and offer genuine feedback. I am continually amazed by your intelligence, strength, and calm wisdom. One of the kindest, most selfless people I know, you are a constant source of love and inspiration. And to Victoria, thank you for loving him so completely. You have the biggest heart, and your undeniable influence in both of our lives allows me to breathe more easily.

Very special thanks to my husband, Brian—the most generous, beautiful, and loyal partner I could hope for—thank you for believing in me from the beginning and giving me the freedom to pursue my dreams. I love you for always loving me exactly as I am and for making our life magical in so many ways.

Denette Wilson, my BFF, soul mate, conscience, co-conspirator, co-adventurer, and guide in this world—you make everything brighter.

Thank you for reading the earliest drafts of this memoir and for being my fiercest cheerleader in everything I do. Thank you for your tireless sense of humor and for always reminding me to handle my shit. I would be lost without you.

Sue William Silverman, thank you for taking the time to so graciously receive my book and provide a testimonial for the cover. Your amazing books helped me change my writing direction and improve my scenes. I am, and always will be, in awe of you.

Marni Freedman, my editor and champion, thank you for your praise, guidance, and encouragement and for helping me realize I was ready for what came next. And thank you for leading me to the San Diego Memoir Writers Association!

Donna and Jeff, the best MIL and FIL anyone could hope for—thank you for raising an amazing human being, for welcoming me into your lives with warmth and hospitality, and for unfailingly encouraging my artistic endeavors with enthusiasm and praise.

Special thanks to my writer-friends Demi Hungerford, Jeanene Burke, Sam Gross, and Robyn Plante, my Blue Crue, for accepting me as I am and for all the writing space, coffee dates, and encouragement as I began my San Diego life. You were the first people who made me feel like I belong here.

To Karen Kimbro Johnson and Lisa King, my wise, intelligent yogi pals and writer gals, I am so grateful for your friendship, writing feedback, and camaraderie on this artistic path.

Cherie Kephart, you took me under your wing and ushered me into a whole new world. Thank you for your honesty and your brilliant editing— and for your beautiful memoir that gave me new hope for what mine could become.

Ashlynn Cubbison, thank you, Bestie, for your inspiration and advice and for always being there to remind me why I wrote this book.

Gina Gonzales-Wagerman and Seth Wagerman, you are two of the best things I ever got from a writers conference. Thank you for your beautiful friendship, wisdom, and light.

Kelly Bowen, my newest creative friend, thank you for your constant support, encouragement, and keen editing advice.

Thank you, Jimmy Pickel, for bringing me back to myself when I'd lost my way and for believing in my writing from the beginning.

Much love and gratitude to my amazing girlfriends who walked in when the rest of the world walked out: Angelina Martinez, Christina Kenny, Crystal Bazzano, Desi d'Amani, Edda Tan, Hallie Smith, Heather Kamei, Katie Cure, Kelly Bloxham, Lara Johnson, Marci Schaefer, Marianna Beery, Molly Dearing, Rebeca Ladrón de Guevara, Stephanie Chute, Teresa Linehan, and Vandra Lochridge. Your acceptance, support, and encouragement have helped me become the person I am today, the person who was finally able to finish this book that took twenty years of heart, soul, and tears. I am honored by and grateful for the laughter, balance, wisdom, and restoration you have brought into my life.

Marsha Jehn, I appreciate your calm and healing guidance. I am so grateful I found you. Rached is smiling down on us with pride and love.

Sandy "Blume" Blumenthal and Micki McAulay, thank you for giving me the opportunity to shine and for pushing me to be strong in body and mind. Your influence in my life is everlasting. And to all of my teammates near and far: thank you for helping me grow into myself and discover what I'm made of.

I am indebted to my read-and-critique friends and editors for their time, advice, honesty, and encouragement. Marcia Hankey, Susan F. Banks, Bev Hamowitz, Anna-Marie Abell, Catherine Shields, Ani Petrak, and Suzanne Park, this book is better because of you.

To all of my Scribophile chapter and beta readers, I appreciate your time, thoughtful feedback, and praise.

Thank you to Kim Keeline, for helping me know what to cut and what to keep.

Sunny Rey and Poets Underground, thank you for welcoming me wholeheartedly and giving me a stage. I am a better, more confident writer because of you. I am honored to cry with you and sit in reverence for the truth you share through your words.

To So Say We All's Jennifer D. Corley and Justin Hudnall, thank you for the VAMP platform and for keeping the community alive through stories.

Jessica Therrien and Holly Kammier, I feel so lucky to have crossed your paths. Thank you for your generosity, friendship, encouragement, and guidance and for providing the ideal home for my story. I love the Acorn team so much.

Debbie Kennedy, thank you for your time and wisdom as you expertly formatted and line-edited this book. I look forward to all of the grammar discussions and font-talk in our future.

Thank you to Damonza.com for your patience and dedication in designing such a stunning book cover. It is perfect in every way.

To all of my writing professors: Thank you for pushing me to be better as I wrote and revised the earliest drafts of this book. Much gratitude to my Chapman University writing professor and advisor, Martin Nakell. You are the first person who made me believe I have what it takes to be a writer. Thank you for giving me the opportunity to discover Italy and the courage to start over.

I am forever grateful for all of my writing students over the years, especially those who expressed excitement over the thought that I would someday publish this book. Thank you for your creativity, laughter, and grace and for challenging me to grow. I hope you will share your amazing stories with the world if you ever feel called to do so.

ABOUT THE AUTHOR

Leslie Ferguson is an accomplished educator, editor, and writing coach. As a youth in foster care, she dreamed about becoming a teacher. After earning her teaching credential from the University of Redlands, she taught high school English at her alma mater for nearly two decades. During that time, she obtained a master's degree in English literature and an MFA in creative writing from Chapman University. Her work has been published in numerous literary magazines and anthologies. A member of Poets Underground, the San Diego Memoir Writers Association,  and the San Diego Writers and Editors Guild, Leslie is a repeat performer at So Say We All's VAMP. She lives with one husband and two cats in the greater San Diego area, where she binge-watches dark character dramas and reminisces about her glory days as an All-American basketball player and collegiate Hall-of-Fame athlete. *When I Was Her Daughter* is her first book.

Visit the author online at LeslieFergusonAuthor.com.

Made in the USA
Las Vegas, NV
28 September 2022

56164213R00185